LOSING THE CLOUDS
GAINING THE SKY

LOSING THE CLOUDS
GAINING THE SKY

Buddhism and the Natural Mind

EDITED BY DORIS WOLTER

WISDOM PUBLICATIONS • BOSTON

Wisdom Publications, Inc.
199 Elm Street
Somerville MA 02144, USA
www.wisdompubs.org

Library of Congress Cataloging-in-Publication Data
Lebendiger Buddhismus heute. English.
  Losing the clouds, gaining the sky : buddhism and the natural mind / edited by Doris Wolter.
    p. cm.
  Published previously as: Lebendiger Buddhismus heute. Bern : Barth, 2002.
  Includes bibliographical references and index.
  ISBN 0-86171-359-1 (pbk. : alk. paper)
  1. Rdzogs-chen. I. Wolter, Doris, 1953– II. Title.
  BQ7662.4.L4213 2007
  294.3'4—dc22
                                2007005588

ISBN 0-86171-359-1

11 10 09 08 07
5   4   3   2   1

Original title: *Lebendiger Buddhismus heute* (Scherz Verlag). © 2001 S. Fischer Verlag GmbH,
    Frankfurt.
Chapters 2, 3, 5, 7, 10, 12, 14, 17, 23, 27, 28, 30, and 31 © The Tertön Sogyal Trust. May not
    be reproduced without permission of The Tertön Sogyal Trust.
Chapter 8, "Distortion," appeared originally in the *Shambhala Sun,* September 1997. It is
    reprinted with the permission of the author.

Cover design by Pema Studios. Interior design by TL. Set in Sabon 10.25/14.5.

Dedication

This book would not have been possible without the inspiration of Sogyal Rinpoche and his tireless work to establish an authentic, living Buddhism in the West. He has my deepest gratitude, and I dedicate this book to his long life and the fulfillment of all his aspirations. May his vision for the transmission of Buddhist wisdom to the people of the twenty-first century continue to unfold and blossom.

I also dedicate this book to my mother, to whom I owe this precious life, and to my son Jasper, who represents a new generation of young people destined to have a decisive impact on this new century. May they learn to act with wisdom and to integrate spirituality into their everyday lives.

PUBLISHER'S ACKNOWLEDGMENT

The publisher gratefully acknowledges the generous help of the Hershey Family Foundation in sponsoring the printing of this book.

CONTENTS

II. Authentic Buddhism Today

III. Bringing the Transcendent into Everyday Life

Editor's Preface

There is no communication in relative truth without understanding everyone's system and idea, so may I adapt to everyone's system, wishing for everyone's benefit.

There is no liberation in absolute truth without release from everyone's system and idea, so may I adapt to no one's system, beyond benefit's wish.
—Thinley Norbu Rinpoche[1]

WORDS CAN ONLY POINT to what is real. But the words of great spiritual masters enable the person who really listens to them to gain understanding in a direct, intuitive way. They reach each person at their own level, wherever that may be, and regardless of whether he or she is a complete stranger to Buddhism, is trying to grasp the philosophical aspects of love and compassion, or has already been practicing for decades. They reach those with faith in any religion—and those who have no faith in any.

While selecting and arranging the texts in this book I was surprised to discover how the themes flow into one another and how the teachings complete and illuminate one another in a wonderful way. If in one context a particular aspect of the teachings is only touched on briefly, more light will be brought to it by another teacher later on, and it will be deepened. Even a basic text on meditation, for example by Sogyal Rinpoche, transmits a taste of *dzogchen*, the highest teaching of Tibetan Buddhism; more complex teachings, such as the one by Khetsun Zangpo Rinpoche, always contain the basic foundations.

Losing the Clouds, Gaining the Sky is a collection of some of the teachings that appeared between 1990 and 2001 in the *Rigpa Rundbrief,* the newsletter of Rigpa, Sogyal Rinpoche's organization in Germany, and many of the pieces also appreared in Rigpa's English-language *View* magazine around the same time. In this forum Buddhist teachers offer insights on the most diverse topics, and alongside the Tibetan masters, some Western students are also represented: Christine Longaker, for example, whose work with the dying is well known, and Patrick Gaffney, the co-editor of Sogyal Rinpoche's famous book *The Tibetan Book of Living and Dying.*

This book, with all the masterly advice and wisdom contained within it, will respond to the real questions that arise for all of us here and now as we traverse our paths of spiritual and ethical development: questions of the relevance of the Buddhist teachings for everyday lives in the West, and of why authentic lineages are so vital for the survival of these teachings.

This book carries with it my hope that it may offer readers an understanding of the Buddhist teachings that is at once profound and fresh, and that for practitioners of long standing its variety will disclose new aspects and connections in the teachings.

Sogyal Rinpoche is the inspiration behind this book. I am grateful for his unstinting efforts to convey the essence of the Buddhist teachings to the West. I am also grateful to Dzongsar Khyentse Rinpoche for his encouragement in this project, and to Patrick Gaffney for his wise counsel in the selection of texts. I received outstanding support in preparing this book from Karin Behrendt, Wolfram Hämmerling, Barbara Nölle, Elisabeth and Heinz Nowotny, Erika Bachhuber, Manfred Bober, Lisa Freund, Pete Fry, Barbara Giehmann, Susie Godfrey, Michael Kömpf, and Heide Schuchardt. The English-language edition benefited greatly from the editorial assistance of Sue Morrison, Jeremy Tattersall, and Julian Chase.

If, in spite of all this support, any inaccuracies or errors remain, they are the fault of the editor.

I. ASPECTS OF THE BUDDHIST PATH

The Foundations of Meditation

Profound peace, natural simplicity,
uncompounded luminosity.
Buddha Shakyamuni[2]

Westerners sometimes view spirituality as something that should come naturally, just of itself. Unfortunately, our habits have for a long time taken us in unnatural directions and have made us too complicated. We need a degree of discipline before we can return to our natural state. The following teachings address this process of re-learning. It is not so easy, for the process goes against some very old habits. But as Shantideva says, "Nothing is difficult when you get used to it." At the beginning, all the most conducive conditions for meditation need to be created: the motivation, the right environment, some spirit of renunciation, trust in the methods of practice, and an ability to concentrate. These work against our habitual patterns, create the space for the veil of delusion to be lifted, so that our true qualities can finally come to light in a natural, unforced way.

1. It's Under Our Very Noses

Sogyal Rinpoche

T HE PROBLEM WITH US, generally speaking, is that we are scattered, everywhere, all over the place. In a country like France, people have a tremendous passion and enthusiasm for the teachings, but after a while it bursts like a balloon; something else comes along and we forget. We are forever carried away by the enthusiasms of the people around us; we are the victims of one fashion after another. We are influenced totally by the latest trend, particularly when we don't have anything we are really following, and we lack stability. We are shaped by whatever those influences might be: good, bad, or indifferent.

The trouble with us is we're not able to keep things or maintain them. They slide through our fingers, and slip away. We lose everything: we lose time, we lose the teachings, and we just forget. I remember people who were strong practitioners long ago and who were constantly practicing. But what happened to them? In those days, at the beginning of their spiritual journey, there was an innocence about them, but then they seemed to mature. Yet what can happen is that, while we mature, something else creeps in. We need to remember that those things that obstruct us from practicing—ego, ignorance, laziness, our habits—are very stable. Very constant. And very skillful. They know exactly how, and exactly when, to catch us.

Of course, as a rule we'll have very sound reasons for not practicing, but however plausible they sound, they may not actually be good reasons. Superficially, perhaps, but what do they really bring us in the end? Behind their eloquence lurks something else, something that we fail to recognize.

Often we're obsessed with novelty. There's a Tibetan saying that if you buy a new *mala* rosary, you get so excited and inspired that you immediately rattle off a million mantras. Your enthusiasm will last that long, and then the mala is forgotten. These days, people are always looking for something new—new people, new experiences—which is a sign that we're lacking something deep down. For example, we've all met people who tell us their life story in the first fifteen minutes. Actually, there's nothing wrong with that—enthusiasm, inspiration, and openness are wonderful—but there's also a lack of stability.

What I'm trying to say is that somehow we don't know how to extract the essence, how to take care of and keep those things that are really good for us. We may have something precious, but we don't know how to keep it; we allow it to be stolen by others. This is something we all need to reflect on.

There's one real danger, one that all of us, but particularly older students of the Dharma, must avoid at all costs. That is of becoming what is known in Tibetan as "Dharma-stubborn." What happens is that, as we hear the Dharma teachings, at the very same time our ego is developing an extremely thick skin. We end up by not being able to be embarrassed by anything; we just don't care any more.

I remember once I was having a debate with someone, and suddenly they realized they had been making a fundamental mistake. Even so, their final argument was, "But don't I have the right to be wrong?" It sounds like a good argument, sure. Of course we have the right to be wrong. But isn't that kind of "right" actually wrong? Because our rights should benefit us, not simply empower us to do anything we like. That's why we need to have discernment.

So as we get older, we ought to be getting wiser. In fact, some older people are much more alive than younger ones—younger in spirit. I think one thing that's very important is that freshness in the Dharma, the beginner's mind—freshness with maturity. Some people, as they get older and receive more and more teachings, become increasingly blasé, flat, and spoiled.

When you know a lot of Dharma, and you're really able to hear it, it will help you transform your life. But along with the Dharma comes other stuff, other stories, particularly ego-stories. As you go through your experiences one after another, ego will start a kind of boxing match with you. At the beginning, you have some energy to fight back, but then ego punches you all over with all its wonderful, heavyweight arguments. You bounce back off the ropes, but ego knocks you about a bit more; you come back, but then it knocks you down. You stagger up, only to be laid flat again. All too soon, you're out for the count. Knocked out. And that's how you stay, unconscious. It's a sort of giving up, a kind of hopelessness. Sometimes, we'll retreat into and take refuge in this hopelessness. And it's not as if intelligent people, with very smart minds, escape either, because the mind is so ingenious in acting against itself. We don't realize what a fantastic job we do in deceiving ourselves. How incredibly clever we are at deluding and fooling ourselves; we don't even recognize it's going on!

In one way or another, this is something we all go through, because one of the biggest problems, you see, is integration—how can we actually follow a spiritual path? These are the real problems. You might say, "Okay, but why go on about it? We all know this, anyway." Because when you hear, if you *recognize,* then it may help you make a real change.

What is it we need to do then? Sometimes, when you look at certain situations in life, it can seem so difficult, so daunting. First, we need to change our environment, that's for sure. But it seems as if there's so much to change, and it feels like what we really need is a completely new "us." What a relief it would be to get a brand new model! There's nothing we'd like better sometimes; but this is too extreme as well. We have a tendency to want *everything* else to be perfect before we can even begin. That's also an excuse: "If only this were right, then I'd be right as well." We impose all kinds of conditions, but that's all they are. They may not be the truth at all.

What it's really all about is how we can transform our minds; and the miracle is how changeable the mind actually is. We *can* change the mind; it's possible. And inspire ourselves. When we see how we've been carrying on, we could think, "My God! What he's saying is exactly what I'm going through right now. It's me he's talking about!" Then, "How terrible I am...maybe there's no hope for me. I've already become Dharma-stubborn. Nobody can save me now. And all these years...all these years of teaching have not affected me one little bit.

What's the use, really?" But getting depressed and repeating this kind of thing to ourselves is just one more excuse, one more evasion.

What I'm saying is that sometimes the solution is very simple. So simple that we can actually miss it. It's under our very noses. There's quite a comical Tibetan story about a man from a country village who traveled all the way to Lhasa, the capital of Tibet, with a team of mules, twenty-two in all. For a Tibetan, Lhasa was an enormous town, and as soon as he saw the Potala Palace he was absolutely mesmerized. He immediately started trying to count the windows, and got more and more excited. Finally he gathered his wits and looked around to check on his mules, but he could only see twenty-one. He panicked and started asking everybody he met, "Have you seen my mule?" Because he'd come from a tiny village in the middle of nowhere, he was convinced that the sophisticated people of Lhasa must speak a different language. He thought they wouldn't have a word for "mule." So he tore up a handful of grass and took a piece of mule dung, and holding them out in front of him, he shouted, "Have you seen the thing that eats this and does this?" On and on he went, asking the same question. Finally somebody said, "But, look! You're sitting on one!" He'd forgotten he was actually riding one of them; the twenty-second mule was right underneath him all the time.

Sometimes the solution is like that, right under our very noses. All the raw materials are at our disposal. When we want to change, we begin by changing the environment of our mind. We can change the environment around us a little as well; we don't have to renovate the entire house, but just a little bit of the decor, here and there. But it's mainly our mind. And how we reorganize our life. And what is so precious here is to look into the teachings, look at your notes, listen to recordings, and then go over them and study them again and again.

2. THE SPIRIT OF TIBET

Patrick Gaffney

Let me begin with a story about something that took place in the Middle Ages in Tibet. Geshe Tönpa was one of the great contemplative masters of the time. One day, he was visited by a monk who was a disciple of some of the other famous teachers, and who had been traveling throughout Tibet. Geshe Tönpa took the opportunity to ask him for news of these other masters.

"What is Potowa doing?"

"He is giving teachings to hundreds of members of the Sangha," the monk replied.

"How wonderful! And what is Geshe Puchungwa doing?"

"He spends all his time making statues and paintings and printing sacred scriptures."

"Excellent! What's happened to Geshe Gönpawa?"

"He does nothing but meditate."

"Marvelous! Tell me about Khampa Lungpa."

"Well, he lives in solitude, and covers his head, and all he does is weep...."

At this, Geshe Tönpa suddenly began to cry and said: "How amazing! This is the one who is really practicing what we call the Dharma...." He knew that the reason Khampa Lungpa was constantly in tears was that he thought of nothing but those who were tormented by the suffering of samsara, and his whole practice was centered on one thing: compassion.

We live in a world today that has very little real compassion. We might even wonder how the twentieth century will be seen when historians look back on it in the future. Will they just see it as a century of genocide and of cruelty, a century in which humans irreparably destroyed their environment? Or will they recognize it as a century when the "developed" world encountered the ancient teachings of the East, including that of Buddha? That encounter has come at a time of unprecedented crisis. The teaching of Buddha, I believe, hands us the tools for our survival, and offers men and women everywhere a way to rediscover the spiritual dimension and take responsibility for their lives and for our future.

All the traditions of Buddhadharma stem from that one full-moon night at Bodhgaya, an event that changed the world, and could still continue to do so. What was it that Buddha discovered that night, two and a half thousand years ago? One of the great Tibetan masters of our time, Nyoshul Khen Rinpoche, describes it:

Profound and tranquil, free from complexity,
uncompounded luminous clarity,
beyond the mind of conceptual ideas:
This is the depth of the mind of the victorious ones.

In this there is not a thing to be removed,
nor anything that needs to be added.
It is merely the immaculate
looking naturally at itself.

The Buddhist tradition of Tibet is based on that same world-transforming discovery, and on the same threefold training that Buddha gave to pursue that discovery to its end: creating simplicity of lifestyle through discipline, awakening clarity of mind through meditation, and seeing directly into the heart of reality with transcendental insight.

Without the fundamental teachings of Buddha, and without the teachings of Mahayana, Tibetan Buddhism would not exist, and so it treasures them as the very ground of its teaching and practice. There is a watchword for a practitioner in the Tibetan tradition: "Outwardly, be a practitioner of the Fundamental Teaching, inwardly be Mahayana, and secretly be Vajrayana." It was part of the genius of Buddha to teach so many paths, to address the vast range of different needs and capacities among sentient beings.

Tibetan Buddhism has a strong sense of the sacredness of the spiritual and welcomes other traditions, much in the spirit of Indian emperor Ashoka, who said: "Let us all listen, and be willing to listen, to the teachings held by others." Looking at the teaching of Buddha like this, what is remarkable is the unity of all its great streams, through the sublime peace and mindfulness of Theravada, to Zen's sparkling insights and unmasking of illusion, to the countless skillful means of the Vajrayana, and the path of mahamudra and dzogchen. Couldn't, for example, Zen master Ikkyu's:

A mind to search for Buddha elsewhere
is foolishness in the very center of foolishness.

step straight from the Tibetan teachings on the nature of mind? And don't the words of the *Dhammapada*:

In this world
hate never yet dispelled hate.
Only love dispels hate.
This is the law,
ancient and inexhaustible.

speak of the essence of the Tibetan understanding of compassion? The light of Buddha shines through all, as if his realization were a great sun, and all its rays the endless expressions of that truth, in different cultures and environments.

The great popularity enjoyed in different countries today by all forms of Buddhism must reflect the great gift that Buddhism is offering the world. Why is Buddhism so relevant? It hands us an antidote to the religion of consumerism, at a time when more and more people are seeing through its tireless labyrinth of illusions. Then, Buddhism points to *mind* as being the crucial issue, and shows that mental peace is the only thing that counts, whatever our technological sophistication. It speaks of responsibility and compassion when many people are being drawn toward helping others and showing their individual engagement in society. Its long-term view and its teaching on interdependence delight environmentalists, while its exploration of mind and its nature holds fascinating insights for the cognitive sciences and for psychotherapy.

Buddhism is a path that appeals not just to the head but to the heart as well, with its skillful methods of compassion and devotion. There are so many means, so many practices, for different kinds of people. And above all, what is so inspiring for many people in the modern world, there is the "good news" that Buddha brought from Bodhgaya: that enlightenment is possible for us all. Each and every one of us has the buddha nature. As Zen master Dogen said: "Only buddhas become buddhas." Or in the words of my master, Sogyal Rinpoche: "Our buddha nature is as good as any buddha's buddha nature."

What is the spirit of Tibetan Buddhism? First there is faith, resilience, and inner strength, an indestructible devotion to the teaching of Buddha. There is wisdom, the whole of Tibetan culture having been based upon the prime importance given to that inner science of the development of the mind. There is a knowledge of the central place of compassion, both in human interaction and on the path to enlightenment. Then, along with the gentleness and softness that so many remark on in the Tibetan people, there is a deep contentment, something we have lost almost completely today. Finally, there is a down-to-earth humor that springs from the understanding that the spiritual path can be followed with joy.

The spirit of the Buddhist tradition of Tibet is embodied in the person of His Holiness the Dalai Lama, who has become in the eyes of so many a great world leader and the champion of human happiness and freedom. His compassion, his patience, and his stand on nonviolence are well known, as are his keen interest in the meeting points between Buddhist wisdom and science, and his concern for the preservation of the environment. The simple majesty of his presence and his message of universal and individual responsibility have moved literally millions all over the globe. His is a message of hope: "I for one believe that individuals can make a difference in society. Periods of great change such as the present one come so rarely in human history it is up to each one of us to make the best use of our time to help create a happier world."

The heart of His Holiness' message is that our future depends, above all else, on our peace of mind, for world peace can only come from inner peace. The Dalai Lama offers us a simple equation. Peace of mind and happiness come from a good heart. Why? For the simple reason that the compassionate heart eliminates the anger, hatred, fear, and jealousy that destroy our peace of mind. He says: "A mind committed to compassion is like a reservoir—a constant source of energy, determination, and kindness. This mind is like a seed; when cultivated, it gives rise to many other good qualities such as forgiveness, tolerance, inner strength, and the confidence to overcome fear and insecurity. The compassionate mind is like an elixir; it is capable of transforming bad situations into beneficial ones."

The ability to transform bad situations could be priceless to us today. The Indian Buddhist master of compassion, Atisha, said:

When the world is full of evil, transform all mishaps into the path of bodhi.

If we look closely we will see that our real enemy, the real source of our suffering, is our ego-clinging, our grasping to a notion of a lasting, independent self. And we will see that our real friend is concern for the well-being of others.

There is an extraordinary painting of Buddha depicting him just before he attained enlightenment. Mara and his demons, desperate to prevent him, fling weapons and missiles at him as they mount their final assault. The Buddha meditates on kindness toward them all. As soon as they come within range of his aura of compassion, their weapons are turned into flowers, their war cries into mantras. What an image that is for us! Difficulties and misfortune can be the opportunity for the transforming power of compassion to arise. No situation, however daunting, cannot be transformed through our vision or attitude. And those who arouse our compassion can become a cause for our attaining buddhahood, and so inspire our deepest gratitude.

It is compassion that frees us from ego-clinging. It is compassion, too, that melts the frozen heart into a stream of understanding and realization. In the Tibetan tradition, it is said that compassion is the

skillful means that arises from the heart of wisdom. For true compassion is always understanding, is always indivisible from wisdom.

It is not possible to separate the gift that Tibetan Buddhism is offering the world from Tibet and its tragic story, a story which is continuing right now. Lands like Tibet or Cambodia are symbolic; let them stand in our minds for all those places where people are suffering. Let us dedicate our practice and our prayers for *all* who are suffering, Buddhist and others, and pray that out of suffering will be born peace, new wisdom, and new courage. Maha Ghosananda is a great Buddhist teacher who, just like Khampa Lungpa in our story, shed many tears, in his case for the people of his country Cambodia. Let his words speak for the world:

> The suffering of Cambodia has been deep.
> From this suffering comes great compassion.
> Great compassion makes a peaceful heart.
> A peaceful heart makes a peaceful person.
> A peaceful person makes a peaceful family.
> A peaceful family makes a peaceful community.
> A peaceful community makes a peaceful nation.
> And a peaceful nation makes a peaceful world.
> May all beings live in happiness and peace!

3. NATURAL GREAT PEACE

Sogyal Rinpoche

THE TEACHING OF THE BUDDHA IS VAST. Just the "Word of the Buddha" alone fills over one hundred volumes. Then the commentaries and treatises by the great Indian scholars fill another two hundred and more, and this is not even counting all the works of the great Tibetan masters. Yet at the same time, the teaching of the Buddha can be essentialized in a very profound way. I remember my master Dilgo Khyentse Rinpoche used to say, "The teaching of Buddha is both 'vast' and 'profound': the 'vast' is the approach of the learned, the pandit, and the 'profound' is the approach of the yogi." When Buddha himself was asked to summarize his teaching, he said,

> Commit not a single unwholesome action,
> Cultivate a wealth of virtue,
> To tame this mind of ours,
> This is the teaching of all buddhas.

To say, "Commit not a single unwholesome action" means to abandon unwholesome, harmful and negative actions, which are the cause of suffering, for both ourselves and others. To "cultivate a wealth of virtue" is to adopt the positive, beneficial, and wholesome actions that are the cause of happiness, again for both ourselves and others. Most important of all, however, is to "tame this mind of ours." In fact the masters, like Nyoshul Khen Rinpoche, often say that this one line captures the essence of the teachings of the Buddha. Because if we realize the true nature of our own mind, then this is the whole point, of both the teaching and our entire existence.

The mind is the root of everything: the creator of happiness and the creator of suffering, the creator of samsara and the creator of nirvana. In the Tibetan teachings, mind is called "the king who is responsible for everything"—*kun jé gyalpo*—the universal ordering principle. As the great guru Padmasambhava said, "Do not seek to cut the root of phenomena; cut the root of the mind." That is why I find these words of Buddha so inspiring: "We are what we think, and all that we are rises with our thoughts. With our thoughts we make the world. Speak and act with a pure mind and happiness will follow." If only we were to remember this, keep it in our hearts, and keep our hearts and minds pure, then happiness would really follow. The whole of Buddha's teaching then, is directed toward taming this mind, and keeping our heart and mind pure.

That starts when we begin with the practice of meditation. We allow all our turbulent thoughts and emotions to settle quietly in a state of natural peace. As Nyoshul Khen Rinpoche said:

Rest in natural great peace this exhausted mind,
Beaten helpless by karma and neurotic thoughts,
Like the relentless fury of the pounding waves
In the infinite ocean of samsara.
Rest in natural great peace.

How do thoughts and emotions settle? If you leave a glass of muddy water quite still, without moving it, the dirt will settle to the bottom, and the clarity of the water will shine through. In the same way, in meditation we allow our thoughts and emotions to settle naturally, and in a state of natural ease. There is a wonderful saying by the great masters of the past. I remember when I first heard it what a revelation it was, because in these two lines is shown both what the nature of mind is, and how to abide by it, which is the practice of meditation. In Tibetan it is very beautiful, almost musical: *chu ma nyok na dang, sem ma chö na de.* It means roughly, "Water, if you don't stir it, will become clear; the mind, left unaltered, will find its own natural peace."

What is so incredible about this instruction is its emphasis on naturalness, and on allowing our mind simply to be, unaltered and without changing anything at all. Our real problem is manipulation and fabrication and too much thinking. One master used to say that the root cause of all our mental problems was too much thinking. As Buddha said, "With our thoughts we make the world." But if we keep our mind pure, and allow it to rest, quietly, in the natural state, what happens, as we practice, is quite extraordinary.

The first practice on the Buddhist path of meditation is called *shamata*, in Tibetan *shi né*, calm abiding or tranquility meditation. When we begin, it is a practice of mindfulness. The practice of shamata can be with an object or support, or without one. Sometimes we use an image of the Buddha as the object, or else, as we will find in all schools of Buddhism, lightly and mindfully we watch the breath. The problem with us is that our mind is nearly always distracted. When it's distracted, mind creates endless thoughts. There is nothing it will not think of or do. If we ever looked, we would see how undiscriminating we are, how often we simply allow any kind of thought to come, and let ourselves get lost in it. It has become the worst of all bad habits. We have no discipline, nor any way of looking into what kind of thoughts we are thinking; whatever arises, we let it sweep us away and off into a spiral of stories and illusions, which we take so seriously we end up not only believing, but becoming as well.

Of course, we should not suppress our thoughts and emotions, but on the other hand we should not indulge in them either. The trouble with us is we have over-indulged in thinking. The result is mental, even physical, illness. Many Tibetan doctors have remarked on the prevalence in the modern world of disorders due to disturbances in the prana, or inner air, which are caused by too much agitation, worry, anxiety—and thinking—on top of the speed and aggression that dominate our lives. What we truly need is just peace. That is why we find that to sit for even a single moment, to breathe in and out and let the thoughts and emotions quietly settle, can make such a wonderful break.

When we abandon ourselves mindlessly to distraction and too much thinking, when we lose ourselves in thought and invite mental problems and anguish, the antidote is mindfulness. The discipline of the practice of shamata is to keep bringing your mind back to the breath. If you're

distracted, then suddenly, the instant you remember, you simply bring
your mind back to the breath. Nothing else is necessary. Even to ask,
"How on earth did I get so distracted?" is just another distraction. The
simplicity of mindfulness, of continuously bringing your mind back to
the breath, gradually calms it down. When you're trying to put an
infant to bed, he will want to start playing with you, and if you give in,
he will get more and more excited, and never go to sleep. You have to
hold him and stay with him, quietly focused, and then he will calm
down. Mind is just the same: however agitated it gets, keep bringing it
back, time and time again, to the simplicity of breathing. Gradually,
mind will settle, in the mind.

Initially, of course, we may feel a little self-conscious, thinking that
when we watch, there are the breathing, the breather, and the breath,
all separate. But slowly as we perfect the practice, and as our mind settles, breathing, breath, and breather shade into one, and finally it's as
if you have become the breath.

What is very important, the masters always advise, is not to fixate
while practicing the concentration of calm abiding. That's why they
recommend you place only 25 percent of the attention on mindfulness
of the breath. But then, as you may have noticed, mindfulness alone is
not enough. While you are supposed to be watching the breath, after a
few minutes you may find yourself playing in a football match or star-
ring in your own film. So another 25 percent should be devoted to a
continuous and watchful awareness, one that oversees and checks
whether you are being mindful of the breath. The remaining 50 percent
of your attention is left abiding, spaciously. Of course the exact per-
centages are not as important as the fact that all three of these elements—mindfulness, awareness, and spaciousness—are present.

Spaciousness is truly wonderful. Sometimes simply being spacious,
on its own, is enough to calm our mind down. Spaciousness captures
the whole spirit of meditation; it is the generosity of the ground of meditation, too. In shamata practice, when we can blend spaciousness with
the focus of mindfulness of the breath, gradually the mind will settle.
As the mind settles, something extraordinary takes place: all the fragmented aspects of ourselves come home, and we become whole. Negativity and aggression, pain, suffering, and frustration are actually

defused. We experience a feeling of peace, space, and freedom, and out of this settling comes a profound stillness.

As we perfect this practice, and become one with the breath, after a while even the breath itself as the focus of our practice dissolves, and we find ourselves resting in nowness. This is the one-pointedness that is the fruition and the goal of shamata. Remaining in nowness and still-ness is an excellent accomplishment, but to return to the example of the glass of muddy water, if you keep it still, the dirt will settle and it will become clear, and yet the dirt will still be there, deep down. One day if you stir it, the dirt will rise again. As long as we cultivate stillness, we may enjoy peace, but whenever our mind is a little bit disturbed, deluded thoughts will set in again.

Remaining in the nowness of shamata will not cause us to evolve, nor can it lead to enlightenment or liberation. Nowness becomes a very subtle object, and the mind that dwells in nowness a subtle subject. As long as we remain in the domain of subject and object, the mind is still within the ordinary conceptual world of samsara.

Through the practice of calm abiding, then, our mind has settled into a state of peace and has found stability. Just as the picture in a camera will sharpen as you focus it, so the one-pointedness of shamata allows an increasing clarity of mind to arise. As obscurations are grad-ually removed and ego and its grasping tendency begin to dissolve, the "clear seeing," "insight" of vipashyana (Tib. *lhak tong*), dawns. At this point we no longer need the anchor of remaining in nowness, and we can progress, moving on beyond our self even, into that openness which is the wisdom that realizes egolessness. This is what will uproot delu-sion and liberate us from samsara.

Let us look at what impact this has on how we deal with thoughts and emotions. To begin with, with no security or ground, we are invaded and scattered by thoughts; this is why in the practice of mind-fulness we focus on one object, the breath. But whatever thoughts arise all arise from our mind, nowhere else, as naturally as the rays from the sun or waves in the ocean. So as we are now in a state of calm abiding, the risings themselves—though never separate from us—will find us different. No longer do we need to be afraid of losing our poise or being distracted; no longer do we need to obstruct the risings, now that the openness of clear seeing of insight has dawned. We have become like a rock weathering all the winds and storms, not like the feather we were before, blown everywhere by the breeze.

All we have to do now is maintain our awareness. As a thought arises from the state of stillness, if we simply recognize it with that awareness, it will dissolve back into the nature of mind. Thoughts and emotions become like the waves on the ocean, rising and sinking back into its expanse, and we become like the ocean itself, vast, spacious, and placid. Nothing remains for us to do apart from maintaining that awareness.

Of course, for beginners the danger is that risings can destabilize us and trigger old habits. The instant an arising is seen as separate, we are lost, and so in that crucial moment before it becomes a thought we must maintain our awareness. So we need to have an awareness of our awareness, a natural remembrance that always brings us back, and without which we will be swept away.

What I am describing here is a process known as stillness, movement, and awareness *(né gyu rig sum)*, which takes on ever-greater depth as you progress through deeper levels of realization. As we develop further, allowing the risings to dissolve and liberate in the light of our awareness, they will only enhance and further the stillness, just as the waves and ripples make the ocean even more beautiful. Through the awareness of clear seeing and the wisdom realizing egolessness, we arrive at the nature of mind. As we progress, we will have profound insights into the nature of reality and into ourselves as well, as increasingly the duality of subject and object dissolves, and we arrive at the state of nonduality.

When we arrive there, we will have arrived at a state of profound peace. Nyoshul Khen Rinpoche used to speak about the natural great peace—*rangzhin shiwachenpo*—the profound peace of the nature of mind, the peace of madhyamaka, mahamudra, and *dzogpachenpo* (dzogchen). As Buddha said, "Nirvana is true peace." When you arrive at the peace of the nature of mind, you discover a vast expanse of great openness. It is like when the clouds drift apart and reveal an endless open sky; as the cloudlike thoughts and emotions dissolve through meditation practice, what is uncovered is the skylike nature of our mind.

Shining in this sky is the sun of our buddha nature—our bodhi-chitta, the heart of enlightenment. The sun brings with it two wonderful qualities: warmth and light. Its brilliant light is like wisdom, and its warmth like love and compassion. If you were to ask, "What is the mind of the Buddha?" it is just this: wisdom and compassion. And, as it is said in the teachings that we all have buddha nature, we all are buddhas-to-be. When we purify our mind, it becomes wisdom, and when we purify our heart, it becomes love and compassion. If you purify your thoughts, that pure intelligence, unobscured by ignorance, is wisdom. When your emotions are purified, they arise as compassion.

So through this practice, we can arrive at the profound purity of the nature of mind, that great peace that Buddha spoke of at the moment of his enlightenment over two and a half thousand years ago beneath the Bodhi tree in what is now known as Bodhgaya. The first words he uttered were "Profound peace, natural simplicity, uncompounded luminosity...." With these words, Dilgo Khyentse Rinpoche used to say, Buddha proclaimed the heart of his enlightenment, which is the state of dzogpachenpo, the great perfection.

That profound peace is what we seek to arrive at through practice. In fact, to "tame this mind of ours" is accomplished completely through realizing that peace. Look at how, when we are moved or inspired by love, we are utterly disarmed. In the same way, when we realize the nature of mind through this practice, it disarms and dissolves our ordinary thoughts and emotions. And a tremendous love and compassion shine through us, just like the sun with all its warmth.

As soon as we connect with the purity of our inherent nature, our buddha nature, what is revealed is our fundamental goodness—the good heart. Kindness, compassion, and love simply exude. And so you are not only in touch with yourself, but completely in touch with others also. You feel a sense of real oneness with them. There is no barrier standing any longer between you and them. Nor even between you and yourself. So often the barriers, and so the problems, are our own; we are at war with ourselves. Now, through this practice, as the grip of ego loosens and our tendency to grasp evaporates, so the conflict, the suffering, and the pain of fragmenting and fighting with ourselves dissolve. For the first time, a deep and fundamental forgiveness for ourselves becomes possible.

At the same time, expectation, fear, and anxiety melt away, and with them all those feelings—of being blocked and closed, of not being in touch with ourselves or others, of being estranged even from our own feelings—that disqualify us from being happy.

It's incredible what this wonderful practice can bring about, and when I hear these teachings of the Buddha, transmitted through the great masters, and when I feel their truth in my own heart, through the little practice that I know, I feel their tremendous blessing. What is extraordinary is that you can actually experience the truth of this teaching. It is not something based on mere belief or faith; it is something you can taste and realize for yourself.

What happens when you experience it? You feel the tremendous compassion and love of the buddhas, and you feel an overwhelming gratitude. And what you want, more than anything else in the world, is to share this, and help all beings everywhere be freed from suffering, and possess this ultimate happiness, this natural great peace, the peace of the buddha. So whenever you experience this kind of peace— even a little—in your meditation, pray from the depth of your heart, just as in the practice of bodhichitta in the Dzogchen Longchen Nyingtig preliminary:

Mesmerized by the sheer variety of perceptions,
Which are like the illusory reflections of the moon in water,
Beings wander endlessly astray in samsara's vicious cycle.
In order that they may find comfort and ease in the luminosity
    and all-pervading space of the true nature of their mind,
I generate the immeasurable love, compassion, joy, and equa-
    nimity of the awakened mind, the heart of bodhichitta.

What you wish is that all beings find peace and happiness, in the true nature of their mind. I feel that in the twenty-first century, what so many people are seeking is to find the truth of themselves. Everybody seems to be asking "Who am I?" yearning to realize their true selves, beyond the ego-self. Through this practice, you can come to experience your true nature, and when you experience it, your greatest desire is for others to find that kind of understanding. Because you know that as well as showing us who we really are, that understanding frees us from ourselves.

It's so important, I feel, that we have a practice like this. We all want peace. We all yearn to feel well, to be a good human being, to have a warm heart, and to be kind. But often we don't know how. There are too many things occupying our minds, and our hearts seem always blocked. We are not free, and amid all the confusion and suffering and pain, we can so easily lose hope and plunge into despair. Yet to hear the wisdom and compassion in these teachings, and to know they are beginning to open the eye of our wisdom and open our heart and mind to our true nature and the true nature of all, can fill us with joy, inspiration, and hope.

Through the practice, we might have a little experience of that peace of mind, but we cannot always remain in that state. We fall back into our ordinary ways and patterns of thinking, which have been waiting to return. Now is the time that we have to be more aware than ever, and remind ourselves constantly that this mind is like a crystal. It is so clear and so pure. Just as a crystal adopts the color of whatever surface you place it on, the mind will become just whatever we allow to occupy it. Mind itself is beyond choosing, beyond duality like good and bad. As Buddha said, "With our thoughts we make the world," and we are the makers of a world that we enjoy or we suffer in, a world of karmic phenomena fashioned by our thoughts and actions.

Yet when you have tasted a little bit of that peace, and gained that insight, you will want to make a pledge with yourself that you will not fall back again. In the Buddhist practice of confession, of acknowledging and healing harm and wrongdoing, there are *four powers*: the power of the presence, which means the presence of the buddhas; the power of regret, which is a feeling of regret about the wrong that we have committed; the power of resolution, which is to resolve that we will never commit it again; and the power of the method, which is the practice, whatever it may be, that we do to purify the harm.

In fact, in dzogchen practice we confess all harm into the dharmadhatu, the all-encompassing space of the nature of mind. We purify all our negative thoughts in the purity of our inherent nature, and all their darkness is purified in its light. As we confess, we resolve not to fall back into the darkness of negativity again, and we resolve to keep our heart and mind pure. Because now we realize more than ever that "We are what we think. All that we are rises with our thoughts. With our thoughts we make the world. Speak or act with an impure mind and trouble will follow...Speak or act with a pure mind and happiness will follow."

However, when through meditation you arrive at the state of goodness of the nature of the mind, whatever you speak is goodness, whatever you see is goodness, whatever you touch is goodness, because goodness is what you are. You are naturally pure, and it cannot but emerge in everything you do, think, and say. When I think of Jamyang Khyentse Chökyi Lodrö, Dudjom Rinpoche, Dilgo Khyentse Rinpoche, and all the great masters, I ask myself how could they always be as they are? How is it that whatever they do benefits beings? The answer is: Because they are always in the state of goodness. That is why they inspire us and fill us with hope. When ordinary people like us see His Holiness the Dalai Lama, it gives us hope in humanity, and to see that there is one such good human being inspires us, in the realization that we too could become a good human being like him. The great men and women practitioners embody that same kind of goodness. And whatever they do is beneficial, on account of the discipline of maintaining purity of mind. They are never corrupted, they are always pure, and they act out of, and remain steadfast, in that goodness.

Sometimes we do feel in touch with ourselves, with others, with the universe, and we really have an opportunity to experience deep, inner peace. Anyone who has had the good fortune to experience a little of this inner peace should resolve, there and then, to maintain it, not only for his or her own sake, but for the sake of the world. When you are in this state, what is extraordinary is that even though you may not do much, your very being can benefit others, even unintentionally, as long as you maintain that goodness and purity of mind and heart, in your motivation and your being. And if you wish to infuse your actions with a special power, you can invoke the blessing of all the buddhas and the masters. It is said that one of the qualities of the buddhas is that as soon as you invoke them, they are there. Sometimes you might think, "How could someone like me possibly merit any of the buddhas' time?" Buddha himself said: "Whoever thinks of me, I am in front of them." And Guru Padmasambhava promised: "I'm never far from those who have devotion to me, but I'm never far from those without devotion either." Such is the compassion of the buddhas.

Good or bad, seemingly, we can receive their blessing. Whatever we may be, it is only temporary; all our delusions are purifiable, because our fundamental nature is good. Clouds may obscure the sky, but all we need to do is go beyond the clouds to realize there is an infinite sky that is never touched by the clouds. The example that is often used in dzogchen is a mirror: Our true nature is like a mirror, it reflects all kind of things, but the beauty is that the reflections never ever dirty the mirror. So whatever we may appear to be, our real nature is pure and pristine. When it is said that we all have the buddha nature, in fact it is true. Even the buddhas, it is said, cannot make buddha nature better, and we sentient beings, with all our confusion and negativity, cannot make it worse. That means that nothing can touch it; it is unchanging; it is uncreated; it is really our true nature, something that can never be tainted or diminished. It is an unchanging goodness.

4. RELATIVE AND ULTIMATE BODHICHITTA

Ringu Tulku Rinpoche

Part 1: Relative Bodhichitta (Lojong Practice)

Bodhichitta

Lojong, which is usually translated as "mind training," is a practice primarily of the Mahayana tradition. It offers us a training in compassion and wisdom that is direct and experiential, and is therefore an excellent way to enhance our bodhichitta. Before talking about lojong, let's first look more closely at the nature of bodhichitta.

Bodhichitta is the key word of Mahayana Buddhism. If we understand bodhichitta, in one sense we understand everything; and if we don't understand bodhichitta, we don't know anything at all. Translated literally, *bodhichitta* means "enlightened heart." *Citta* means heart and mind, so it is not merely the thinking mind, it is much larger than that. *Citta* is the mind that experiences, and it includes all our thoughts, emotions, and feelings.

The Sanskrit *budh,* which means "to know," "to understand," or "to have insight," is the root from which the word *bodhi* is derived. *Bodhi* means enlightenment, so a buddha is someone who has attained bodhi. Therefore bodhichitta is "the heart of enlightenment," or rather "the heart *for* enlightenment," because this better expresses the element of aspiration.

The four limitless aspirations

At first we see bodhichitta as an aspiration for enlightenment. Bodhichitta begins as a fervent wish to be without problems, suffering, and pain, and to enjoy happiness, peace, and well-being. Ultimate happiness is happiness that endures, and that is exactly what we wish for ourselves. However, we don't want these good things for ourselves alone; we want our children, parents, and friends to share the same happiness. I know I wouldn't like it if all the people who are really dear to me were suffering while I, and I alone, had perfect happiness.

If we continue this line of thought, it is clear that everybody in existence has their own near and dear ones, and that all beings are in this way connected with each other. Consequently we wish that not only ourselves, but that all sentient beings could be free from any and every kind of suffering. We wish that everyone, all of the innumerable beings throughout space, not merely all human beings, might be free from difficulty and frustration.

We also wish for all sentient beings the highest kind of happiness, peace, and well-being. Whatever the best and most profound happiness is, that is what we wish them. And we don't want them to enjoy that happiness for only a short while; we want them to enjoy it for the rest of time.

These wishes are called *the four limitless aspirations,* and they are based on bodhichitta. The first is that our wish is extended to absolutely every being, since there is no limit to the number of sentient beings. Secondly, we wish that all sentient beings may be free, not just from gross suffering or from subtle problems, but from every conceivable kind of pain. The third wish is for them to attain the best kind of contentment possible. Fourthly, we wish this not just for a short time but for all time.

Compassion that is free from any limitation or reservation whatsoever is called bodhichitta. It is the complete opposite of small-mindedness. Bodhichitta is ultimate and absolute compassion, and it can be generated more genuinely if we develop both our compassion and our wisdom. *Compassion* is wishing for happiness and the absence of suffering for ourselves and wishing that we can bring these qualities to all others. We don't wish that only others might experience goodness; compassion benefits us as well.

Compassion for ourselves
People sometimes misunderstand the nature of compassion. Some people even come to me and say, "It's just too heavy to be compassionate

all the time. I have to be nice and always smile at everybody and let everybody do whatever they want with me. I have to be a doormat that everybody can walk over, and I'm not even allowed to get angry about it. I shouldn't ever feel any selfishness, desire any goodness for myself, or pursue any self-interest whatsoever. I should want goodness for everybody except myself. Maybe you can practice that kind of compassion, but for me it's just not possible."

According to my understanding, compassion for beginners means wishing goodness for ourselves as well as everybody else. It's not possible to have zero self-interest or to care nothing about our own needs. There is nothing wrong with caring for ourselves. However, looking after our interests and our interests alone, and caring for all sentient beings as well as ourselves are two very different things. Of course we should care for ourselves. If we don't, who will?

Not wanting others to experience suffering and wishing them happiness is grounded in our own experience of taking care of ourselves. We don't want suffering, we want happiness. If we didn't feel this, how could we possibly wish the same for others? If we don't care for ourselves, then as long as we remain in a samsaric state of mind, caring for others is almost impossible. We begin the practice of compassion by looking after ourselves. Just as we wish good things for ourselves, all other beings wish for exactly the same things, so, by extension, it is easy to wish everybody else happiness and freedom from suffering, too.

Of course we have a lot of negativity—many problems, faults, and weaknesses. The same is true for everyone. Everybody can be selfish, greedy, afraid, angry, and spiteful. This is reality and something we need to see and accept, because it is the basis of compassion. Everybody suffers from negativity, including ourselves, and that's why we wish everybody well. If everybody were already perfect, there would be no need. However, they all have problems, so we pray that they might be freed from them.

Understanding this makes things a lot clearer. Most of the problems we encounter in our daily lives—at work and in relationships—result from our expecting other people to be better than they actually are. We also set the same high standards for ourselves. This creates a lot of trouble because neither are we as good as we expect ourselves to be, nor is anybody else as good as we believe they should be. We get disappointed with ourselves and disappointed with everybody else, too.

If we realize that everybody has weaknesses, we no longer expect too much, and things become much easier. In fact, we will often be pleasantly surprised, because everybody can be nice sometimes, and that's much better than we expected. It's only if we assume everybody should be the embodiment of compassion, completely pleasant and generous, that we don't notice when somebody is good to us. So the secret of living in harmony with other people is to consider that they are all very bad!

In the same way, the secret to being satisfied with ourselves is to see how bad we are, because then we can work with ourselves. If we occasionally see a little bit of an improvement, it will make us happy. If we are normally lazy and we do some work, we can feel very good about it. On the other hand, if we see ourselves as a really good, hard-working person, even if we work really hard we are not impressed.

Attachment and aversion

Why we do we suffer? How did all our misery and problems come about? When we look into ourselves we slowly discover that what determines our suffering, and also our happiness, is the way we label and respond to our experiences. We might, for example, find something to be very good at one time but experience the same thing as very bad on a different occasion. How we feel about a situation is how *we* feel—at least for the moment—it's *our* experience.

All spiritual paths tell us that we have to deal with our way of experiencing the world. We are, of course, affected by external circumstances. Although we can change some of these circumstances, we can't change them all. We have a much better chance of success changing the way we experience things, however, so whenever we have the opportunity to transform something about the way we see things, we should take it. In lojong mind-training practices, as in Buddhism more generally, we examine our experiences and reactions. Usually we discover that our responses are not very compassionate.

Generally, we react according to what we experience through our five senses: sight, hearing, touch, taste, and smell. When we see or hear something beautiful, we experience it as truly pleasant, and our reaction is to want that beautiful thing. The moment we want something, we have created a problem, because we're not going to be happy until we have it, and we then have to do something in order to obtain it. Not having what we want causes us suffering. We are compelled to run after what we want and sometimes endure many hardships to attain our goal. And even if we succeed we are not entirely happy, because we're afraid of losing what belongs to us.

When we encounter something unpleasant, we don't want anything to do with it. Again, this causes us trouble because we have to find a way to get rid of this terrible thing. This takes time, but we make the effort because we're unhappy; we're suffering because we have something we don't want. Even if we manage to get rid of the problem, we are afraid that the unpleasantness might return, and other problems will arise in any case.

These two ways of reacting are called attachment and aversion. Both responses cause us a lot of problems, but this is, unfortunately, how we react. Therefore we need to transform the way in which we respond, for our own good. If we can learn to manage the way we react inside, we can create genuine happiness and put an end to our suffering.

Relative bodhichitta

Lojong provides us with two ways of finding happiness: relative bodhichitta and ultimate bodhichitta. Relative bodhichitta may be easier to explain, but it is not easier to accomplish. Although the teaching describes ultimate bodhichitta first, the main practice is contained within the method of relative bodhichitta, so we will focus on relative bodhichitta first. But to really practice it properly we will need to have at least some understanding of ultimate bodhichitta.

What is the root cause of attachment and aversion? Aversion comes from thinking that something is not good and therefore we should not have it. At the root of this aversion is fear. Fear also causes attachment—we think that if we don't hold onto what we're attached to something bad will happen to us. Fear comes in many guises: the fear of not getting something we want; the fear of losing something we possess; the fear of getting something unpleasant; the fear of not being able to get rid of something unpleasant or of the unpleasant thing returning. Fear is at the root of attachment and aversion.

The story of Gihoja

The only way to work with our fears is to face them. There is no other way, because the more we fear our fears, the stronger and more horrendous they become.

A Tibetan man was once traveling high up in the mountains where it is freezing cold and ice forms quickly. One night, he went to sleep on a high plateau in an area said to be haunted. In the middle of the night, he heard a thin, shrill voice, calling his name from far away: "Gi, Ho, Ja." He listened with all his concentration and heard the voice again: "Gi, Ho, Ja."

He was really frightened. How could anybody in this uninhabited, remote place call out his name? Who knew his name in the first place? He was a stranger in these parts. It had to be a ghost or demon. So he listened again. He heard the same thing and was terrified.

He leapt up, dressed, saddled his horse, and rode as fast as he could away from that evil place. After some time he stopped and listened, but still he heard the sound of his name: "Gi, Ho, Ja." Looking behind him, he saw a horde of people racing toward him in the darkness.

He rode on for a long time, as fast as possible, before daring to stop again. When he did, the unearthly voice seemed even closer, and his pursuers were still hot on his trail. He rode at full pelt the whole night. Finally, he reached his home and climbed, exhausted, into bed. But he could still hear the same sound: "Gi, Ho, Ja."

This time he concentrated very carefully on the sound, and he slowly realized that it had been coming out of his own nose. His nose was congested and the air was icy cold, so when he breathed, it made a really strange sound: "Gi, Ho, Ja." Then he looked behind him and saw that the fur inside his coat had frozen into some very odd shapes, which he had mistaken for people chasing him.

Tonglen

When we are frightened, everything that happens makes us more and more afraid. If we suffer from vertigo, we have to confront it by visiting high places. The same principle applies to fear: we have to face it. Lojong gives us a way of doing that. There are many preparatory practices, but the main practice for facing our fear is called *tonglen*.

Tonglen means "giving and taking"—taking what we don't want and giving away what we do want, which is the complete opposite of our normal behavior. Usually we are reluctant to accept what we don't like, and we don't want to let go of what we like. In tonglen practice, we ground our activity in compassion, giving away everything that is pleasant and taking on everything unpleasant.

This is not an intellectual exercise. When we work with ourselves, we have no choice but to work experientially. It is not enough merely to say that we should avoid attachment, aversion, fear, hatred, or anger, or that we should be very compassionate. A conceptual understanding is easier to understand, but it only works on a conceptual level. If we want to change our way of reacting, we are obliged to work experientially.

Therefore, as we breathe in, we visualize ourselves receiving the problems and negativity of every being. To do this we need courage, and we also need to understand the essence of ultimate bodhichitta, which I will explain below. We receive the negativity in the form of smoke. As we breathe in, the smoke enters our heart and confronts our ego, which is afraid of receiving negative things. The negativity eats away at our fear and aversion, and when all our fear is removed, wisdom emerges. The peaceful, enlightened state of our mind, that aspect of ourselves that is free from fear, is revealed in the form of bright light, as strong as sunlight. In the face of such a powerful light, the darkness and negativity we have breathed in vanishes. Even a cave that has been sealed off from sunlight for thousands of years will be flooded with light when we turn on a lamp—light and darkness cannot coexist.

Our fearlessness, which is ultimate bodhichitta, is revealed after negativity has been removed. The rays of light that stream from the sun of bodhichitta are suffused with peace, happiness, joy, and a genuine sense of well-being. As we breathe out, we give all this freely to all sentient beings. We visualize that the light rays touch and transform all beings, who benefit in exactly the same way we do.

We repeat this practice over and over, but we don't necessarily need to do it every time we breathe during the practice. When we are not afraid to receive negativity, we are rid of our own fear, and when we are not afraid to give away everything positive to others, we are freed from the fear of loss. As we continue to work on our attachment and aversion, our compassion and wisdom grow, and we wish for the same beneficial changes to take place in everybody. We send out healing light, not to just one or two people, but to all sentient beings. The greater the expanse into which we send our love, the stronger it becomes.

QUESTION: *How often should we practice tonglen? Should we only do it when we feel strong?*
RINPOCHE: We should practice tonglen when we feel good about doing it, but it depends on how we understand the practice. If we are feeling afraid, we can't do the practice well. This practice works with our fear, however, so feeling a little fear is natural.

QUESTION: *Could I do this practice if I am ill?*
RINPOCHE: Perhaps I shouldn't say this, but tonglen is said to be very good for improving our own health. Lojong was brought to Tibet by Atisha and became widely studied and practiced there through the efforts of Geshe Chekawa.

At first Geshe Chekawa taught tonglen to only a few, because he felt that the practice might be too exacting. In the region where Geshe Chekawa lived was a large encampment of lepers, and he resolved to help the lepers by teaching them tonglen. The lepers practiced diligently, and many of them were completely cured. Geshe Chekawa became renowned as a teacher of lepers.

Geshe Chekawa used to teach in a tent. One day, the geshe's brother hid behind his tent and listened to the teachings in secret. His brother had always been a hard, angry person. Seeing his brother slowly become a better human being, Geshe Chekawa wanted to discover the reason behind his transformation. It was when he found out that his brother always listened to the teachings without anyone knowing that Geshe Chekawa realized people could practice tonglen on their own and heal themselves. As a result, he began to teach tonglen more widely, and to healthy people as well.

We shouldn't practice tonglen purely for our own benefit, but it is said to have a very good effect on our health.

QUESTION: *When we have a health problem, can we integrate it in our tonglen practice?*
RINPOCHE: The main thing we work with in tonglen practice is fear. Someone suffering from a particular illness can consider that they are taking on that illness from everyone who has contracted it so that nobody suffers from it any more. If we have the flu, we take everybody's flu onto ourselves and thereby extinguish it. When the flu is purified, we send the "flulessness" out to others.

QUESTION: *How can I practice tonglen in daily life? I am a taxi driver and meet many people and much suffering. It's too difficult to visualize when I'm driving, so I just try to be open, to take on the negativity, and to be the other person.*
RINPOCHE: We purify things through prayer, by wishing for all the suffering of sentient beings to be replaced with positivity. As we breathe in, we take in the negativity and give back healing and peace. We can accept the help of Avalokiteshvara, the buddha of compassion, by visualizing him in our heart. Light radiates out to the other people, and all their negativity is pacified. This is a very good way of responding to somebody's suffering. The emphasis is more on reacting and wishing the other person well rather than the visualization. There is no need to spend a long time establishing the visualization. Just feel Avalokiteshvara's presence while driving. It doesn't take a long time to get angry driving a taxi, but you don't need much time to generate compassion either. This, essentially, is how you can practice tonglen in daily life.

Part II: Ultimate Bodhichitta

The Buddhist view is that most of the problems in our psyche originate with our inability to let things come and go. Tonglen helps us work with these emotions. Most importantly it gives us confidence in dealing with emotions. We no longer believe that sadness, fear, or anger are so terrible, or that negative emotions should be avoided at all costs. Thinking that unpleasant emotions should be avoided does not make them disappear. Trying to push our negativity under the carpet does not help because it is still there; we only pretend it doesn't exist. In such circumstances, one tiny incident can drive us berserk. This is not the way to work with emotions.

We need to practice with every rising in our mind. Our consciousness is like the sun, and the sun's rays are everything that rises in our consciousness. Because we have such a clear and bright awareness, it's natural for all kinds of things to manifest. We can't expect, or accept, only the pleasant manifestations, or reject all unpleasant experiences. As the sun is here, its rays must also be present. We can't stop the rays or say that we only want the sun without any heat.

Whether a thought is a problem for us depends on how we react to it. If a negative emotion arises and we follow it, we fall into a trap. The emotion takes on an overwhelming power, and we suffer as a result. If, rather than follow the rising, we let go of it, then there is no problem. If we allow water to flow, it becomes a river, continually moving; it irrigates and allows things to grow. If we stop the river, we create a flood. At some point we have to release the water because we can't hold it back forever.

The flow, or the risings in our mind, is not the problem. The way we react to the rising is the problem. Therefore we need to realize that thoughts come and go, moment by moment. This is a very important point. We usually think that the emotion we are feeling is one continual event.

To think that we are angry and that we have had this anger inside us for a long time is a mistake. It's just our own action, repeated over and over. Everything is momentary. It's rather like somebody shocking me by saying, "You are a scoundrel," and then he says it again, and I'm shocked and angry all over again. Our reactions are not one enduring event; that is merely how we perceive them.

When we work with our emotions, it is easier to work in short periods of time because everything rises moment by moment. In this moment, whatever is happening, look at the mind, see a thought emerging, and let it go. In the next moment some other feeling or emotion arises, and we let go of that too. This is a truly profound method of working with ourselves.

In tonglen practice, we let go of whatever we wish to keep and accept whatever we wish to resist. In a way, it is a very simple practice, but it is also really quite difficult. Just like two rams running headlong into each other, colliding and locking horns, we are rushing headlong into confrontation with our ego. What ego doesn't want, we want to accept; what it wants, we want to give away. In this respect tonglen practice is not very easy at all.

People are sometimes frightened of this practice because they think that if they receive all these terrible things, terrible things will happen to them. It might therefore be easier to begin by focusing the practice on ourselves. We can, for example, divide ourselves into two aspects. As we breathe in, one part receives all the problems of our past, present, and future, and as we breathe out, it sends back positive things to the aspect that was holding those problems.

Wisdom and ignorance

The deepest way of working with our fears, however, is to work with ultimate bodhichitta. Relative bodhichitta is compassion, and ultimate bodhichitta is wisdom. What is wisdom? Wisdom is not information; it is direct perception, seeing things as they really are, without any distortion. Wisdom is experiencing ourselves in a natural way, without the interference of any conditioning, neurosis, or pattern whatsoever.

From a Buddhist point of view, what causes our attachment, aversion, and fear is the opposite of wisdom—ignorance. Ignorance is failing to see things directly and perceiving them in a distorted way. It is seeing ourselves in a distorted way too, which means that we don't really know who we are. This is why we cannot be wise, why we experience attachment, aversion, and fear, and why we remain in samsara.

Let's look more closely at this distortion. What is it that we label "I" or "me"? We may point to our body and say, "This is me." But is this body really "me"? And is "me" just one entity?

The body is formed from many parts, and each part consists of thousands of millions of cells, which are all in a state of constant change. Once I went to the doctor to have my blood checked. He took a tiny drop of blood, put it on a glass slide, and looked at it through a microscope. The magnified image of the blood was visible on a screen. It looked like outer space—things moving here and there, some with halos, some like planets, and one absolutely huge microorganism. There was a whole universe in that single drop of blood. While we tend to think of our body as one entity, it is actually a multiplicity of things. We also tend to say, "my body," or "my hand," as if my hand were somehow me. If I amputate my hand, then it can't be "me" anymore. Therefore, my body is not me.

What about my mind? Am I my mind? What is my mind? If we look for our mind inside or outside our bodies, we won't find anything. Of course we are conscious, but consciousness changes all the time—one moment we say something, and next we think something, then we perceive something, and then we are aware of our perceptions.

There is no independent consciousness; consciousness is interdependent. There are six types of consciousness: those of the eye, ear, nose, tongue, body, and mind. To have a visual consciousness, we need eyes. If we had no eyes or if there were no object to see, we couldn't see. Consciousness is formed out of many things; it is not independent or unchanging. Emotions likewise come and go continuously; they too are not single or ever-present.

If we look deeply, we find that we are very complex. We are made up of a huge number of interdependent parts, which Buddhism classifies within the *five aggregates*. There is no single, complete, and independent self that I can point to and call "me." Failing to understand this fact is the nature of our distortion.

We tend to see that which we label "me" as independently, rather than interdependently, present. If something is independent, it must be separate from everything else; it can't be formed out of many things being brought together. It must be singular. If we see the self like this, we believe in the reality of "I" and that "I" am here somewhere, even if we can't say for certain where. We point to our head, our hands, our thoughts, our emotions as separate elements, yet we still feel that the self is present.

Sometimes people say that because they feel, there must be an "I" that feels, and because they can see, there must be a see-er. From the Buddhist point of view, this is merely an assumption, because we can't locate the one that thinks or sees. This assumed identity, the thinker, is what we call the ego, and it is the cause of all our problems. If we believe that we exist as an independent entity, then it follows that everything else is "other." Everything that is "other" is either something for us or against us, good for us or bad for us. If it is good for us, we must have it, and we feel attachment. If it is not good for us, we feel aversion. We confront everything, except the self, in one of these two ways. The natural result of attachment and aversion is conflict and suffering. As long as we see ourselves as independent entities, we have no other way of reacting.

When we examine ourselves closely, we find no single independent self. We are interdependent, changing, moving, and fluctuating. The self is a continuum, more or less like a flowing river. We might see a river and think that it has been there for thousands of years, but the water was flowing the moment that we came across the river, and in the next moment that same water is no longer there. We think of this as a river because it is a continuum.

We are also a continuum. If we see ourselves like that, we don't need security or something to hold onto. The river flows; it doesn't hold onto its banks, and it couldn't even if it tried. The more we try to hold onto the banks, the more problems we have. Like the river, we can't do it. This is our dilemma: we are like a river, but we don't want to change, or flow; we want to hold onto things and not let them go. But the river flows without anything going wrong. In the same way, if we let ourselves flow, we won't have any problems either.

Not understanding the way we are and believing there is something we must secure and something we must fear, then everything becomes a threat to us. Thinking that some things should not be here and that others should be gives rise to suffering. Therefore, understanding ourselves as we actually are is of utmost importance if we want to be free of fear. What is there to be afraid of?

Seeing and experiencing our true nature clearly and deeply is what we call freedom. There is nothing to secure, fear, or protect, and therefore there is no enemy. Fear comes from believing that something must be prevented or something must be destroyed. There is nothing to be destroyed, which is why Milarepa said:

> In horror of death, I took to the mountains.
> Again and again I meditated on the uncertainty of the hour
>   of death.
> Capturing the fortress of the deathless unending nature
>   of mind,
> Now all fear of death is over and done.

If we know that everything is always changing, then even death is not so frightening.

Therefore, if we can clearly understand ourselves to be as we actually are—as interdependent, as cause and effect—we will not see ourselves as separate from the nature of things; there is seeing, but no one separate from the seeing who sees. When we see exactly what we are, we don't have to react in our habitual ways. Nothing in us can be destroyed, and this frees us from fear. As we no longer respond with attachment or aversion, we are enlightened.

Enlightenment is a realization, and freeing ourselves from suffering is a realization. It is not something that we obtain, or something that we never had before; it's just that we see clearly how things really are. Nothing, other than the way we perceive, has to change. This is what wisdom is, and this is why Buddhism considers wisdom so important and emphasizes the need to realize the nature of mind: it frees us of our suffering. When we see—directly, experientially—that there is nothing to fear, we are liberated.

While essential, a full understanding of the nature of mind is very difficult to attain. It requires us to work with ourselves, to see things in a way that we are not used to. Driven by fear and habit, it is very difficult to rid ourselves of that assumption that everything is separate from us. However, even a little bit of understanding of our true nature helps us apply the lojong teachings.

Since there is nothing to fear, we can receive everything, and there is no problem with sending out goodness either. Each one of us is limitless because there is nothing to be destroyed. We will never become nothing because there is nobody to become nothing. It's not that we don't exist; we do exist, but we exist in a way that is different from the way in which we think we exist. If things existed independently of one another, there would be a beginning and an end. Because there is no one independent entity, there is no beginning, no end, and nothing to fear.

Seeing the truth of this is the realization of ultimate bodhichitta. When even a small amount of ultimate bodhichitta arises in us, relative bodhichitta arises in us naturally. If we have no agenda of our own to pursue, the only thing left to do is to care for others, and this gives rise to genuine, completely unselfish compassion.

Until that time arrives, our compassion will always be a little bit selfish, but that is quite acceptable. We are ourselves, and the way we are geared, patterned, and conditioned is selfish. Our selfishness prevents us from being free, but if we start by deciding to be supremely beneficial for ourselves by attaining complete freedom from fear, we will then be able to benefit others as well.

QUESTION: *How can we bring things we have understood intellectually from our minds into our hearts?*
RINPOCHE: Because of the way terms are translated, people can sometimes misunderstand what is meant. A scholar might say that Western people believe that mind resides in the head, whereas Eastern people think that mind is located at the heart, but this is not true. The Tibetan word *sem* and the Sanskrit word *chitta* do mean "thoughts," but they also mean "emotions, feelings, and everything that you know." *Sem* means "the totality of our consciousness."

When a scholar seeks a translation of *sem* or *chitta* by asking somebody or by looking in a dictionary, the answer he or she will usually get is "mind." The problem is that in the West, the word "mind" does not always mean only thoughts and thinking. Similarly, Eastern people also consider that we are thinking with the heart as well as with the head, but they do not see the heart as the totality of mind.

Somebody once said that the longest journey is the one from the head to the heart, and it is true. It is difficult to bring the understandings of the mind to the heart. Bodhichitta has to do with experience, with the heart, but the first step is for us to understand this intellectually with the head because it is easier to understand intellectually. However, we can't say that intellectual understanding is not experiential at all. It is an experience, it's just not deep experience. All of us are capable of understanding something intellectually and of then reacting in a way that contradicts our understanding.

To deepen our experience, we need to practice. Practice means repeating something, or reminding ourselves of something over and over, which is why practice is sometimes known as *mindfulness and awareness*. This is the only tool we have for bringing the understanding of the head to the heart. We repeat and remind ourselves again and again. The understanding slowly becomes more and more familiar, and then the familiarity becomes habitual. Finally, if it is the correct understanding, it becomes natural. Even an incorrect understanding can become habitual, but only a correct understanding can become natural.

QUESTION: *Whenever we speak about selflessness in connection with the five skandhas, I grasp at* alayavijñana, *the "store consciousness," and think if there is an "I," it must be alayavijñana. Why is alayavijñana not the self?*

RINPOCHE: Alayavijñana is a continuum. What I am in this moment creates what I am in the next moment. There is no one thing that is there all the time. We can use many different names to describe this continuum, but if we analyze or examine it, we fail to find anything. Even this moment is causing the next, but there is no single thing here. Nothing goes from here to there; it's merely that this moment creates the next moment. Therefore whatever you call it, it's not like the thread in a mala—there is no thread. One moment produces something else. The *Abhidharmakosha* gives these five examples:

If I recite *Om mani padme hum hrih* and someone learns from that how to recite it, how did the mantra go from my mind to theirs?

When I look into a mirror, my face is in it. How did it get there? If my face were not there, there could be no reflection.

If I light one candle from another, is this second flame the same as the first flame? And if I light more candles, is the last flame the same as the first, or is it another flame?

If I press a seal into some sealing wax, the imprint of the seal is different from the seal, but the seal and the imprint are interdependent.

Milk is not yogurt and yogurt is not milk, though there can be no yogurt without milk. How does milk turn into yogurt?

These five examples illustrate that when changes take place in our consciousness, when, for instance, we take rebirth, nothing goes from here to there. The same is true of changes taking place moment by moment: it is a continuum—cause and effect.

If I become enlightened and see myself completely clearly, my wisdom is very sharp. When we say that our samsaric state of mind reacts with attachment and aversion, and that there are, in reality, no concepts, no dualistic view, and no attachment or aversion in the enlightened mind, this can be misunderstood. We might think that no concept means we have no thoughts, or that no duality means that we can't distinguish between ourselves and other people. We might think that no attachment and aversion means that we have no feelings, that we're like vegetables. This is completely incorrect. Wisdom is an experience of complete naturalness within the process of changing and being. There is nothing to hold onto or reject, so it's complete and natural clarity. Vajrayana calls this *clear light* or *luminosity*.

The complete clarity of the wisdom state is said to be a hundred thousand times clearer than what we experience right now, because there is a complete absence of confusion. We see everything from all angles, so there is no need for attachment or aversion. Because of its complete clarity, awareness, and vibrancy, the experience of wisdom is sometimes called the *diamond mind*. It is neither dull nor lacking in feeling.

From the experiential point of view, the nature of the wisdom mind is changeless. *Alaya* is changeless nature, the primordial state of pristine wisdom. In terms of our experience, there is no change, there is nothing. From an analytical approach, we can't find anything either. Because there is nothing, this experience is a little difficult to conceptualize. If you conceptualize it, then it becomes another concept just like the self, or like proudly saying, "This is my buddha nature, this is my alaya," or, "My alaya is bigger than his." If this were our experience, our way of reacting would be the same as it was before because we would not be able to keep our alaya intact.

The Master in Vajrayana

The best spiritual friend is the one
who attacks your hidden faults.
Atisha[3]

Probably no single theme is discussed more often and more
intensively among all the lineages of Buddhist practice in the
West than the need for a teacher on the spiritual path. Dilgo
Khyentse Rinpoche expressed himself very clearly on this
subject: "No single buddha of the past, present, or future
attained or will attain enlightenment without relying on a
spiritual teacher. Whichever of the nine vehicles of Buddhist
teachings one practices, one has to rely on a spiritual teacher,
take his or her teachings, and practice according to his or her
instructions. There is no other way."[4] Dzongsar Khyentse
Rinpoche expresses it in drastic terms: "The outer guru is
necessary in order to awaken your wisdom mind, to manip-
ulate your ego—and to crush it." And Francesca Fremantle
even compares a realized teacher to a live electric cable: dan-
gerous to all who venture too close, especially the ego.

Gampopa, the great master of the Kagyü lineage of
Tibetan Buddhism, explains that we need a master, or "spir-
itual friend," because, although we carry within us the qual-
ities needed to realize wisdom, we do not know how to
dissolve the "veil of negative emotions and our primitive
ideas of reality." He gives three similes for what a teacher
represents: "The spiritual friend is like a leader or pathfinder
in unknown lands, a companion in dangerous regions, and a

ferryman for crossing great rivers."⁵ The contemporary Buddhist scholar Alexander Berzin comments on this in the following way: "As a navigator, the spiritual teacher gives correct information for the student to be able to find his way on the path. As a companion he stays close by him on the journey so that he doesn't get lost. As the steering ferryman he contributes energy that drives the student to reach his destination."⁶ Berzin emphasizes that this relationship with the spiritual friend is indispensible in the Mahayana and the Vajrayana and therefore recommends modern students in particular, with their "do-it-yourself mentality," to gain deeper understanding of this subject.

Because of the key position the master holds, critical understanding must be employed from the earliest steps on the path. In the first instance, the teacher must be examined in the light of the four reliances taught by the Buddha:

> *Rely on the message of the teacher, not on his personality;*
> *Rely on the meaning, not just on the words;*
> *Rely on the real meaning, not on the provisional one;*
> *Rely on your wisdom mind, not on your ordinary, judgmental mind.⁷*

The next step is, among other things, to check the motivation of the teacher and to see if it is really based on compassion. Sogyal Rinpoche says:

> *One of my teachers, Nyoshul Khen Rinpoche, told me someone once asked him, "What are the qualities needed to be a Dharma teacher?" He replied: "To have a pure motivation." The prime concern of Tibetan masters will always be that (1) the source of the transmission is pure, and (2) the motivation to teach is pure—the bodhisattva ideal. The key qualities in a Dharma practitioner which I know a teacher will always look for, with an eye on the continuity of the*

lineage, are that he or she is a good human being: reli-
able, genuine, with their basic character and being
tamed by the Dharma teaching itself, and with their
motivation being one of bodhicitta.[8]

These crucial points are echoed in several other teachings in
this collection.

The function of the teacher or master in Tibetan Buddhism is multilayered. Four kinds or levels of teacher are
described. In the first instance there are the teachings themselves, the Dhama, the word of the Buddha and of other realized beings. Second, the human person of the teacher is also
looked on as a master. Third is the master in the form of a
universal principle—life itself can teach us and can be a manifestation of the master. Finally, the true master is our own
ultimate nature, our pure innermost awareness. The Buddha
is not outside of us but is in fact the nature of our mind.

Difficulties arise when we think we can begin straight
away at the ultimate level. Sogyal Rinpoche pointed to this
when he wrote:

> Recognizing who is and who is not a true master is a
> very subtle and demanding business; and in an age like
> ours, addicted to entertainment, easy answers, and
> quick fixes, the more sober and untheatrical attributes
> of spiritual mastery might very well go unnoticed. Our
> ideas about what holiness is, that it is pious, bland,
> and meek, may make us blind to the dynamic and
> sometimes exuberantly playful manifestation of the
> enlightened mind. As Patrul Rinpoche wrote: "The
> extraordinary qualities of great beings who hide their
> nature escapes ordinary people like us, despite our best
> efforts in examining them. On the other hand, even
> ordinary charlatans are expert at deceiving others by
> behaving like saints." If Patrul Rinpoche could write
> that in the nineteenth century in Tibet, how much

more true must it be in the chaos of our contemporary spiritual supermarket?[9]

This chapter does not cover the entirety of Vajrayana Buddhism; rather, it is concerned with the significance of the master on this path. The Vajrayana works to transform our energies and our perception. The figure of the spiritual master helps us to achieve this transformation of perception into pure vision, or the pure perception of an enlightened being. The master is looked upon as the embodiment of enlightened qualities, and we practice with him or her and strengthen our purer way of seeing until we can also perceive this original purity in other beings. In the practice of guru yoga, simple human emotions are used and transformed in a union of our mind with the wisdom mind of the master. Ultimately, we reach a stage of practice where dualities such as higher and lower, practitioner and nonpractitioner, are dissolved.

5. THE GURU PRINCIPLE

Sogyal Rinpoche

WHEN WE TALK ABOUT THE LAMA, the master, or the guru principle, it is important to remember that the guru is not merely a person. The guru represents the inspiration of truth; he embodies the crystallization of the blessing, compassion, and wisdom of all buddhas and all masters.

As my master Jamyang Khyentse Chökyi Lodrö used to explain, our true nature is buddha, yet from beginningless time it has been obscured by a cloud of ignorance and confusion. But despite this obscuration, our buddha nature, or the truth within, has never surrendered to ignorance, and rebels against its confusion. This is our inner teacher or guru, the active aspect of our buddha nature, which from the very moment when we became confused has been working for us to bring us back to our true nature. It has never given up on us; in its infinite compassion, it has been tirelessly working for our evolution, not only in this life, but in all our past lives, using all kinds of means and situations to teach us and guide us back to the truth. Even from an ordinary point of view, we realize that life is always teaching us. And though it may be a teaching that we often do want, we cannot run away from this truth, for life continues to teach us. This is the universality of the guru.

As a result of our past aspirations and prayers, and our purified karma, this inner teacher actually begins to manifest more clearly and take shape in the form of the *outer teacher,* whom we actually encounter. In fact, the outer teacher is none other than the spokesman of our inner teacher. He teaches us how to receive the message of our inner teacher, and how to realize the ultimate teacher within, restoring a belief and confidence in ourselves and thereby freeing us from the suffering that comes from not knowing our true nature.

The outer teacher is a messenger, the inner teacher the truth. If someone wants to reach you on the telephone, for example, they call your number. In the very same way, the buddhas call you through your buddha nature, your inner teacher. He is the direct line, but until you know how to listen and hear, it is your outer teacher who answers the phone. They work through him, to you. It is important not to lose the sense of this connection between the inner and outer teacher. The outer teacher is teaching you how to find yourself, how to find the buddha in you. He is introducing you to yourself, and until you find the buddha within, he is that substitute.

In the dzogchen teachings Padmasambhava embodies this universal principle. He is regarded as the incarnation of the buddhas of the past, the representative of the buddhas of the present, and the source from whom all the future buddhas will come. He is the timeless guru, within whose being all masters are embodied. Many of the great masters of the Tibetan tradition have drawn inspiration from him and are his emanations, like the rays flowing from the sun. So if you connect with any one of them, they will eventually lead to him. His human connection with you is your teacher. It is through your teacher that you can recognize Padmasambhava.

For whatever you consider Padmasambhava to be, or whatever you consider your master to be, is what dzogchen is. That absolute state of dzogpachenpo is the wisdom mind of your teacher. So you do not regard him as an ordinary human being. What he embodies is the truth or wisdom that he touches and inspires in you. So for you he comes to embody the wisdom mind, so much so that just to think of him crystallizes all the teaching and practice into an essential flavor. The master is not separate from the teaching; in fact, he is the energy, truth, and compassion of the Dharma. He is the embodiment of dzogpachenpo, so whenever you think of your master or Padmasambhava, it invokes this blessing into your presence. This is the principal source of inspiration for dzogchen practice.

As Kalu Rinpoche said in his last public teaching:

What we call the buddha, or the lama, is not material in the same way as iron, crystal, gold, or silver. You should never think of them with this sort of materialistic attitude. The essence of the lama or buddha is emptiness; their nature, clarity; their appearance, the play of unimpeded awareness. Apart from that, they have no real material form, shape, or color whatsoever—like the empty luminosity of space. When we know them to be like that, we can develop faith, merge our minds with theirs, and let our minds rest peacefully. This attitude and practice are most important.[10]

We need to humanize the truth in order to make it accessible to us. Without that, how could we possibly understand the absolute? For us, the guru is the human face of the truth. As Dilgo Khyentse Rinpoche says, "there is no buddha who became enlightened without having relied upon a spiritual teacher." You cannot realize the absolute within the domain of the ordinary mind. And the path beyond the mind is through the heart and through devotion. As Buddha told Shariputra, it is through devotion, and devotion alone, that one realizes the absolute. Nyoshul Khen Rinpoche points out:

According to dzogchen, and the special approach of the great dzogchen master Shri Singha, there is a way of recognizing the nature of mind solely through devotion. There are cases of practitioners who simply through their heartfelt devotion attained realization, even though their teacher had already passed away or was nowhere near them physically. Because of their prayers and devotion, the nature of mind was introduced. The most famous example is that of Longchenpa and Jigme Lingpa.[11]

Dzogchen cannot be realized merely with the intellect or the thinking of the ordinary mind, but only through purity of the heart. For dzogchen is beyond mind; it is the wisdom of rigpa, which can only be transmitted via a closeness of the heart between master and disciple. Devotion is naturally inspired when a teacher is able to open your innermost heart and offer you a glimpse of the nature of your mind. From this comes a tremendous joy, appreciation, and gratitude to the one who has helped you see, and to the truth that he embodies.

That heartfelt, uncontrived, genuine feeling is true devotion. True devotion is not some kind of adoration or worship on a mundane or conventional level, but simply the natural ability to invoke the warmth and blessing of the truth in times of need, through a genuine and pure devotion. It comes from having seen the view, and from this also comes tremendous compassion. As Nyoshul Khen Rinpoche explains: "Once you realize the true meaning of emptiness or dzogpachenpo, effortless compassion arises for all beings who have not realized it; if crying could express that compassion, you could cry without end." These three—the view, devotion, and compassion—are indivisible, one flavor: the taste of Dharma.

6. SAINTS OR SCOUNDRELS?

Francesca Fremantle

"*What criteria can we use to assess whether or not a master is genuine?...True teachers are kind, compassionate, and tireless in their desire to share whatever wisdom they have aquired from their masters, never abuse or manipulate their students under any circumstances, never under any circumstances abandon them, serve not their own ends but the greatness of the teachings, and always remain humble. Real trust can and should only grow toward someone who you come to know, over time, embodies all these qualities*"[12]

The bases on which teachers are judged in the Mahayana are unequivocal. In the Vajrayana the same principles hold as far as motivation and experience are concerned, but it is much harder to assess the master on the evidence of his outer behavior because of the variety of means he may use in that path. Provocative methods may be necessary to jolt us out of deep-set habits, and from the outside the master may appear to have little concern for the student at all. Francesca Fremantle discusses here some of the aspects of the complex Vajrayana path that can be incomprehensible to those looking on from the outside and lead to misunderstanding.

THERE HAS BEEN A LOT OF CONCERN and a continuing discussion in some quarters about the ethics and behavior of Buddhist teachers in the West. Some of this concern relates to certain Tibetan lamas so, without going into details of individual cases, I would like to express some thoughts about the function of the teacher in Vajrayana.

All forms of Buddhism contain multiple models of the student-teacher relationship, depending on the personalities and expectations involved. Sometimes the teacher appears as a father or mother figure, sometimes as a demanding leader, and sometimes on a more egalitarian level as a spiritual friend and guide. One frequent analogy is that of a doctor, and the Buddha himself was known as the great physician. But in tantra, whether Buddhist or Hindu, the teacher is perceived in a rather different way, and I prefer to use the Sanskrit word *guru* in this context.

The essence of tantric practice is the transmutation of energy. Through it, the negative emotions of samsara, arising from greed, hatred, and ignorance, are transformed into the positive qualities of the awakened state. In Vajrayana or tantric Buddhism, "the Diamond Vehicle," there is a realization of not only the wisdom and compassion of enlightenment but also its power. *Vajra* means "the diamond-like, brilliant, indestructible nature of ultimate being." The tantric guru is regarded as someone who is in direct contact with the immense power of the awakened state, and who is able to transmit this in a meeting of minds when the disciple is open enough to receive it.

All kinds of extraordinary things happen around an accomplished guru. He or she is like a live electric cable, dangerous to approach too closely. Both the external world and one's inner state can be affected in strange ways, and one begins to look at the world from a different perspective. A genuine tantric guru has great power, and so, if it is not firmly based on a realization of emptiness and motivated by compassion, such power could be wrongly used. There is no doubt that this occasionally happens, and there have always been scoundrels who masqueraded as saints, as well as saints who, for their own reasons, pretended to be scoundrels.

Much of the recent criticism leveled against masters in the West, however, seems to stem from a lack of knowledge of tantra and its methods. Situations in the relationship between guru and disciple sometimes may look like abuses of power from the outside but are really quite the opposite.

Vajrayana teaches that we can attain liberation in this very life. Of course, this is only a possibility, not a promise! From the ego's perspective, it is actually more of a threat. If we really think about the implications, surely very few of us would be willing to submit to what is necessary. All the same, even though few practitioners contemplate such a goal, this is the inspiration behind tantric attitudes and practices.

Liberation means the complete letting-go of self, the overturning of all our ordinary habits of thinking and feeling. How can this come about without a drastic upheaval, an inner revolution? Such a process demands total commitment, as well as the good fortune, through previous preparation, of meeting someone capable of doing whatever is required to help us. The guru may have to use all kinds of means to expose our hidden weaknesses, hesitations, and resistances, and enable us to overcome these obstacles. As a Tibetan text says of the archetypal guru, Padmasambhava, "He subdues what needs to be subdued, he destroys what needs to be destroyed, and he cares for whatever needs his care."

Devotion to the guru is very important because only a student who feels genuine trust and confidence will be able to remain open and responsive under all circumstances, without at some point giving in to the instinct for self-protection. At the beginning, a questioning, critical mind is very necessary; doubt and even cynicism are regarded as promising starting points. Repeated warnings about the dangers are always given, and would-be students are told that it is better not to set foot on the path of tantra than to give up later on. But although we hear these warnings, we somehow manage to persuade ourselves that it will never happen to us. It seems impossible that I, my precious self, might be made to feel rejected, manipulated, or insulted!

If this happens, then even though we have previously made a decision to trust the guru no matter what, we somehow feel quite justified in changing our minds. Or we may wonder: "Did he do that for my benefit or his?" Then another ego trap lies in wait; we think: "Even if he hurts me I can take it, because he's doing it all for me; it shows he is really interested in me." Ego is reinforced, and even more drastic shock-treatment may be necessary. Eventually, if we are to continue working with the guru, we realize that the only way is to give up our attitude of criticizing and judging altogether, and simply accept whatever happens as a teaching.

This may look like blind faith, but nothing could be further away from it. Blind faith and blind obedience have absolutely no place in tantra. They are indeed nothing but forms of spiritual blindness that prevent us from seeing clearly. To reach the clarity of vision that lies beyond self, we have to give up one of ego's firmest footholds, our sense of self-righteousness. The student really should have no concern with the guru's actions, but only with his or her own state of mind. At that point the guru's motive is no longer relevant. We realize that the whole universe is our teacher; whatever occurs, good or bad, right or wrong, becomes inspiration for our practice.

I do not want to give the impression that the tantric path consists of nothing but hardship. The overwhelming experience is of joy and wonder at the sacred world revealed by the practice. All the Vajrayana teachers I have met show extraordinary kindness, understanding, and compassion. Provocative methods may be useful at certain times, but they are not appropriate for everyone; some people only develop through gentleness and encouragement.

It is said that the love between guru and disciple is greater than in any other human relationship. The openness and intimacy that take place in this relationship can, of course, provide another kind of opportunity for misunderstanding and abuse. But even the most experienced teacher cannot always predict a student's reaction. If a student does become disillusioned, for whatever reason, and blames the guru, then we should take into account the experience of fellow students; if they have no complaints and are making progress, it is very unlikely that there has really been an abuse of power. Only those who are close to the guru really have the chance to observe the depth of his or her compassion and insight; it cannot be judged by others.

Good teachers are always learning from experience and from their students. At the same time they have their own development to complete and their own problems to deal with. They may be following a path that is beyond the understanding of their students, let alone the outside world. The tantric ideal is to welcome whatever occurs and to enter fully into all kinds of experience with an inner attitude of nonattachment and equanimity. There is even a practice, which has a very long history in India and also exists in certain Western traditions, of deliberately attracting disgrace and blame to oneself. This is why genuine tantric gurus who are criticized will never reply or justify their actions. Whether deserved or undeserved, praise and blame are equal when their essential emptiness has been realized.

The tantric teachings contain a vast range of methods suitable for various personalities and ways of life, and gurus have many different styles of teaching. They may all inwardly have transcended worldly concerns and values and be totally free in spirit, but only a tiny minority defy convention outwardly to the extent of appearing to society as mad or bad. Very few indeed follow William Blake's maxim: "The road of excess leads to the palace of wisdom."

Such gurus could be regarded as the most compassionate of all, for they are willing to take risks, even at the cost of their reputation, to enable both themselves and others to go beyond their limitations. Let us treasure these rare and unique teachers! No one is forced to become their student or is likely to do so unwittingly. As for their impact on the wider sangha, do we not need someone to shake things up occasionally, and put the cat among the pigeons every now and then?

7. THE GURU QUESTION

Gyalwang Drukpa Rinpoche

This interview takes some of the themes of the previous chapter deeper. It shows what it means for a master or guru to be seen not simply as an expert in spiritual experience but, through the skill-ful means of the Vajrayana, to be looked upon as a buddha. It also becomes clear here that devotion to the master, such as in the practice of guru yoga, has nothing to do with hierarchical behav-ior. Rather, through the union of our mind with the wisdom mind of the master, we attain the same level as him—a truly revolu-tionary way of dissolving all differences.

QUESTION: *You have often said that when you teach Buddhadharma, you seek to put across a message that is universal, one that cuts across cultural and geographic barriers. However, one of the main principles in Tibetan Buddhism is that of the guru, or lama, and this seems to press strongly against many ideas in Western culture. Maybe it is because the guru is actually culturally specific that it has no precedent in the West and that some Westerners have difficulty in relating to it. So is the guru a cultural phenomenon or a universal principle?*

RINPOCHE: That's an interesting question; nobody has asked me this so directly before. I don't think the guru should be looked at as a cultural thing; it should definitely be treated as a spiritual and universal issue. Otherwise you would imply that the entire practice of Buddhism, espe-cially the practice of Vajrayana, is just a cultural development. I always say that if you go too much into the cultural aspect of a religion and get stuck there, that approach becomes a spiritual poison. That kind of notion will definitely paralyze you. Don't get me wrong: there are many beautiful cultures in the world, but they are beautiful in a different sense. We should not confuse spiritual practice and culture.

If you are asking whether the guru principle is designed only for Tibetan culture and society, it is not. It is universal. Why? Because the authentic guru is nothing other than the universal truth. We are not really talking about the human body of the guru you are looking to or sitting in front of; we are talking about the ultimate goal of the spiritual path itself. This is what the guru principle represents. However, until you realize the nature of your mind, you need support from a human being in the form of instructions on meditation and so on. Whoever can give this kind of guidance skillfully is known as a guru. But this is what I would call the conventional guru—the relative, external guru—as distinct from the ultimate guru, which is the enlightened mind.

The conventional guru is someone who leads you in the right direction. Without him or her we would all be lost; we don't have wisdom, so we are unsure what to do or where to go. This is why we need a guru. I don't think that is special to Tibetans or to Tibetan culture. Everybody, everywhere, needs such guidance, no matter whether they are Tibetan, Indian, British, or French—culture really doesn't matter. Wherever you come from, you need spiritual guidance. And since the actual meaning of the guru is the realized state of mind, there is no reason why we cannot say that this is a universal principle.

QUESTION: *Traditionally, when we decide to follow the Buddhist path, we take refuge in the Buddha, Dharma, and Sangha. We take the Buddha as our guide. So why is Buddha not enough?*
RINPOCHE: We don't know who Buddha is. Who is Buddha? Where is Buddha? That's exactly the point. We need a human connection in order to know the Buddha. It's quite unfortunate, I know, but what to do? We cannot find Buddha by ourselves. "Buddha" actually means enlightenment, the enlightened mind. As we are not yet enlightened we are lost, so we need the help of a skillful human being who is smarter than us, who can give us true authentic guidance. This person is what we call the guru. He or she may only be the conventional guru, but we need this guru all the same.

QUESTION: *So what is the relationship between the conventional guru and the Buddha?*

RINPOCHE: The conventional guru is the guide who leads you to the actual guru, which is enlightenment, the buddha within you. You have to realize buddhahood for yourself; the poor guru cannot do it for you, he can only give you guidance.

In Vajrayana we always say that the guru has to be seen as a buddha. Again, this is not cultural, it should be seen in a universal way. It means that, in terms of helping us realize our buddha nature, the guru is as kind to us as the Buddha himself. I know that the idea that the guru or lama is a buddha can lead to tremendous confusion unless you know what it means. So, first of all, what do we mean by buddha? Buddha is enlightenment. And secondly, what do we mean by guru? The guru in human form, the conventional guru, is the key person who guides you along the spiritual path, so you come to know or realize your own nature, the ultimate guru, which is buddhahood. Rather than make a long sentence, we express this in an abbreviated form and simply say that the guru is buddha.

QUESTION: *There are two points here, aren't there? The guru is the key person who leads you to the buddha nature, but also the guru is considered to have many of the qualities of a buddha.*

RINPOCHE: Yes, you can say that too. By "buddha qualities" we mean that he or she has skillful methods to share with us, and has great compassion to share with us. So yes, you are quite right, you can call the lama a buddha from many points of view.

QUESTION: *We also take refuge in the Dharma. Although the Buddha has passed away he left his teachings. Is it not enough to follow the guidance the Buddha himself has left us?*

RINPOCHE: No, it is not enough. Why not? The difficulty is that you may get lost—not "may," but rather it is 95 percent sure you'll get lost. Why? Because we may be very smart in other senses, but very unfortunately we are extremely ignorant in terms of spirituality.

It is true, we take refuge in the Dharma. But what exactly is Dharma? We can read Buddhist texts, we can do chanting and other practices if we want, but will this bring us a good result or a bad one? We don't really know what will come of it. This is another reason we need a guru.

Above all, as I said before, we need a guru to lead us in the right direction. Dharma is a direction. Dharma is not a book, and ultimately Buddhist books are not Dharma, they are just paper and ink. Scriptures are what we would call conventional, relative Dharma, but for them to help you, you need the skill and understanding to know how to go through them. It is precisely this skill that is imparted by the guru, and learning this skill is the authentic way of taking refuge in Dharma. In fact this is basically why the guru is so important: because he shows you the *path* to buddha, and the path is another name for the Dharma.

These difficulties arise because of our ignorance. If we were really smart, why would we need a guru? We have our own, authentic guru within—enlightenment, the primordial buddha—so why rely on an external one? That's exactly the point. But unfortunately we are nowhere, we don't know that primordial buddha, we have not realized our buddha nature, therefore we still need guidance from a human being who has the qualities of the Buddha.

QUESTION: *At a recent conference, some Western Buddhist teachers said that Buddhism is entering a new phase in the West where the master is no longer so important. Buddhism will develop in a more egalitarian way based on mutual support between sangha members and on active service within the community (engaged Buddhism). Maybe the model of the Vajrayana guru doesn't fit the Western mentality? If this is a cultural barrier, how can we cut across it?*
RINPOCHE: I don't think the Vajrayana guru is a barrier. Actually, the guru principle is extraordinarily effective in helping us to understand the universal truth. Of all the different teachings of Buddha, the Vajrayana teachings especially provide a very real possibility to attain the universal truth. I see the Vajrayana as a great door to universal truth. It takes you out of all types of relative blockage. For example, the Vajrayana doesn't let you become blocked with the idea of the guru; and if your enthusiasm at becoming a Buddhist leads to you becoming attached to Buddha and Buddhism, the Vajrayana doesn't accept that

either. Vajrayana has many deities—wrathful deities, peaceful deities, female deities, male deities—but as soon as you are attached to them, you are not a practitioner of Vajrayana. You are not to be attached even to your enlightenment.

In Mahayana Buddhism, of course, attachment is equally discouraged, but not to everything. Mahayana discriminates between those things to which we should not be attached, such as beautiful women and men, flowers, wealth, health and so on, and pure things, such as Buddha and Dharma, toward which attachment is allowed. So I think Vajrayana is the quickest way to get into the universal realm.

Finding a guru takes skill. When the Buddha gave Vajrayana teachings, he knew the risks involved; therefore he himself said you have to take your time to find a guru. You shouldn't just say, upon meeting a lama, "I like him very much, he's such a nice chap. He welcomes me warmly, he's obviously a good person, he's the man I want as a spiritual guide." No, this is not good enough. There are hundreds of thousands of nice guys in the world; you can't be so naive.

If Westerners are disillusioned with masters now, it is their fault. They are so hungry for a spiritual touch that as soon as a "master" comes, they take to him or her and don't check first. Some simply fall in love. People are so hungry, firstly for spiritual guidance, and secondly for emotional support. They cannot now blame their problems on the culture of Tibet.

QUESTION: *You said on one occasion that the difference between emotion and devotion is that emotion is misunderstanding and devotion is understanding. Could you say more about that?*

RINPOCHE: You develop devotion once you have taken many years of your life, and considerable trouble, to check that the person who claims to be a master is indeed an authentic master. You don't choose him as your teacher because you are attracted to him or to Buddhism. You test him first. But it is important to know how to test. In fact, there is a wisdom in knowing how to test. It is not the sort of test you give a student at the end of a university course, or a sort of job interview to see whether someone is rich, well educated, or computer literate. You need some spiritual wisdom before you can check a master, and intellectually you have to be informed. This preparation comes through listening to basic Buddhist teachings or reading spiritual books. Then at least you have an understanding of what is meant by a guru, and what a master's qualifications have to be. So you develop devotion on the basis of understanding.

When I say that emotion is misunderstanding, I am thinking of someone whose reaction to a master goes something like this: "I just met you today and I fell in love with you because you smiled at me, or you hugged me, or whatever. I sense you are the man, the guide, the guru, who I have been looking for all these years." But at that moment of reaction, such a student is not checking to see what is really going on inside. Instead, he or she is simply slipping into emotion. This is a mistake.

QUESTION: *You said that the guru is the gateway to the universal dimension. Could you also say that he is the gateway to the absolute?*
RINPOCHE: The guru will open the door for you, open the door of your understanding. The guru will discriminate for you, pointing out misunderstanding and pointing out understanding. It's as though he is drawing a map for you. He is able to do this because he is experienced. For example, I don't know London and am completely lost there. Even if someone lends me a car, I can't go anywhere because I don't know the city. A spiritual master has to be as expert in spiritual experience as a London taxi driver is in knowing all the roads and short cuts. Only someone with that degree of experience is able to lead you.

The universal truth I am referring to is the ultimate state of life and of the world. This is really difficult to express in words. It is something that is beyond what we are seeing right now. This is the relative level, and that is the ultimate level. The relative level is the level we normally relate to, but ultimately there is no truth in it.

QUESTION: *Are there two things here—a truth that applies universally and our experience of that truth?*
RINPOCHE: Yes. There is the experiential point of view and the universal point of view. In philosophical terms, it is the difference between tathagatagarbha and dharmakaya. The universal point of view is primordially there, whether you experience it or not.

QUESTION: *The main practice in Vajrayana is guru yoga. Could you say in a nutshell what the point of guru yoga is, and how it works?*

RINPOCHE: The point is to realize buddha nature, enlightenment, the universal truth, which is primordially there within yourself. But guru yoga is just a technique: it is not a universal technique but rather a particular Vajrayana technique that relates only indirectly to the universal. The practice of guru yoga—the recitations, the visualization—is just relative, conventional. We live in the conventional world, so we practice conventionally. Guru yoga is actually a process of cleaning the mirror of *rigpa*, our intrinsic, pure awareness, and that process is known as *blessing* (Tib. *jinlap*). You can use different names for this, but we use the word blessing. The reflection of your face is already there, in the mirror, and through this process you will be able to see it clearly. This is the point.

QUESTION: *So you think it is a mistake to give up on the guru?*

RINPOCHE: Yes. Some masters are taking advantage of the situation too, of course. It's too easy to be a master in America, for example. Hundreds of disciples can gather around a master as soon as he teaches in America. It is fine to have thousands of fans if you are a rock star, but for a spiritual teacher that is not the point.

I want students to have enough knowledge to check me, and to take time to check me. People are too quick in this modern world; their mind is very computerized, life is very fast, and they think there is no time to check. So people complain about masters and decide they don't need one and can practice by themselves, because the buddha nature is within them anyway. Unfortunately, it will never work. On the other hand, if you take time to check, you will find there are hundreds of genuine masters. If you are careful you will never be cheated.

8. DISTORTION

Dzongsar Khyentse Rinpoche

Dzongsar Jamyang Khyentse Rinpoche challenges us as Western Dharma practitioners to become aware of the distortions that we impose on the Buddha's teachings through our cultural arrogance, our deceitful ego, and just plain ignorance. He maintains that the successful transmission of the subtle and challenging practices of Buddhadharma requires careful study and clear acknowledgment of our habitual mental patterns—and it is precisely in this task that the teacher becomes essential as someone who draws our attention to these mental patterns.

This piece is a clear-sighted, sometimes sharp, yet also humorous response to the many attacks that the Vajrayana was subjected to, especially in America in the early and mid-1990s. Christians, feminists, psychotherapists, even Western Buddhists— all had their views on the "dangers" of the teacher-student relationship. Yet we are challenged here by Dzongsar Khyentse Rinpoche to remember that criticism is worthy of attention only when it emerges from a deep and intimate knowledge of the terrain.

TRANSPLANTING ANYTHING from a foreign culture is a difficult process that may corrupt what is being imported. Buddhism is certainly no exception; in fact, among imported foreign goods, Dharma is perhaps the most prone to corruption.

Initially, to understand Dharma even on an intellectual level is not at all simple. Then once we have some understanding, to put Dharma into practice is even more subtle, because it requires that we go beyond our habitual patterns. Intellectually, we may recognize how our narrow-minded habits have brought about our own cycle of suffering, but at the same time we may also be afraid to engage wholeheartedly in the process of liberating these habits of ours.

This is cherishing of ego. For even if we think we want to practice the Buddhist path, to give up our ego-clinging is not easy, and we could well end up with our own ego's version of Dharma—a pseudo-Dharma that will only bring more suffering instead of liberation.

For this reason, most Oriental teachers are very skeptical about exporting Dharma to the Western world, feeling that Westerners lack the refinement and courage to understand and practice properly the Buddhadharma. On the other hand there are some who try their best to work on the transmission of the Dharma to the West.

It is important to remember that a thorough transplantation of Dharma cannot be accomplished within a single generation. It is not an easy process, and as when Buddhism was brought from India to Tibet, it will undoubtedly take time. There are enormous differences between the attitudes of various cultures and different interpretations of similar phenomena. It is easy to forget that such supposedly universal notions as "ego," "freedom," "equality," "power," and the implications of "gender" and "secrecy," are all constructions that are culture-specific and differ radically when seen through different perspectives. The innuendoes surrounding a certain issue in one culture might not even occur to those of another culture, where the practice in question is taken for granted.

In recent years there have been numerous critiques of both the Buddhist teachings and certain Buddhist teachers. Unfortunately, these often reveal a serious degree of ignorance about the subject-matter. Many Tibetan lamas adopt the attitude that "it doesn't matter," because they genuinely don't mind such attacks. I think the perspective of many lamas is vaster than trying to keep track of the latest likes and dislikes of the fickle modern mind. Other Tibetan lamas adopt the attitude that Westerners are merely spiritual window-shopping, telling the younger lamas like myself, "See, we told you! They are not here for the Dharma. For them, we are a mere curiosity." In an attempt to adopt a good motivation, I would like to propose some alternative perspectives.

Certain critiques of Buddhism actually enhance my devotion to the teachings and to my teachers, because I feel the Dharma defies any such criticisms. But I also feel that some of these writings can be harmful in their effect. There may be many beings whose connection to the Dharma is just about to ripen, and these writings can jeopardize their opportunity. In our lives we encounter a multitude of obstacles and difficult circumstances. But the worst possible obstacle is to be prevented from engaging in an authentic path to enlightenment.

In this age, when people naively jump to conclusions based on the writings of those who try to warn about the hazards of guru-disciple relationships, such critiques may result in the tragic destruction for many people of their only chance of liberation from the ocean of suffering. In the sutras, it is stated that someone who rejoices even momentarily over something that leads to such a lost opportunity will not encounter the path of enlightenment for hundreds of lifetimes.

Generally, I think that when we want to expose a fault or present an opinion, two attributes are necessary: one should know the subject thoroughly, and one should not oneself have the faults that one is criticizing. Otherwise, one will be, as the Tibetan proverb describes, "a monkey who laughs at another monkey's tail." Let us not forget that as human beings we are victims of our own narrow-minded interpretations. We should not give so much authority to our limited points of view: our interpretations and subjective perspectives are limitless and almost always stem from our own fears, expectations, and ignorance.

It would be of great amusement to many learned Tibetan scholars if they could read some of the presentations written by Westerners on such subjects as Buddhism or gurus. It is like imagining an old Tibetan lama reading Shakespeare's Romeo and Juliet or listening to a beautiful aria. He would most probably think the former uninteresting and that the latter sounded like a cat being skinned alive!

It is better not to distort things with our limited interpretations at all, but if we have to, then at least we should be more aware of how powerful and one-sided our interpretations can be. For example, I could claim all kinds of things about the way that Westerners approach the study of Eastern cultures. I could easily put forward an interpretation, one that might seem entirely valid, that claims Western conceptual frameworks stem from a basic attitude of arrogance in the way that they construct themselves and others.

In almost all departments in Western universities that allegedly teach Buddhism, the teachers usually have to hide the fact if they happen to be Buddhists themselves. Do the mathematics teachers hide the fact that they believe in the logic of mathematics? Western scholars need to be more questioning about their own rigid biases that prevent them from being able to appreciate other perspectives. I find heartbreaking the imperialist attitude that arrogantly isolates one aspect of Eastern culture, analyzing it at a careful distance, manipulating and sterilizing it to fit Western agendas, and then perhaps concluding that it is now suitable for consumption.

Another example of the hypocrisy involved with this kind of attitude is the Western "benevolent" wish to "liberate" Eastern women from the clutches of what is imagined to be the oppressive tyranny of a misogynist system, resembling the Western missionaries wanting natives to adopt Christian morals and values. In the West, amongst other things, women are photographed naked and the pictures are published in magazines. Many other cultures would regard this as exceedingly embarrassing, as well as extremely exploitative and oppressive of women. So from their point of view, Western criticism of another culture for its subjugation of women is a highly contentious matter.

Surely no culture should claim to have the deep appreciation and understanding necessary to produce a thorough and justified critique of an important aspect of another's culture (especially when the topic is as sophisticated and complex as Buddhism) without having the humility to make the effort to accurately and deeply learn about that topic on that culture's own terms.

Sometimes it might help Westerners to develop more respect and appreciation for the East if they remember that three thousand years ago, when the East was flourishing with philosophy, arts, languages and medicine, the Western natives still hadn't had the idea to brush their own teeth! And in many cultures' perspectives, so-called Western science and technology has not really done much besides destroying the world's resources. Ideas such as democracy and capitalism, as well as equality and human rights, can be seen to have failed miserably in the West, and to be nothing but new dogmas.

I find it difficult to see the advantage of incorporating these limited Western value systems into an approach to the Dharma. These certainly do not constitute the extraordinary realization Prince Siddhartha attained under the Bodhi tree twenty-five hundred years ago. The West can analyze and criticize Tibetan culture, but I would be so thankful if they could have the humility and respect to leave the teachings of Siddhartha alone, or at least to study and practice them thoroughly before they set themselves up as authorities.

If people could put some effort into being respectful and open-minded, there is so much knowledge available that could liberate them from all kinds of suffering and confusion. It is only now that I have come to realize the significance of the great respect that the Tibetan translators and scholars of the past had toward India, their source of Dharma and wisdom. Instead of being critical or even resentful of their source, they called it "The Sublime Land of India." This kind of attitude is very different from the Western shopping mentality that regards the Dharma as merchandise and our own involvement as an investment—only wanting to accept what sits well with our habitual expectations and rejecting what we don't find immediately gratifying.

This is not to say that Westerners should not be critical of the Buddhist teachings. On the contrary, as the Lord Buddha himself said, "Without melting, beating, weighing and polishing a yellow substance, one should not take it for gold. Likewise, without analysis one should not accept the Dharma as valid." Logical analysis has always been encouraged in the Buddhist tradition, and Buddhism has always challenged the promotion of blind faith.

The difference lies in the attitude you take towards the criticism. In the process of analyzing that "yellow substance," the analyzer must not only maintain an open mind, but also acknowledge that he/she may not have an adequate knowledge of the subject matter. That is the whole point of analysis. Otherwise we are just seeking confirmation of what we already believe. Being skeptical and seeking faults are two completely different things.

Nowhere is the difference between these two attitudes more obvious and more important than when it comes to criticisms of the guru in Vajrayana Buddhism. Unfortunately, the guru is a must for Vajrayana practice. However, all great masters and teachings repeatedly advise that one should always be skillful in checking the lama before one takes him as one's master. We have that option, and we should take advantage of it. It is vital to study the teachings extensively in order to be prepared to take on a teacher. In fact, some of the Vajrayana scriptures mention that one should check a potential teacher for twelve years before becoming his student.

However, I think it is also important to remember that Buddhism is not only Vajrayana. There are other paths such as Theravada, which is the foundation of all Buddhist paths. This is a straightforward path, which does not spark off all kinds of mystical expectations. What sometimes seems to happen is that people want to practice Vajrayana because they see it as something exotic, when in fact they would be better off with the sanity and simplicity of the Theravada.

In Vajrayana, in order to enable the guru to help us and work on our dualistic ego-centered preoccupations, we are supposed to think that the guru is no different in wisdom than the Buddha. This is the highest form of mind training. We are literally making a hero out of someone who, because he sees our potential, has no qualms about challenging and even abusing our narrow-minded and habitual patterns. This is a very radical, difficult and revolutionary method. From a conventional point of view, or from the point of view of ego-cherishing, the whole notion of the guru-disciple relationship is something almost criminal. Yet the point to remember is that the only purpose of the existence of the guru is to function as a skillful means to combat habits of dualistic conceptualizations, and to combat the tricks and tenacity of ego-clinging. In this way the guru is a living manifestation of the teachings.

It needs to be emphasized that it is our perception of the guru that enables the guru to function as a manifestation of the Dharma. At first we see the guru as an ordinary person, and then as our practice develops we start to see the guru as more of an enlightened being, until finally we learn to recognize the guru as being nothing but an external manifestation of our own awakeness or buddhamind. In a subtle way then, it is almost irrelevant whether the teacher is enlightened. The guru-disciple relationship is not about worshipping a guru, but providing the opportunity to liberate our confused perceptions of reality.

Looking at it from the teacher's point of view, if someone assumes the role of a teacher without being qualified, the negativity of this deception obviously will remain within their mindstream. It is important to understand that unless a lama is completely enlightened, he or she must carry the burden of what they do. Obviously, if he is an enlightened being, he has no karma, but if not, the consequences of his actions will come to him; his actions are his responsibility. From our point of view as students, if we have chosen him as our teacher, we should just learn from him, according to whatever path we wish to follow.

The principle of guru and devotion is much more complicated than creating a role model and worshipping him or her. Devotion, when you really analyze it, is nothing more than trusting the logic of cause and effect. If you cook an egg, putting it in boiling water, you trust the egg will be boiled. That trust is devotion. It is not blind faith or insistence on the illogical. The Buddha said, "Do not rely on the individual, rely on the teaching." Yet it seems that we nonetheless decide to continue judging individual teachers without remembering the wider perspective and context of the purpose of the teachings.

One issue that can be controversial, and that has attracted a great deal of attention, is that in the Vajrayana pleasure such as sex is not rejected as a threat to spiritual practice, but rather is used to enhance spiritual purification. While this may sound fascinating, it is important to remember that such practice requires an immense theoretical and practical grounding, without which, when viewed from the outside, it is easily misinterpreted.

Vajrayana male-female symbolism is not about sex. The practice can only exist in context of a correct view of the unity of compassion and wisdom. Furthermore, as the tantric path works on a personal and non-conceptual level, it is not possible to make judgments about a practitioner. Tantra transcends completely the conventional idea of a man and woman having a sexual relationship. It is about working with phenomena to bring about the extraordinary realization of emptiness and bodhicitta in order to liberate all beings from samsara. To expect a yogin or yogini, who is aspiring to go beyond the chauvinism of the confused mind, to worry about sexual rights issues seems absurd in the context of such a vast view.

Yet for the neophyte Westerner, certain Tibetan traditions must be very annoying, and seem sexist or male chauvinist. Western perspectives on sexual relationships emphasize "equality," yet this is very different from what is meant by equality in Vajrayana Buddhism. Where equality in the West stands for two aspects reaching equal footing, in Vajrayana Buddhism equality is going beyond "twoness" or duality all together.

If duality remains, then by definition there can be no equality. I think social equality between men and women is less important than realizing the equality between samsara and nirvana which, after all, is the only true way to engender a genuine understanding of equality. Thus the understanding of equality in Vajrayana Buddhism is on a very profound level.

The notion of sexual equality is quite new in the West, and because of this there is a certain rigid and fanatic adherence to the specific way it should be practiced. In Vajrayana Buddhism, on the other hand, there is a tremendous appreciation of the female, as well as a strong emphasis on the equality of all beings. This might not, however, be apparent to someone who cannot see beyond a contemporary Western framework. As a result, when Western women have sexual relationships with Tibetan lamas, some might be frustrated when their culturally conditioned expectations are not met.

If anyone thinks they could have a pleasing and equal lover in a rinpoche, they couldn't be more incorrect. Certain rinpoches, those known as great teachers, would by definition be the ultimate bad partner, from ego's point of view. If one approaches such great masters with the intention of being gratified and wishing for a relationship of sharing, mutual enjoyment etc., then not only from ego's point of view, but even from a mundane point of view, such people would be a bad choice. They probably will not bring you flowers or invite you out for candlelit dinners.

Anyway, if someone goes to study under a master with the intention to achieve enlightenment, one must presume that such a student is ready to give up his or her ego. You don't go to India and study with a venerable Tibetan master expecting him to behave according to your own standards. It is unfair to ask someone to free you from delusion, and then criticize him or her for going against your ego. I am not writing this out of fear that if one doesn't defend Tibetan lamas or Buddhist teachers, they will lose popularity. Despite a lot of effort to convince the world about the pitfalls of the Dharma and the defects of the teachers, there will still be a lot of masochists who have the misfortune to appreciate the Dharma and a crazy abusing teacher who will make sure to mistreat every inch of ego. These poor souls will eventually end up bereft of both ego and confusion.

I know there are plenty of people who will disagree with much of what I have said. For as much as I am set on my interpretations, so are others set on theirs. I have met great teachers whom I admire enormously and although I may be a doomed sycophant, I pray I will continue to enjoy the company of these teachers. On the other hand, people may have other ideas and be happy with them. My practice is devotion to the Buddhist path; others may chose doubting the Buddhist path. But as Dharmakirti said, ultimately we must abandon the path. So I hope in the end we will meet where we have nothing to fight over.

> Mind's ultimate nature, emptiness endowed with vividness,
> I was told is the real Buddha.
> Recognizing this should help me
> not to be stuck with thoughts of hierarchy.

> Mind's ultimate nature, its emptiness aspect,
> I was told is the real Dharma.
> Recognizing this should help me
> not to be stuck with thoughts of political correctness.

> Mind's ultimate nature, its vivid aspect,
> I was told is the real Sangha.
> Recognizing this should help me
> not to be stuck with thoughts of equal rights.

> One cannot disassociate emptiness from vividness.
> This inseparability I was told is the Guru.

Recognizing this should help me
not to be stuck with depending on chauvinist lamas.

This nature of mind has never been stained by duality,
this stainlessness I was told is the deity.
Recognizing this should help me
not to be stuck with the categories of "gender" or "culture."

This nature of mind is spontaneously present.
That spontaneity I was told is the dakini aspect.
Recognizing this should help me
not to be stuck with fear of being sued.

—Dzongsar Khyentse Rinpoche

II. AUTHENTIC
BUDDHISM TODAY

Glimpses of Buddhist View(s)

To study the Buddhist way is to study oneself.
To study oneself is to forget oneself.
To forget oneself is to be illuminated
by the ten thousand dharmas.
To be illuminated by the ten thousand dharmas
is to free one's body and mind—
and the body and mind of all beings.
Dogen Zenji: Genjo Koan[13]

There are many ways to explain the basic views of Buddhism, and some of them are given in this section. Dzogchen Rinpoche addresses the fundamental questions of "What is the Buddhadharma?" and "What does it mean to be a buddha?" We get a sense of what meditation practice is and the understanding of consciousness that underlies it. Key Buddhist ideas, such as relative and absolute truth, dependent origination, and shunyata, are also examined in this section. Philippe Cornu gives a brief overview of Buddhist thought and offers fascinating connections with Western thought, not least the increasingly obvious parallels between modern Western science, philosophy and ethics, and this 2,500-year-old science of the mind. Chökyi Nyima Rinpoche shows how the Buddhist teachings on emptiness are not just theory but come vividly alive in his interactions with his students in investigating the reality of emptiness in the very moment.

Another key theme in this section is the great importance of receiving teachings from a pure lineage and of passing on that pure lineage. As Sogyal Rinpoche says, "Suppose, for example, we alight upon some aspects of the teachings which seem inconvenient and we assume they are cultural paraphernalia. How can we be sure we are not making a huge mistake, and they might be in fact an integral part of the teaching?"[14] Much of what is said in this book could apply equally well to other traditions: Zen, for example, faces the challenge of preserving its authenticity in the midst of a fast-growing body of teachers who never received training in a Japanese monastery, let alone followed a teacher for any long period of time, and who use Zen methods removed from their spiritual context.

Orgyen Tobgyal Rinpoche, at once one of the strictest defenders of the purity of the lineage and also a master of great humor, does not hold back in his criticism of the Western habit of making things more complicated than they need to be, and even speaks of "perverse" and "false teachings." Among younger lamas, Dzogchen Ponlop Rinpoche and Dzigar Kongtrul Rinpoche also seek to defend the authentic teachings with all the power at their disposal. Dzigar Kongtrul Rinpoche, whose teachings will appear in later sections, speaks unambiguously on how important both study and practice are in this respect: "The present generation, especially, carries enormous responsibility, since the Dharma is only just coming to the West and setting down roots. If this generation just invents anything it wants, then future generations will have no basis or example to build on. This generation therefore has a significantly greater responsibility than any future one. This is why study is so very important. Through study, through listening to the teachings, we learn how to reflect; through correct reflection we learn how to meditate; finally, through meditation we have genuine experiences and learn how truly to embody the teachings. Only in this way can we preserve the Dharma and be of real benefit to ourselves and to others, accomplish good work, and truly serve the Dharma and all beings. And that is the real reason why we practice Dharma, why we study and practice—why we concern ourselves with the path to enlightenment."[15]

Dzogchen Rinpoche

> *Dzogchen Rinpoche belongs to a younger generation of lamas who have gone through a formidable traditional education but who also have a considerable experience of Westerners. In this teaching he conveys the foundations of the Buddhist worldview and ties this in with varied advice on the importance of the authenticity of teachings, a subject that appears later in this section. A special quality of Dzogchen Rinpoche's teaching is his emphasis on the equal value of the various methods of practice, and his concluding words are important: "The purpose of practice should be to tame our own mindstreams."*

Dharma is like medicine

The teachings we receive are part of Dharma's nectar. The Dharma, we are told, is like medicine, and no one medicine is used for all purposes. Specific medicines remedy specific illnesses: if we have a stomachache, we take one medicine; if we have a headache, we take another; and if we have a fever, we take a third. If we take headache medicine for a stomach pain, we are clearly making a mistake. In the same way, there are different stages to the practice of Dharma, and each stage has a particular method of application. We should apply the teachings appropriately, according to our circumstances.

The medicinal methods of the Dharma have been authenticated through use; they have been proven to work over a millennium, from the time of Guru Rinpoche and the early masters of the ninth century down to the present day. The teachings of the early translation school, the Nyingma, present a peerless body of philosophy and practice, but it is important to remember that the generations of masters who transmitted those teachings in an unbroken lineage to the present day never treated their inheritance as mere theory. It has never been enough to know that a particular text contains teachings whose origins stretch back a thousand years and more. This fact does authenticate them, but it is the way in which the teachings have been practiced and realized by learned and accomplished masters over generations that makes them truly significant.

Generation after generation of accomplished masters put the theory found in the teachings into practice and thereby attained the rainbow body. They have left us a path that we can follow, a legacy of methods that have been proven time and again. To make progress on our path, we are best served by following these proven methods rather than trying to come up with something for ourselves that is new and unproven. Appreciating our good fortune in receiving these teachings, we should put what we have heard from our teachers into practice.

It is often said that it is important to see the spiritual master as a buddha. This is a crucial point and is not a question of one culture enforcing its customs or traditions on another. The reason we consider our spiritual master as a buddha is that holding this view benefits the student. We receive power and blessing by viewing our masters purely, as buddhas.

How then should we practice the Dharma? Our practice should be an expression of our devotion and of our motivation for enlightenment. The Dharma is not meant to be studied merely as an intellectual exercise or academic pursuit; it is meant for practice, for expression in faith and devotion. We can study various disciplines and fields of knowledge, but our concern should be the ultimate point of our studies. When we are concerned solely with the things of this world and lifetime, we fail to arrive at any profound conclusions. The Dharma should go beyond these shallow goals and bring us to some final point, some ultimate purpose. This is the reason for practicing the Dharma, and the way in which our practice should proceed.

Ego and the skandhas

The Buddhadharma is a process, one through which we train and tame our own mindstreams. One approach is to go to the root of what we mean by "I," our sense of self or individual self-identity. We cling to our sense of self like shipwrecked sailors clinging to a raft in the middle of the ocean. The problem with this self-identity is that the raft is going to fall apart, it is never going to prove as durable and reliable as we would like it to be.

The "I" or "self" is the way in which the mind perceives its own mind-body aggregates, or *skandhas*. These components of experience are by their very nature subject to destruction and dissolution. They do not last; they fall apart. The mind perceives the skandhas as a single entity called the "self" or the "ego" because there is a strong conviction in the mind that the ego exists, and not because there is really an ego there.

Nagarjuna, the great Indian Buddhist master, said that while our sense of self is false, the actual essence of our mind is buddha nature. Another way of saying this is that we all, as unenlightened beings, have the capacity to be buddhas.

Buddhahood is a state in which all suffering has been removed, in which there is only unchanging happiness, well-being, and bliss; it is the *path of no more learning*. Nothing more is to be learned because we have attained unchanging and ultimate buddha nature. This is clearly not the state of being that we currently experience, which is full of suffering and subject to impermanence and change. If we attain buddhahood, the final goal of the path, we attain a lasting and unchanging happiness, untainted by any suffering or flaw.

Surely this is what we are all hoping for when we undertake the path of Dharma. Whatever name we give our path, we are all seeking happiness. If we want to be truly happy, we should be seeking lasting happiness rather than temporary happiness.

Even though our lives are filled with suffering and pain, we do experience temporary states of happiness, but they are superficial. We may enjoy the benefits of our activities for a while, but things always change. Perhaps we are very skillful in our business—we might even cheat people out of enormous sums of money and make a great deal of profit. We might even feel good about that. But the karma we accumulate through cheating people ensures that this happiness is temporary, and the suffering that will result when the negative karma ripens is guaranteed.

All over the world, people spend most of their time trying to ensure themselves happiness by investing their money and engaging in business. We try to secure continuing profit and the benefit of perpetual happiness for ourselves. But the happiness that we gain from this kind of activity is only temporary and fails to last. What continues is suffering.

Not only does Dharma show us the origin of temporary suffering and happiness, it also shows us the source of lasting happiness. This is why the Dharma is sacred—not because of a set of esoteric rituals, but because it shows us why we suffer and how we can create lasting happiness.

Buddha nature

Nagarjuna says that the mindstream of every unenlightened being is permeated by the heart essence of buddhahood. The fundamental nature of our mindstreams is *tathagatagarbha,* or buddha nature, the seed and heart essence of an enlightened being. It is this quality that gives us the capacity to become buddhas.

How do we know that this is our fundamental nature? Can someone verify this for us, or is it just somebody's opinion that we all blindly follow? We have the examples of countless individuals who have gained certainty about their own buddha nature by following a path that has brought about their enlightenment. We have many testimonies. It isn't just an opinion or a theory; it has been proven time and again. The fundamental essence of our nature, the basic birthright of all sentient beings, is buddha nature.

If this is so, what can we do about it? Ultimately, we recognize our buddha nature by experiencing it directly. The difference between an ordinary being and a buddha is simply the recognition, or lack of recognition, of our buddha nature. Given that the potential for us to be buddhas exists, all that is necessary is for us to recognize it. Upon the direct recognition of our potential, we attain buddhahood. Without that recognition we remain in a state of confusion, the state of an ordinary being. From the point of view of the extraordinary teachings of the early translation school of the Nyingma, this is the only difference between buddhas and ordinary beings.

What we are looking for is proof. In Nagarjuna's works is a verse that attests to buddha nature being at the core of the minds of all beings. In addition, the dialectical approach of the Sutrayana schools reason that all sentient beings have the potential to become buddhas because the nature of their minds already is buddha nature. Therefore, sentient beings definitely have this potential.

Practitioners follow the path set forth in the teachings. However we proceed, we should do so on the basis of conviction. One approach is that of the yogi or yogini, someone who emphasizes meditation as the main way in which to follow the teachings. Others are more inclined toward the scholarly approach of the pandits, which emphasizes the study and contemplation of the scriptures, and proceed with their practice on that basis. Followed intelligently, both paths are perfectly good.

We should remember, however, that the Buddha said that, like gold, his teachings should be examined and evaluated and that our understanding of them must be refined, just as gold is refined. Buddha is saying that we shouldn't follow him blindly and accept without question whatever he says. We should determine its truth for ourselves. We don't just accept anything put in front of us as gold; we analyze, assess, and evaluate. We need conviction that what we are putting into practice works, that it really is authentic, that it really is the gold that it is claimed to be.

Such conviction can be achieved through analytical, meditation, which makes use of our ability to reason. Alternatively, we might arrive at that same certainty through the more intuitive meditation where the mind simply rests in its own nature. Historically, both approaches have been employed, and both are valid.

The purpose of practice is to come to a direct understanding and realization of the nature of mind; but as ordinary, worldly individuals we are not going to have that direct authentic perception straight away. To refine our understanding, we are obliged to follow a process of training. The practice of Dharma gradually hones our minds to the point where we can directly recognize the nature of mind.

Absolute and relative truth

If we are to train our minds by applying the Dharma, we need to know what constitutes Dharma. The Dharma can be understood on two levels: the relative level of reality, and ultimate reality.

The Tibetan term for conventional or relative truth, *kundzob,* refers to everything that is part of our ordinary experience—what we ordinarily see, hear, and understand about things constitutes relative or conventional truth. Actually, "truth" is a bit of a misnomer, because the implication of the term *kundzob* is one of falsehood. It is something that is not the case, like a lie that is told in order to confuse people. In the same way, the relative perception of our ordinary mind is a state of mind under the influence of confusion and misperception.

Döndam is the ultimate perception of reality, the very nature of things. It is not influenced by *kundzob,* and so it is not so easy to have direct access to it. The absolute cannot be directly introduced to us within the context of our ordinary confused mind. Again and again, the teachings explain that the ultimate does not exist within the sphere of ordinary mind. A frequently used example is of someone showing the position of the moon by pointing his or her finger at it. The moon has nothing to do with the finger; the finger is simply the means through which the moon is indicated. If we get caught by conventional experience we are still looking at the finger, and we are not going to see the moon of ultimate realization. Conventional perception can point us toward the ultimate through interdependence, but it does not constitute the ultimate.

Everything that we experience is interdependently connected with everything else. To put it simply, the only way we can talk about what is in one place is by referring to something in another place. The one relies upon the other. The concept of something "over there" and something "over here," of "far away" and "near," is based on the relationship of one thing to another, so things are interdependently linked.

The only way we can talk about conventional experience and ultimate reality is through interdependence. When we use these two truths, which are almost completely opposed to each other, we are using the fact that interdependence exists on a conceptual level, even though that may have nothing to do with the ultimate state of things. If we use interdependence skillfully, we can distinguish between the absolute and the conventional and also directly experience absolute nature.

The heart of our practice is the use of the relative truth of interdependence to arrive at our ultimate nature. The lower yanas call absolute nature the actual nature of things, the way of abiding *(nelug)*, or emptiness *(tongpanyi)*, and the higher yanas refer to the absolute as *rangzhin rigpa*, the naturally occurring nature of mind, or as Samantabhadra. The purpose of our practice is to recognize ultimate reality directly, which is in stark contrast to conventional experience.

Death and impermanence

How do we put this into practice? It is vital to understand how wrong and problematic it is to trust in our physical body, our embodiment for this life. We are just like those people on the raft desperately hoping that the raft is not going to fall apart and that they are not going to drown. The raft may hold together for a while, but we don't even know for certain that it is taking us in the right direction.

We depend on our body—this physical existence that is the support for our current experience—as though it were indestructible, but just as we have no idea when the raft is going to break up, we also have no idea when we are going to die. We can't say when death and impermanence are going to take their toll. This is a crucial point for all Dharma practitioners. We all currently enjoy a human existence, but we have no clue how much longer we will be alive.

Such contemplation may frighten us, but it makes us respect the inevitability of change. It is rather like the police enforcing the law. The reason we can have laws, and why they can be upheld, is that people fear the consequences of violating our laws. When we meditate upon impermanence, we are appointing our own police force to "enforce" the truth of impermanence as a motivation for us to practice. We remind ourselves of death so that we can develop a healthy concern and respect for the fact that we could die at any point, and that we need to make use of whatever time is left to us.

I use the example of the self-appointed police force because when sentient beings like us realize that there is no time to waste, when we are under a certain amount of pressure, we work with diligence and enthusiasm. When we think we have all the time in the world, it is much easier for us to be lazy and to procrastinate.

Death and impermanence are emphasized in the teachings because they are one of the best ways of motivating ourselves to practice. Contemplating death and impermanence is very sobering. It reminds us that we currently have an opportunity that we may never have again, and we need to use that opportunity while it is still available.

It is all too easy to slip into the self-delusion of thinking that we will get around to practicing tomorrow, next week, or even next year. All too easily we can find that we never get around to practicing. But recognizing the inevitability of death and impermanence reminds us that the pressure is on and that we cannot delay. Meditation upon death and impermanence is one of the best teachers. It is one of our best friends on the path, because it will always chastise us for laziness and remind us there is no time to waste.

This contemplation is not only about the our death, it is also about the fact that so many things change throughout our lives, even before we die. We can witness the truth of impermanence in relation to nations, communities, and families.

Everybody trusts that some kind of stability and predictability can be assured, whether it is in building a home or going to war, but the way in which events unfold is completely unpredictable. We tend to live our lives as if we could always predict their outcome, but we can't. We forge a connection with someone, certain that this relationship is going to last for the rest of our lives, only to separate in a year or two. This happens not because there is anything inherently wrong with any particular situation, but because the nature of all phenomena is not one of permanence, stability, and predictability, but of impermanence.

The more we understand, in conventional terms, that it is in the nature of things to be impermanent, unpredictable, and without guarantee, the more relaxed and spacious we can be. We no longer need to impose a false sense of predictability on unpredictable events, or force permanence onto situations that are by their very nature impermanent.

The more we see that impermanence is the nature of things, the less disturbed or overwhelmed we are when inevitable change occurs. We no longer find change so surprising, and we suffer less. If we insist that whatever happens to us must be good, and base our activities on the belief that whatever we do is going to work out perfectly, we are setting ourselves up for future suffering. When things prove themselves to be impermanent, our whole idea of how things are supposed to be falls apart, and we suffer. People can even drive themselves mad when they insist on a certain view of reality that is contrary to the way things actually are.

It is crucial that we understand that this world functions through impermanence. Good things happen, but they are impermanent; bad things happen, and they are also impermanent. There is no stability at all, no predictability, and no certainty.

To benefit from the medicine of Dharma fully, we should apply the teachings skillfully to every aspect of our lives. A basic flaw in the way people follow the Dharma is that they fail to use it in the way it is intended. As long as things are going well, it is easy to meditate on compassion for all beings and to cultivate patience. But the moment something goes wrong we become irritated; bodhichitta flies out the window, and we completely lose our patience. Clearly, this is an example of not taking the medicine properly. We should take our medicine at the right time, and the right time to meditate on compassion and patience is when we are actually angry.

When we study and practice the so-called lower and higher yanas, we might hear that the most sublime, or the pinnacle of all teachings are those of dzogchen, and this is true. The "lower" yanas of the *shravaka* and bodhisattva paths, the "higher" paths of the tantras, and the "pinnacle" path of dzogchen are distinguished from one another in this way. This gradation shows the various ways in which it is appropriate for beings of differing propensities to proceed upon the path. Ideally, a practitioner proceeds from the lower levels of practice to the higher levels, and then to the summit. This does not mean that the lower levels of practice are to be disparaged or ignored. We should not focus on the higher paths at the expense of the lower paths; a lower path may well be most appropriate for us at the moment. We should practice according to our own capacity.

The lower paths seem stricter in their guidelines and rules and in the way one proceeds with the practice, whereas the higher levels of practice seem to be more spacious, open, and unstructured. But this spaciousness is something that is arrived at as a result of passing through the various levels of understanding. What is appropriate on the lower levels of practice may not pertain to the higher levels, and what is appropriate to the higher levels may be completely unworkable on the lower levels of practice; but again, that doesn't mean that any of these paths should be discarded. Unfortunately, people tend to think that a higher path must be a better path, and that the other paths have no real purpose, but this is simply not true.

The Buddha's teachings answer the needs of every kind of person. Everybody has a certain caliber, a certain disposition and capacity for understanding. The Buddha taught in ways that meet all these needs, and it is important for us to see the common purpose and validity of each and every path.

It is also important not to mix the paths up. Any one individual can progress through the yanas, but that doesn't mean that the person should then rid himself or herself of the understanding and insight gained through studying and practicing them. We also need to respect that the principles of the lower yanas are incorporated into the higher yanas, and that the teachings of the higher yanas do not fit into the context of the lower yanas.

We start to apply the Dharma by hearing the teachings, then by contemplating them, and finally by meditating. If we haven't gone through the process of hearing and contemplating, what do we have to meditate on? This progression is absolutely necessary. Once we have heard and studied the teachings, contemplated them, and put them into practice through meditation, we gain the realization that the teachings can confer, and display the signs of accomplishment.

There are many people today who say they practice but who sit around with their mouths open doing nothing, who go through the motions of practice without ever really practicing. Don't ever think that this is practice. Practice properly. Now that the teachings are starting to spread to this part of the world, make sure that they spread well. Make sure that, to the best of your capabilities, you practice well. People who claim to be practitioners can often indulge in very ordinary activities. They fight, they squabble, they get involved in petty disagreements, controversies and infighting. Let us remember that the purpose of practice should be to tame our own mindstreams.

10. KARMA, TRUTH, AND EMPTINESS

Philippe Cornu

BUDDHISM HAS MANY DIFFERENT WAYS of explaining the nature of life, and the relationship between a person and his world. It begins with a very straightforward observation: everything is transitory. Everything we perceive in our daily lives—from the most fragile of creatures to trees and to the planet itself—is subject to a continuous process of birth, growth, and death. Nothing escapes the law of impermanence.

When we look at this more closely, we can see that the birth or arising of phenomena results from certain factors that come together at a particular moment in time, and that constitute the causes and conditions of each arising. Let's take the example of a seed. Although the seed is the main cause of a new plant, it cannot produce the plant by itself. The seed will have to fall into the earth, will need some rain to moisten the soil and decompose its outer casing, and will also need some warmth to grow. All these other factors we call secondary causes, or conditions, and their meeting is essential for germination to be successful.

How does the plant grow? The seed no longer exists once the plant breaks through the soil, and yet there is an obvious link between the preceding thing (the seed) and the new thing (the shoot). Buddhists would say they belong to the same causal series. But we have already seen how this causal series itself depends on many other phenomena, such as rainfall, sunshine, and so on. By extending this example we find that all phenomena exist in dependence upon other phenomena. There is no such thing as an autonomous and independent entity. This is what we call the law of interdependence, or dependent arising. It is one of the basic principles of Buddhism, and one of the most far-reaching.

Not only do things change over relatively long but humanly perceptible periods of time, they also change much more intrinsically, from moment to moment. A familiar example of this is a river that looks as though it is always the same river even though the water is changing at every moment. Buddhists assert that all phenomena are impermanent not only on the macro level, but on the micro level as well.

Karma

Interdependence, then, can be seen through the universal play of cause and effect. However, when interdependence applies to beings like us who are endowed with a mind and with a will, we call it *karma*. So what is karma exactly? In the first instance, it is a moment of volition, an impulse of the mind. This impulse sets thinking in motion, and thinking in turn sets the body or speech in motion. The initial impulse therefore ends in an action, but this action is not random or neutral. It is a cause that affects the object to which it is directed, while at the same time leaving a subconscious trace in the person who carries it out.

Imagine the case of a thief who steals someone's wallet. The theft upsets the victim and causes him or her a certain amount of suffering. The thief's act has therefore had a negative effect. At the same time, it leaves an indelible trace in the thief's consciousness, a trace the thief may not be aware of or remember, but that will nevertheless condition his or her future behavior and experiences. Traces like this can create habits, so if the thief steals often, he may develop a subconscious tendency to steal regularly. Furthermore, once the appropriate secondary conditions come together later on, the trace will ripen into an experience identical in nature to the original act. So, for example, the ex-thief is likely to be robbed himself, or to suffer from poverty.

Karma is considered to be the main factor conditioning future interdependent situations. And since the actions that link people are countless, they give rise to countless interactions between those people in the future. In a world where everything is interdependent, carrying out an action is no small undertaking!

The person and the outside world

According to Buddhism human beings have three "doors"—body, speech, and mind—that act as gateways between ourselves and the world. The body is in certain respects a physical container for the mind and a contact point between oneself and the surrounding environment. Speech, which is connected to breath and to the voice, allows communication to take place between inner and outer worlds. Finally, the mind, which is intangible, appears to "reside" in the body and give it consciousness. It is clear that the first two "doors" are under the control of the third, the mind, which is not only captain of the ship but also interprets the messages relayed from the outside world through the five senses.

Yet Buddhism tells us that the mind is ignorant and deluded, confused and turbulent. We only have to sit down for a few minutes on a meditation cushion to realize how true this is. But if this is the case, how can we possibly rely on our mind's interpretation of the world?

Buddha explained that, in its confusion, our mind attributes a certain reality to the notion of "I" as separate from the external world. It then attempts to maintain the reality of this "I" against all the odds. In order to do this, it develops a complex strategy for survival. For example, it craves what it finds attractive and wants to have it. On the other hand, anything it finds repulsive or threatening it pushes away in anger, hatred, or disdain. Anything that falls into neither of these categories it will blithely ignore. The problem is that these three basic emotions—desire, anger, and ignorance—are the fuel of our actions; in other words, of our karma.

What is the confusion that lies at the root of this process? It is basically our feeling of separation between ourselves and the world, or, to put it another way, the sense of subject-object duality. We think that the subject, I, grasps an object that is external to it. But is there really a world outside of our consciousness?

Even within Mahayana Buddhism, each philosophical school has a slightly different answer to this question, so there is no single "Buddhist" view. Maybe the most relevant here is that of the idealist Chittamatra school, which interprets Buddha's statement that "all phenomena are mind" to mean that all phenomena are of the same nature as the mind and merely appear to the mind, and so do not truly exist as external events. The *Lankavatara Sutra* says that "consciousness is the spectator, the spectacle, and the dancer at one and the same time," which is to say that in any experience we have, whether in waking life, dreams, or any other state, nothing comes from outside of the mind that perceives it.

This is not to deny that phenomena appear to our minds, simply that rather than existing separate from our minds, they are in fact produced in dependence on the ripening of karmic traces left in our consciousness by past actions. These appearances are perceived by the sense consciousnesses (sight, hearing, taste, smell, and touch) and mistakenly identified as separate and external. Because of this we react to them as "objects" through our emotions, and these reactions cause us to create yet more karma that leaves yet more karmic traces, and so on, endlessly.

As long as our minds are not totally purified of karmic traces, our actions and reactions are unconsciously conditioned, though not wholly determined, by these traces. The same is true, of course, for everyone. The act that I carry out in relation to someone else, therefore, involves causes in myself but also involves causes in the other person—karmic traces in his own consciousness that lead him to suffer my action. Over countless lives, we have in this way woven innumerable connections with innumerable beings, and we will continue to meet these beings as long as our traces have not cleared. This vision of interaction avoids us falling into the solipsistic trap of thinking that nobody exists other than ourselves.

Relative and absolute truth

There are other views in Buddhism that do accept the existence of an external world—the Vaibhashika and Sautrantika schools, for example. As for the Prasangika Madhyamaka School, its Tibetan Gelug proponents reject the Chittamatra view, while its Tibetan Nyingma advocates accept it—but only as what they term "relative truth."

The beauty of the Madhyamaka school is that it falls neither into eternalism (thinking that things exist substantially and inherently) nor into nihilism (asserting that nothing exists at all). It proposes a "middle way" between such extremes by distinguishing relative truth from absolute truth. This distinction is an important key for understanding the Buddhist perspective.

We have already seen that all phenomena are impermanent and dependently arising. The characteristics of impermanence and inter-dependence are what is meant by *emptiness* in Buddhism. Emptiness has often been taken as a synonym for nothingness, particularly in the West, but this is a mistake. Emptiness does not "empty" objects of their content nor deny that they appear to us; rather, emptiness is the ultimate nature of everything. It prevents us from believing that things have a permanent and indestructible essence or an underlying sub-stance or being. It is in this respect that the Buddhist approach is so revolutionary.

For ordinary human beings, things appear to us through our senses, and we take what we perceive to be real. This is what is called *relative truth*: we share a common understanding about how things are—what a table is, what a chair is, and so on—but if we subject our perception to analysis, we find that things have no hard core, no substance. It is the absence of inherent existence that is called *emptiness,* or the absolute truth of things. Relative and absolute truth seem at first to be mutually contradictory, but actually they are inseparable: even though things may not exist inherently, they nevertheless appear to our senses, and even though they appear to our senses, they are nevertheless empty. The essence of appearance is emptiness.

Madhyamaka masters show the truth of emptiness through precise logical reasoning, yet reasoning is only a bridge toward that primordial wisdom that is beyond logic and conceptual understanding. This is a crucial point, since emptiness and wisdom are not "objects" that can be grasped by the intellect. As soon as all our concepts have dissolved, the ordinary mind dies and our primordial, nondual wisdom is revealed. According to the Nyingma and Sakya schools, it is this pri-mordial wisdom that actualizes emptiness.

For the Madhyamikas, then, whether we believe the external world exists (the realist view) or does not exist (the idealist view) is of little importance. Both options are simply a matter of choice on the level of conventional or relative truth. Either way, the world is empty on the absolute level.

Action

What role does action have in an impermanent and interdependent world? Buddhism emphasizes two practical points.

First, rather than setting out to conquer a world considered *a priori* to be external, as we have done in the West, the Buddhist approach is to privilege the action of looking inward. Buddhism subordinates any description of the world, and any activity in the world, to the need to first understand our own minds. The appearance of the world, after all, is conditioned by the states of mind of those who experience it. It follows that, for a Buddhist, it is simply naive and deluded to try to secure happiness solely by mastering external circumstances. This is rather like a dream in which we cut back the undergrowth only to find that it has grown again even more than before. As long as the dreamer doesn't realize he is dreaming, he believes it is real and will exhaust himself trying to improve the storyline.

Buddha taught that everyone, every single being in the universe, suffers, and that this suffering is caused by our deluded minds. To suffer means to be out of place, to miss the point. We could say that Buddhism is a comprehensive therapy in which healing and mental health are understood on the highest level. Merely healing a few neuroses is not enough to bring about liberation. Even people who are psychologically "normal" are deluded. Ultimate healing can only come about through the path of meditation, through working on ourselves; there is no external savior. Each one of us, guided by an experienced teacher, has to come to know our own mind and gradually reduce our suffering by clearing our ignorance.

Second, we have also seen how strong and close are the ties between ourselves and all those around us. It is therefore inconceivable to work on ourselves to the exclusion of others. Once we realize that others suffer just as much, if not more, than we do, then we naturally aspire to help them out of suffering too. It is therefore wrong to brand Buddhists as being uninterested in society, even though their approach is not to launch themselves into social action straightaway but first to find a place of inner strength in order to ensure that their action will be truly effective in the long term. The Dalai Lama and Thich Nhat Hanh, for example, both work actively for peace in the world, but both emphasize the need for inner peace as a prerequisite for true outer peace. If we are to have deep and impartial compassion for those we wish to help—and this is the only healthy basis for social action—then it can only come from within.

Dialogue with the West

Over the last twenty years or so, a number of Western scientists and thinkers have entered into dialogue with Buddhist masters and scholars. These exchanges have been promising, although often compromised by assumptions and naiveté on both sides. Scientific research in quantum physics, astrophysics, and thermodynamics, for example, requires a high level of mathematical abstraction that Buddhist thought, being more qualitative than quantitative, has not developed. If we are not careful, dialogue in these fields can lead to gross errors, such as believing that the void of quantum theory is equivalent to the emptiness of Buddhism. One can only compare like with like, and this would be mixing physical and philosophical orders of reality.

Perhaps the most fruitful areas of dialogue have been in philosophy and in epistemology, or theory of knowledge. This is not without its difficulties, however. For centuries, Western culture has been founded on Aristotelian philosophy that posits the existence of an *a priori* external world, made of phenomena that have an essence. It is this view that has enabled the West to gain mastery over the material world. In the seventeenth century Francis Bacon encouraged people to dominate nature, and the Enlightenment was all about a rationalism that sought to conquer and triumph over the material world.

There have always been other currents of thought in Europe—the skepticism of Pyrrho, the humanism of Giordano Bruno, the empiricism of David Hume, the epistemology of Karl Popper and Thomas Kuhn—but until recently their supporters have been less influential. However, relativity and quantum theory have caused philosophers to question their old notions of linear reasoning and scientific objectivity. Heisenberg's uncertainty principle, for instance, and quantum theory have shattered the idea that a researcher is objective: the observer influences his object and modifies the result of the experiment. So how can we observe our world objectively while still belonging to it? Only a totally closed system would be free of an observer's influence, but paradoxically it would then be impossible to observe and would therefore be nonexistent for the researcher.

Although our old ideas have been shaken at their foundations, and although the notions of interdependence and subjectivity are now widely accepted by Western thinkers, the implications of these "new" notions have not yet been fully drawn out—namely, the absence of duality between subject and object, the role of the mind in shaping phenomenal reality, and the universal responsibility that flows from this. Buddhist philosophy therefore has an important contribution to make to Western thinking at this juncture, since all these implications have been elaborately developed by Buddhist scholars for two and a half thousand years.

It is not surprising that our old certainties cannot be swept away easily, especially when they have given rise to such impressive technical feats. But, in fact, the key may lie not so much in sweeping away a particular way of thinking and replacing it with a Buddhist one, or any other for that matter, but rather in reassessing the objectives behind scientific research and social action, and in deepening them.

Western researchers are more and more concerned with the ethical dimension of their work. How is mankind affecting the evolution of the world it inhabits? How far can we go? In this respect it can be helpful to reflect on the interdependence between human beings, on the importance of compassion, and on the fact that we live in a world of mutual solidarity. We know that our mistakes can have repercussions on the entire planet. Now, more than ever, individual responsibility cannot be separated from universal responsibility. Maybe we have outgrown the era of external conquests and should now look inward so that our actions can finally bring about lasting happiness for everyone.

11. Cutting Dualistic Thinking

Chökyi Nyima Rinpoche

In September 1994 Chökyi Nyima Rinpoche made a brief visit to Cologne with his father Tulku Urgyen Rinpoche. The following teaching was given to a small group that had gathered informally in a private flat. The unforced atmosphere and the direct way in which Chökyi Nyima Rinpoche worked directly with his audience, drawing them into his reflections or challenging them with provocative remarks, are clearly in evidence in this teaching. Rinpoche addresses himself to many aspects of Buddhist thought with a playful light touch, and he seems here to be most concerned with loosening views that have become tightly held.

THINKING IS A SUBTLE FORM OF SUFFERING. What exactly do we spend our time thinking about? We might think about how to enjoy life and how to function, or even that we can't achieve anything without thinking. We might well believe that thinking is very important. We think in a certain way and then head in a particular direction, and that is why we are how we are. But are we happy, and are we perfect? If we were already perfect then we would not need to search for anything. This simple fact tells us that thinking is the real creator of suffering. Even considering something to be pleasant or good ends in suffering because it arouses our attachment and desire.

While most of us consider roses to be beautiful, some of us will think that they are ugly, and a few will remain neutral or indifferent toward them. Whatever opinion we hold on the subject of roses, however, our opinion is the product of thinking. If I give a rose that is almost fully blossomed to someone, would he or she think that this is good or bad? And if I give this same flower to someone in ten days' time, what would he or she think about my gift? When we receive something beautiful we feel pleasant, because our desire has been aroused. When we feel desire, we believe that we lack something and this can cause us pain and suffering.

If I were to bring a reeking garbage can closer and closer to someone, he or she would become irritated or perhaps even angry. And if I made someone a gift of something that he or she finds to be not so interesting, his or her feeling would be unclear. These are the three ways in which we normally respond to the world: with attachment, anger, or ignorance.

Do you agree? You should test out these pronouncements, especially if you don't believe what I say. The Buddha's teaching is a very open one; students should investigate all of these ideas carefully. Only then will they gain clarity and really learn. If all we do is just agree with what someone says, our insight won't be complete.

Thinking is emotion and is also dualistic, which means that thinking obscures the truth. What is truth? Truth is suchness, "as-it-isness," and is beyond ideas and thoughts. According to the tantric teachings, an idea is an obscuration of the truth; you might even say that an idea is a sin. There are many kinds of thought: some ways of thinking are good, some are bad, while others are neutral. From the perspective of the tantric path, however, even "good" thinking is subtly dualistic. As long as we are thinking, ego is involved, and ego-clinging, holding onto a false idea of self, is the cause of suffering. It is awakened mind, or egolessness, that is the cause of liberation.

We should reflect on the following four points, which are sometimes called the *four seals,* and which initially we will understand only intellectually: everything is impermanent; negative emotion is suffering; all phenomena are empty; and liberation is peace.

Perhaps we can all agree by now that everything is impermanent and that negative emotions bring suffering. The third point is that all phenomena are empty, but this is not how we usually perceive things to be. Buddha says that the self does not exist, that our true nature is egolessness, and whoever believes that the self or other phenomena exist is mistaken and confused. So, who is right—the Buddha or us?

Perhaps we believe that we are right. After all, we can touch things, so how can anyone say that they are empty? How can anyone logically explain that anything that we perceive through the five senses is empty?

For example, when we look at a friend we see his or her face. No one doubts a face, and seeing means seeing, it doesn't mean failing to see. If we can see someone's face, it implies that whatever lies behind that face also exists. But when we look at a face, even though it appears to us that we see the whole face, we actually cannot focus on one part of the face, such as the eyes, unless we fail to see another part, such as the chin. We do not see the entity that we call the "face," we only see part of it. If we look at one side of it, we fail to see the other. If we look at the tip of the nose, we can't see the ears, and if we look away we cannot see a face at all.

Even though we cannot see atoms, regardless of how small something might be, everything must have at least five sides: South, East, North, West and middle. If we were to look at only one side, we would fail to see the other four sides. And not only that, we will see that this one side also has at least five sides to it. If we examine things thoroughly in this manner, it becomes very difficult to identify anything as existing.

There are many ways to prove that things are empty. Modern scientists are discovering things, such as the nonexistence of time, which are actually referred to in the teachings of the Buddha. How can time not exist? Isn't this a very strange and shocking suggestion? What does time mean? The past, present, and future are now. How can we pinpoint or prove that? Time means change, but we cannot pinpoint where time changes. Why? The present must relate to the past and the future. In fact, there is no "now" without referring to the past or the future. If this is the case, we should separate "now" from the past and future, but if we do that, where is now? It seems that time, the self, and phenomena exist, but the Buddha called this, the way things appear, confusion. Seemingly, whatever exists is confusion.

Who are we? We are not our name, but if that is so, who are we? Words like "I" and "me" are only words, and our name is only a label. The same is true for objects: a "chair" is not a chair. The word "chair" is a label that we give to a particular type of object. Even to describe it as "a particular type of object" is also an example of labeling. To say that an object is literally a "chair," that the word is somehow identical to the object it describes, is not logical. So, what does the label mean? Where is the real chair? Is it the leg, the seat, or the back of the chair? To find out what it really is, we must examine it very carefully.

In the same way, can we say that we have a body or that we are a human being? Is the body the human being? Are we our body, are we our mind, or are we our name; who are we? It is very important for us to find the answer to this question for ourselves. We may think our mind, body, and name belong to us, but they are not what we are, and this demonstrates why the Buddha teaches egolessness, that the self does not in essence exist.

If we first understand the wisdom of egolessness intellectually, the second step is to examine the stages of egolessness in order to experience this wisdom for ourselves. When we recognize the wisdom of egolessness, then there is no longer any hope or fear, and this is what is known as *buddha nature*.

Why is it important to realize buddha nature? What does *buddha* mean? To be a buddha means our negative emotions totally collapse, once and for all, and our wisdom and compassion expand. Whoever accomplishes this is a buddha. This is the outer meaning of buddha: a person. The inner meaning of buddha is that everyone has buddha nature and that everybody can be a buddha. The teaching of the Buddha is what we follow in order to recognize our buddha nature and is the basis of our study and practice. This is the method and wisdom of the Buddhist path. Even though it is sometimes not so easy or beautiful, method is extremely important. When a chair is not stable, we can fix it by putting a small piece of wood under one leg, and this is an example of method.

So what is meant by method here? The logic and truth we encounter through contemplating the four thoughts—the preciousness of our human birth, impermanence, karma, and the suffering of samsara— inspire us to practice and encourage us in our search for the truth, but these contemplations alone will not bring us liberation.

Is the practice we do, such as refuge, bodhichitta, and dedication, nothing more than a tradition, a law, a religious rule or discipline of

Buddhism? Buddhist discipline is not only traditional, it is also deeply logical. Refuge and bodhichitta are our head and hands, renunciation is our feet, and the heart is the nonconceptual state of mind.

So, what is buddha nature, and where can we find it? Buddha nature is present whenever dualistic mind is absent. When one thought has ceased and another has not yet risen, there is a gap, and a chance for us to see our buddha nature. Unfortunately, the gap may be very small because we are not in the habit of remaining in that state.

How can we recognize our buddha nature? There are four kinds of teacher that can help us. The first kind is an experienced, qualified living master who has realized his or her own buddha nature. The second teacher is good, authentic Dharma books. These two types of guru are ones we need to come across during the course of our life, while the third teacher is life itself. Life is dualistic; it is strange and it is fun; it is empty and it is not empty; friends become enemies and enemies become friends; good becomes bad and bad becomes good.

But each of these three teachers is only temporary. The ultimate teacher lies within ourselves; it is the same as the wisdom of egolessness, buddha nature, and the suchness of absolute truth that is beyond all concepts. If suchness had no special qualities, we would not need to discuss it—or practice it. Suchness is omniscient and has an infinite capacity for reason and impartial loving-kindness. Suchness is blessed with two kinds of wisdom: the knowledge of how everything is and the ability to discern what is not true.

Ego does not have any of these qualities. Ego's love is a love based on selfishness. We often tell people that we like them because we need them and are happy that we have them. Love based on ego is not so pure, whereas the loving-kindness of suchness is pure, because it is not dualistic or conditional. Although it has many different names, such as mahamudra, dzogpachenpo, and madhyamaka, the suchness that we need to realize has only one meaning. The essence of mind is empty, the nature of that emptiness is clarity, and the union of emptiness and clarity is uncompounded.

To recognize this innermost essence of our mind, we rely on a teacher and authentic Dharma books. Until we have recognized our inherent nature, even if we were to win power over the whole world, we would still experience difficulties and suffering. In the ultimate state there is no thinking, so there is no hope and fear. For as long as we continue to think, we will endure hope and fear, and the result of feeling hope and fear is suffering.

To return to our natural state, we receive and contemplate the teachings of the Buddha, and we need to engage progressively in the various levels of practice. But when we recognize the wisdom of egolessness, there is really no practice left to do. Reaching this ultimate state of suchness is not dependent on study alone; faith and compassion also have a great influence. When we feel devotion and loving-kindness, our mind is pure and perceives purely. A pure mind is a clean mind, and a clean mind can encounter clarity.

Thinking is emotion, and it is also an obscuration, so how can we rid ourselves of obscuration? Although liberation and being a practitioner are clearly two separate things, the practitioner's way of thinking is not identical to the conventional way of thinking. Many great Kagyü practitioners say that they like thoughts because more thoughts bring greater wisdom; a thought comes, and that thought is changed into a state of wisdom. Great practitioners know how to be with their thoughts. Their devotion to the teacher and the teaching is very deep, because it is the teacher and the teaching that made them aware of how the mind works.

It goes without saying that the most important teacher is the Buddha, but our karma is such that we did not meet the Buddha, so for us the messenger is our teacher. Without a master we could not possibly realize the nature of mind, so if and when we reach that point of recognition, it will not be possible to put our appreciation and devotion for our teacher into words, and our devotion for our teacher will be unshakeable and unending.

QUESTION: *How can I find my teacher?*
RINPOCHE: The ultimate teacher, and our ultimate destination, is the wisdom of egolessness. However, if we want to cook really well we need more than a cookbook; we need to learn from an experienced cook. In the same way, if we want to recognize the nature of mind, it's very important to find and follow a spiritual teacher.

All over the world people are searching for a spiritual path. Some believe that they need to search tirelessly for their teacher, who they imagine will be a truly exceptional person, surrounded by color and pulsating energy or displaying magical powers. I have come across people who have been searching everywhere for ten years and still haven't found their teacher. Others don't want to search at all; they meet someone and assume that he or she is their teacher. Some people are prepared to rely on almost anybody, but sooner or later they might come to realize that they are not following a genuine teacher. Therefore, we should adopt the middle way in our approach to finding a teacher.

We should also know what to look for in a teacher. A teacher needs to be both sharp and kind. If the teacher has a sharp mind and a good heart, then he or she won't mislead us. A teacher must have recognized the nature of emptiness, as whoever realizes his or her buddha nature is endowed with the qualities of wisdom, discernment, and loving-kindness.

QUESTION: *You said that thought is emotion. Could you explain that a little more?*
RINPOCHE: First of all, thinking that something is good is emotion, because it is an expression of desire. Even relative bodhichitta involves thinking, and so relative bodhichitta is also an emotion. In the teaching of the Buddha there is a very important distinction between relative and absolute bodhichitta. Absolute bodhichitta arises out of the wisdom of egolessness. Thinking obscures the truth of the nature of mind, and it also confuses ordinary mind.

QUESTION: *Did you say that from the Kagyü point of view, thinking is also wisdom?*
RINPOCHE: No, the *essence* of thinking is wisdom. If we don't recognize this, thinking is just thinking, and we cannot really handle our emotions. Genuine practitioners are not so easily thrown by thoughts, whereas we accumulate more and more conflicting emotions and increase the strength of the samsaric mind. Practitioners follow their spiritual path and have responded to the teachings on how to manage

emotion, so they know how to practice with rising thoughts. Practitioners are not yet liberated, but they are on the path to enlightenment. They still experience powerful emotions, such as anger, but they do not respond to their anger as we do; they do not continue with or become distracted by their anger. Through their practice, they have learned to manage their emotions, whereas we are stuck in our habitual tendencies. This is why we need to learn how to manage our emotions, which we do by engaging in practice.

QUESTION: *When I look at my mind I see thoughts, and when realized beings look at their minds, they see wisdom.*
RINPOCHE: Yes, at the moment, as we have not realized the wisdom of egolessness, our mind is controlled by the ego, and whatever thoughts we register rise out of our dualistic mind. We think in terms of I and you, good and bad, right and wrong. We have received teachings on how to cut through dualistic thinking and attain the wisdom of egolessness. If our fixation on duality collapses for one whole day, we will become a buddha. Even a bodhisattva has to deal with emotions, so for us we need to be mindful in order to remain undistracted by our thoughts. Mindfulness is the method of practice, while thinking that we want to practice mahamudra is not practice at all; it is a desire, an idea, a hope, and it will not lead us to wisdom.

From the perspective of ultimate wisdom, buddha nature is extremely simple—there is absolutely nothing to do! If we believe that we're supposed to have some experience, we assume that that there is "something" to experience. But that is a false assumption. Wanting to experience something is a dualistic idea. There is nothing to experience. So what should we be doing?

Here's an example: can you see space? Space means openness. Although we don't see a particular object "space," there still is something to see, but it isn't a "thing," and yet we still see it. When we say that we experience emptiness, what is that? It's very hard to find an adequate example. Experiencing the quality of space is similar. Do we perceive space? We have to say yes, because this openness—in which we can actually move—is space. We may be able to say "I see the space" because there are no walls preventing us from doing so. We can open the door and enter a room because we know that there is space there. This means that we perceive this openness, and yet there is nothing concrete to hold on to. There is no object, no *thing*ness, and yet we can have an experience of it. It is in this way that we can see space, and that is a simile for the experience of emptiness.

If we say that we want to experience emptiness, we often start with the assumption that we're supposed to experience something concrete, or some feeling such as happiness or joy. Various feelings may arise, but these feelings are bound up with the ordinary, dualistic mind: "That is good, that is bad." Any grasping onto these is not the ultimate state of wisdom; they are just experiences that pass away again.

Experiencing emptiness is like experiencing the openness of space. But that is just an example, a simile, and is not the same. An example can only be an approximation. Reality cannot be explained.

12. Pure Buddhism, Authentic Transmission

Orgyen Tobgyal Rinpoche

> *Orgyen Tobgyal Rinpoche, was one of Kyabje Dilgo Khyentse Rinpoche's closest students. Renowned for his commitment to upholding the Khyentse lineage, Rinpoche is particularly well-known as a Vajrayana specialist. During his visit to Lerab Ling in the summer of 1997, Rinpoche—who was translated with great panache by Chökyi Nyima (Richard Barron)—spoke candidly about the transition of Tibetan Buddhism from the East to the West, putting the current situation into historical context, and offering Western Dharma practitioners some very practical advice.*

I N BUDDHISM, OUR TEACHER THE BUDDHA taught a system that doesn't require blind faith from those who practice it; rather, we are encouraged continuously to examine the teachings thoroughly. The Buddha presented the Buddhadharma in such a way that—whether you are approaching it from the ordinary perspective of an unenlightened person or with the omniscient wisdom and awareness of an enlightened being—the more you examine and scrutinize the Dharma, the more benefit and value you find there, as well as more and more reasons for practicing it. The Buddha even promised us that this is the case.

As we study the Buddha's teachings, it is important that we understand them both from the point of view of scriptural authority and through our own powers of reasoning; we need to follow both approaches. But of the two, the most important kind of understanding for us to achieve is the understanding we arrive at by applying reason and logic to the teachings ourselves; all the great pandits (scholars) of

Indian Buddhism and all the learned masters of Tibet agree on this unanimously. If the final authority we rely on has nothing to do with our own powers of reasoning—that we simply assume something is true because our root lama says it is so, or we accept something blindly just because we're told that God or Brahma said it was true—then something fundamental and vital is missing.

Buddhism has a rich vein of authentic scriptural material—the authentic words of the Buddha as well as the commentaries of great masters. Beyond these texts, the primary practice of Buddhism is that of applying logic and reason in order to confirm, experientially, the conclusions stated in the scriptures. Without this, we cannot progress, at least as far as Buddhism is concerned. And in my opinion, without personal exercise of reason, we don't have the Dharma.

However, I don't want you to imagine that the truth of the teachings is easy to prove and that absolutely anyone will be able to do it. That's not what I am saying at all. Complete understanding of the entire canon of the Buddha's teachings is by no means simple, and an ordinary person will certainly not be able to get it right away. Even though the powers of reasoning are an important factor, it's not that simple; understanding does not happen automatically.

What, then, does a Buddhist practitioner need most? Authenticity— to be a true Buddhist. If those who teach or practice the Dharma are not truly Buddhist, then we are faced with a situation quite different from the one we have been talking about. A teacher who claims to be Buddhist but teaches something other than Buddhism creates a different situation, a contradiction, making the kind of authenticity that can be proven by our powers of reasoning impossible.

The authentic Dharma

The Tibetan Buddhist tradition traces its origins back to India, which was where the Buddha taught. Tibet's indigenous religion was, and is, Bönpo; the Buddhist teachings were brought to the Land of Snows from India around 1,200 years ago.

The teachings of the Buddhadharma are primarily what we refer to as the *three yanas:* the so-called *path of the shravakas,* or the Hinayana path; the Mahayana path of the bodhisattva; and the Vajrayana path.

Each of these three yanas involves a *view,* a system of *meditation,* and a system of conduct, or *action.* As these teachings spread in any given culture, certain customs and traditions will develop as a matter of course, but it's important to understand that the differences between the teachings of each of the three yanas exist only because of the diverse levels of understanding of those receiving the teachings. There are no contradictions within the teachings themselves; there are only differences in emphasis.

The Buddha taught so methodically and thoroughly that he was able to give all these very distinct teachings extremely precisely. Traditionally, a simile is used to describe the clarity of the Buddha's presentation. If you put a tiny grain in the palm of your hand, you will be able to see it quite distinctly; the Buddha taught with the same sharpness and clarity. So, the Buddha's teachings are well thought out, and their presentation is extremely well formulated. There is nothing willy-nilly or half baked about any of it, and you won't find any lack of depth in the Dharma.

Taking the broadest possible view, the Buddha is said to have given some 84,000 collections of teachings. These can be summarized and categorized into nine yanas, or more concisely into the three yanas we have already spoken about. These three yanas can be categorized even more concisely into two approaches: the approach of the sutra path, based upon causes leading to results; and the path of the tantras, based upon those results. There is such harmony within all these teachings that if we examine just a single verse of any aspect of the Dharma, it is possible to determine the level to which it applies. We can see exactly where that one verse fits into the entire spectrum of the Buddha's teachings.

The actual words of the Buddha, what he said during the years he lived in this world, have also been carefully categorized: the Vinaya, or the ethical codes of Buddhism; the Sutras, the discourses of the Buddha; and the Abhidharma, the higher metaphysical teachings of the Buddha. They haven't been mixed together into a messy kind of stew. Instead, they are presented systematically and with exquisite accuracy and precision.

Taking the words of the Buddha as their basis, the great Indian pandits further elaborated them in treatises, or commentaries, on the enlightened intent underlying his original words: these explanations are wholly in accord with the way the Buddha gave his teachings. Choosing their own particular strengths as their subjects, Vasubhandu commented on the Abhidharma; Nagarjuna wrote his famous works concerning the madhyamaka, or middle-way, approach; and Dharmakirti commented on how to attain states of valid cognition and insight. Many of these great masters of the past were encyclopedic writers, and their commentaries can run to hundreds of volumes. But without exception, they were all commenting on the original teachings of the Buddha, not establishing a new school. Not one of these masters ever declared, "This is Dharmakirti's Dharma," or, "This is Nagarjuna's Dharma"; it was always the Buddhadharma as explained by a master. In fact, if you look at the first page of any one of these texts, you will see a statement to the effect that it is commentary on an aspect of the Buddha's intent.

The process of transmission

So, to come to my key point: now that the Tibetan tradition of Buddhism is coming to Europe and the Western hemisphere, we need to make sure that what takes root here is authentic; that it is in accord with the scriptural sources of the tradition, and that what is being transmitted is an authentic transmission of the Buddhadharma.

If we are going to have Buddhism at all, it should be a pure, clean Buddhism, completely in accord with the three yanas as taught by the Buddha. If what is taught is not in accord with the three yanas as taught by the Buddha, it's not pure, clean Buddhism. If we try to mix Buddhism with other religions, we don't have pure, clean Buddhism. We may swap terms with other religions, we may see others try to incorporate Buddhist terminology into their schools or find that other schools' terminology creeps into the Buddhist schools, but that's just swapping words. It doesn't have anything to do with what the tradition of the Dharma actually is. This is an important point.

In Tibet you will find a great many ancient texts that have been translated from Indian languages, and the first thing you will read is the title of the text in its original language. No one in Tibet is astonished by this; it seems perfectly natural to honor the authentic origins of the tradition. As the Tibetan presentations of Buddhism are translated for the modern world, we must make sure the transition is accomplished as authentically as it was in Tibet. A confusing, mixed-up process of transmission would not be good or useful, and we won't have the true teachings of the Buddha here in the West unless real care is taken.

This is particularly important as there seem to be a number of people setting themselves up as lamas whose teachings have nothing to do with any of the yanas of Buddhism. This is not a good development. I find it distressing that such a shocking lack of authenticity so often creeps in because no attention is being paid to authoritative transmission.

The teachings rely upon those who transmit and uphold them, on the masters who pass on the lineage. Throughout the world, spiritual masters of a wide variety of different spiritual schools uphold their respective teachings: this is wonderful, it is to be praised and admired. However, if those who don't understand how to uphold the teachings authentically—but act as though they do—are teaching, it will bring about ruination of the teacher, of the teachings, and of the country in which the teaching takes place. There are many stories cited in the teachings that confirm this. Without authenticity, everything falls apart.

Buddha himself spoke of the danger of people setting themselves up as false teachers. There are many prophecies in the Buddhist tradition warning that, particularly during times of spiritual degeneration, individuals will appear whose perverse aspirations allow them to manifest as though they were authentic spiritual teachers, but who teach wrongheaded Dharma, leading beings to the lower realms. Traditionally, it is understood that especially during times of transition, like today, there is always the danger of perverse teachers teaching wrongly and confusing and harming people.

That is not to say there is not room for skillful means in presenting the teachings in a manner appropriate to the situation. But ultimately a teacher's methods must accord with the principles of the three yanas as taught by the Buddha.

Authentic teachers

Traditionally, both in India and Tibet, you have to follow a strict process of education before becoming a teacher. First you must, yourself, rely upon a teacher. Once you have found an authentic teacher who holds an authentic lineage, you receive teachings from him or her, you contemplate the teachings you receive, then you put them into practice, developing your own meditative experiences and realization. In this way your mind will be liberated to a greater or lesser extent, and before you teach others you must have achieved a level of liberation yourself. Having done so, you are then in a position to benefit others as a teacher. Never in the Buddhist tradition have teachers who have not themselves relied upon a teacher and an authentic spiritual practice sprung up from nowhere, like mushrooms on a lawn.

When you examine a spiritual mentor to determine his or her authenticity, don't focus entirely on how learned he or she may or may not be. The main issue is whether or not the quality of bodhichitta has blossomed in the heart and mind of the teacher. Is the teacher's activity based on self-interest or on an uncorrupted and altruistic selflessness? If someone claiming to be a teacher acts selfishly, however much they may speak about altruism and compassion, you will not have found the qualities required of a true teacher.

I've heard a lot about various famous modern teachers here in the West who have attracted large numbers of students. But when I've asked who their teachers are, the information has often been rather vague. No one really knows who their teachers are. Then I started to look into what kind of teaching these famous teachers are giving, and, frankly, it seemed to be no more than a bit of this and a little bit of that, a chunk of Hinduism here, and a dollop of Buddhism thrown in there for good measure. Don't you think that's a little odd?

If you are going to teach the Dharma, that's exactly what you have to do. You shouldn't be thinking about what people want to hear, what you should say to make them like you, or "Am I a great teacher?" That's entirely the wrong motivation for a teacher.

It is as important for the spread of the Buddhadharma from Tibet to the modern world as it was when the teachings first came from India to Tibet that teachers present the teachings of their lineage authentically. In order for that to happen, there has to be a lineage, and a lineage depends on an authentic, methodical process of transmission.

13. THE BUDDHIST VIEW OF REALITY

Dzogchen Pönlop Rinpoche

What is Buddhism?

Many people regard Buddhism as one of the world's great religions. However, according to the teachings, scriptures, and practices of Lord Buddha Shakyamuni, it is not really appropriate to label the spiritual path called Buddhism a religion. The conventional understanding of the word religion does not really apply to the practice and view of Buddhism.

So, what is Buddhism? There is no such word as "Buddhism" in the original teachings of Buddha. They are free from the concept of "-isms" and notions of religion, belief, and dogma. My experience and understanding of this path is that it is a science of insight, an inner science or a science of the mind. It is a pure and genuine philosophy of life.

Central to most religions is a belief in a certain power, external to us, that controls the world. Such a belief does not exist in Buddhism. We cannot employ Buddha, or any of the other enlightened beings, to make us happy or to clear away our suffering. In Buddhism, this responsibility falls on our own shoulders, a fact that clearly illustrates that Buddhism is a path and science of insight.

In Tibet we call Buddhists *nangpa*. *Nangpa* literally means "insider," although some people translate it as "internalist." The spiritual practice of this particular tradition focuses on our inner self and existence, and the essence of mind.

The practice and view of Buddhism are mainly concerned with the mind. Buddhism does not maintain that our world and existence are controlled by a supernatural being or by any supernatural power outside of our own mind. The whole world, whether it is positive or negative, happy, sad, or suffering, is simply a creation of our own mind. Nobody else created this world for the purpose of our suffering or happiness; it is our own creation. Neither Buddha nor any other enlightened being possesses the power to control our world and life.

Therefore, ideas such as pleasing Buddha to create happiness, or acting in a way that displeases Buddha and creates suffering, are not part of the Buddhist path. Buddhism is a path of individual liberation and freedom. If we want to free ourselves from pain and suffering by means of this path, we have to work on ourselves. If we want to enjoy the wealth and happiness of liberation and freedom from suffering, we have to involve ourselves in creating that happiness and in making that vision materialize.

Working with our mind involves working with both aspects of mind: the fundamental nature of our mind, and the temporary nature of our mind. Buddhism addresses both these aspects as well as our entire way of life. Therefore, it is free from the constrictions of religious dogma, cultural expression, and any one language. Buddhism simply and straightforwardly focuses on the nature of our existence.

We could say Buddhism is like pure fresh water, free of any color or shape. If we pour this water into a Tibetan cup, it takes the shape of the cup, of that culture, and it reflects the color of that cup or culture. The color and shape of whatever hand is holding the cup of water is reflected in the water, or you could say that although the water adapts those colors and shapes, the water is totally free of those shapes and colors. If you pour this water into a French wine glass, its shape will also change into that of a French wine glass, and will adapt to the hand that holds the glass.

Just as the nature of water is free from shape and color, the spiritual path known as Buddhism is free of any particular culture or language. But we can't say that we don't want the container, that we just want the water, because there is no way you can transport or hold the water, or use it well, without a container. How can we say that we don't want the bottle, that we just want the water? How can we benefit from the water if we have no bottle? Irrespective of the type of container the water comes in, we still need a container.

We simply can't say that other cultures and languages are garbage and not needed, or demand to have the water without any container. If we throw the bottle into the garbage and just pour the water into our hands, it won't serve its purpose; it will trickle onto the ground, and this precious pure water will be wasted.

So, if we don't like a particular container, we must choose another one. We should ensure that this alternative container is clean and undamaged, so that the water will not seep out as soon as it is poured in. We must master the technique for transferring the water from its original bottle into our chosen vessel, and be certain that we have transferred every last drop before discarding the original bottle.

Before we throw the old bottle into a recycling machine we should make sure that our new container is good enough to transport the water, and then transfer the water from the bottle destined for the garbage sack into a precious vase of our own choosing. This is how Buddhism has traveled from the original source and bottling plant in Northern India to Tibet, on the roof of the world, to China and Japan, and to other continents, where various appropriate containers were created for this thirst-quenching water.

It took over two hundred years for Tibetans to prepare the container for their Indian "water," and it may take a similar length of time to transport this water into other cultures and languages, but that is not a problem. We have to start somehow, because if we think Buddhism takes two hundred years to establish and decide to ignore it, the translation will never take place. It is important to start somewhere, and so it is worth preparing a clean container and transferring the water into our own cultural and linguistic container.

At the same time we must be patient. We can't simply rush in and declare that we no longer live in medieval times, that we live in the fast-paced world of high technology, and that the transference will not take anything like two hundred years. We might expect it to take only two, or at most twenty years, but this is not the case. Even though we live in the high-speed era of technology and we have access to all sorts of swift-acting media that enable us to produce computerized Dharma, video Dharma, audio Dharma, fax Dharma, and Internet online Dharma, our problem is that we don't have time.

We have stacks of media equipment and all the high-tech help we could ever want, but where the transportation of Dharma is concerned, we are traveling at the same speed as the great translator Marpa did when he walked to India. Marpa dedicated his time fully to the path of spirituality and to the transportation of this water, whereas we don't have anything near that amount of time available to us. The obstacles or blockages we need to overcome are different from those that Marpa was confronted with, which were mainly to do with limited technology. He could not fly or take a train from Tibet to India; he had to walk.

Two truths, relative and absolute

The Buddhist view of reality can be summarized in two main points: relative truth and absolute truth, the view of relative or conventional reality and the view of ultimate reality.

According to Buddhism, the fundamental nature of reality in our relative, conventional world is suffering and impermanence. The reality of the world that we experience, live in, and struggle through is one whose nature is impermanence and suffering. Most of the time we don't even want to think about it or hear someone talking about suffering or impermanence, so our normal method of dealing with relative reality is to ignore it.

Lord Buddha's message was that ignoring our suffering does not help us to overcome our suffering or help us make our world a better place to live. The best method for dealing with suffering, according to Buddhism, is to discuss, reveal, and go into the depths of it. By going through the depths of suffering, we can gain the wisdom of ultimate truth.

Ignoring our suffering doesn't help us on any level. In our regular life we employ various simple methods for ignoring and evading our suffering. For example, if we have a little disagreement in our family, we might take refuge in a bar. We have a drink and think that we are getting rid of our suffering, but in actual fact, after receiving the "blessings" of the bar, we might jump into a car, and drive at high speed through the streets. We might even drive on the wrong side of the road, crash into another car and break our legs, fracture another person's head, and wreck our own car. Both drivers could end up in the hospital and face high hospital bills. So just by ignoring our little problem, we get into another much bigger problem. Such are the consequences of ignoring our suffering.

The three sufferings

What is suffering? We might think that we have had enough of suffering and that we don't want to talk about it any more—that we already know what suffering basically is. Buddha's answer to this question is that there is one word that describes the origins of suffering, and that one word is *fear*. Each of the innumerable kinds of suffering are expressions of fear.

What is this fear? The fundamental expression of this fear is of losing something that is valuable to us, such as our precious human birth, and the second kind of fear is getting something that we do not want, such as an illness.

There are three fundamental kinds of suffering: *all-pervasive* or *self-existing suffering,* the *suffering of change,* and the *suffering of suffering.* Self-existing or all-pervading suffering is the fundamental fear that pervades every aspect of our existence, irrespective of whether our lives are full of suffering or happiness. Happiness is merely a superficial façade, because behind this happiness lurks fear, the fear of losing our happiness, that some unknown factor may destroy our happiness. So, to a certain degree, happiness is an even greater form of suffering.

The suffering of change and the suffering of suffering are also pervaded by fear. The traditional simile used to illustrate the suffering of change is to suppose that we are attending a marriage ceremony and the house suddenly collapses in an earthquake.

The suffering of suffering can be explained by imagining that we are already suffering from a disease like diabetes or cancer, and on top of that we get a headache, and one of our wisdom teeth is not growing properly. Then we go to a bad dentist who makes us suffer even more by making mistakes while treating our wisdom tooth.

So these are the three sufferings, which according to Buddhism are a fundamental aspect of our existence.

Impermanence

Another reality in our lives is impermanence. When we look at a candle, we can see that the flame is continuous, but this continuity depends on discontinuity: the stability of the flame depends on the discontinuity of the candle. When the fire burns faster, the flame becomes more stable, as it consumes more candle wax, so the continuity of this flame depends on the discontinuity of the candle. This example also describes the nature of our existence. The continuity of our future and the continuity of the present moment exist only because of the discontinuity of our life, which changes from moment to moment.

Our existence in relative reality is subject to both suffering and impermanence. Impermanence can be seen as a candle burning lower and lower until it disappears, which is like death. The candle does not disappear in an instant; it disappears in every moment, just as we die from moment to moment. Death occurs in every instant, and we also take birth in every instant. We live in a world of impermanence, the second characteristic of our relative existence. To acknowledge suffering and impermanence is the purpose of our practice, and seeing suffering and impermanence clearly is the wisdom of relative truth.

Absolute reality

Absolute or ultimate reality can be variously described as egolessness, selflessness, or emptiness, and this is what Buddhism holds to be the fundamental reality of our world. Whether we characterize this world as full of suffering, impermanence, or happiness, and whether it is good or bad, ultimately none of these qualities exists. Our very own self does not exist either. This is the basic nature of reality, the essential nature of the entire world. There is no fundamental ground of existence. Existence is totally nonexistent, empty of self and ego, of suffering and impermanence. We can come to understand egolessness through analyzing the Mahayana Buddhist view of the lineages of Nagarjuna and Asanga, which offer a detailed analysis of how seemingly existing phenomena do not exist at all.

A simple illustration of ultimate reality is the dreaming state when compared to the perception of a person who is fully awake. When we are in a deep sleep and dreaming, everything in our dream seems to be real. We might dream that we are in a zoo and see a tiger breaking out of its cage and then chase after us. We are running away from a dream tiger, yet we still experience the reality of running for our precious lives.

As long as we are in the dream we consider the dream to be real, and that there is no existence separate from that of our dream. Perhaps a friend hears us talking in our sleep, "Oh, a tiger," or, "Help! I'm dying!" and as this friend is very compassionate, he or she wakes us up by shaking us or by throwing a bucket of water over us. When we have woken up we will appreciate our friend's action, because we no longer have to try and run away from a tiger and don't need to fear any more for our life. We see that there is no tiger, that we were not running away from it, and there wasn't even any zoo. The city that we ran through was merely part of a nightmare.

Right this minute, we are going through a nightmare called samsara. It is a different kind of a dream, a human dream. We go through all sorts of dreams, but when we wake up from this thick state of ignorance, we find none of these dreams actually exist. That is the nature of ultimate or absolute reality. Ultimate reality is the state of being fully awakened. From the view of the absolute nature of reality, nothing exists; there is no ego or self and no phenomenal world. Our world is currently a dream, or perhaps a nightmare that is produced by the sleep of our ignorance.

Relative reality is like our dreams, and our fully awakened state is absolute reality. We should not mix these two realities together. When we differentiate these two aspects of reality we can understand them without confusing their qualities.

QUESTION: *I feel that I have often experienced this state of awakening from the dream state, but sooner or later I realize that I was awake for only a short time and that I have become fully caught again. How can I recognize the point at which I come out of the dream state into absolute reality?*
RINPOCHE: The basic sign of us waking up is egolessness. When we realize that there is no ego, we are fully awake. Basically speaking, we go through different stages of waking up. Our dream experience becomes lighter and lighter, and we gradually seem to lose the rigidity

of our dreams, which is akin to entering a state of lucid dreaming. Then we wake up.

But when we wake up in the morning and see that it is still early, the sky is gray, and it is raining a little bit, we don't so much feel like waking up, because the real world doesn't feel like much fun at the moment. Our bed is still warm and cozy, so we go back to sleep. We want to go into another, better dream, or continue the dream we were just having. By the time we wake up again it could be lunch time. Maybe we get up, have a snack, and go back to sleep again. This is what the process of waking up is like. We need a real willingness in order to wake up, a decisive will.

Wisdom-Jewels of Twentieth-Century Tibetan Masters

*It's not appearances that bind you,
but your attachment to them.*
Tilopa, to Naropa

This section contains teachings from some of the greatest masters of the previous century. Each of them played an important role in the lives of the younger generation of teachers who appear in this book.

Jamyang Khyentse Chökyi Lodrö was the childhood master of Sogyal Rinpoche, who calls him "the foundation of my life" and "the living example of someone who has realized the teachings and perfected the practice."[16] *Sogyal Rinpoche associated him with the very atmosphere of practice and of the teachings, and his being and his activities deeply influenced him as a young lama. At the end of the 1950s Sogyal Rinpoche left Tibet with him, and in Sikkim, shortly before his death, Jamyang Khyentse advised the young Sonam Gyaltsen (Sogyal) to go to Dudjom Rinpoche.*

Dudjom Rinpoche was at that time the head of the Nyingma School of Tibetan Buddhism. It was almost by chance that Sogyal Rinpoche discovered his inner quality: as he was translating for one of Dudjom Rinpoche's Western students, who were rare at that time, he was so gripped by the profundity of the teaching that he later requested personal teachings from the master, which he received.

In the meantime, Dilgo Khyentse Rinpoche had been

spending decades in retreat and had ripened into an extraor-
dinary teacher. After Dudjom Rinpoche's death Sogyal Rin-
poche placed himself under Dilgo Khyentse Rinpoche's
spiritual direction. During the same years he also established
a long and profound connection with Nyoshul Khen Rin-
poche, from whom he received numerous extensive teach-
ings up until the latter's death in 1999.

These teachings are about how we investigate the mind,
and how we realize its nature. Teachings such as these need
time to be read and ingested. If we just gulp them down or
read them through the telescope of intellectual distance, they
will have no influence on us and will not reach us in those
places within, where they can take effect. We need to
approach them with open hearts.

14. Meditation and Peace

Dudjom Rinpoche

WE HUMAN BEINGS ARE composed of body, speech, and mind, but it is this mind of ours, which we call "The king who does everything" or "the universal ordering principle," *kunjé gyalpo,* that dominates the body and speech and bosses them around. The creator of happiness is the mind, and the creator of suffering is also the mind.

How does happiness come about? When we look after our own mind, and carefully leave it in a state of peace, then happiness will arise.

How does suffering come about? Since mind's desires are insatiable, when it hankers after the objects of desire, this gives rise to all sorts of disturbing emotions, like anger and aggression, which in turn generate a host of negative thoughts. These drive us into all kinds of endless activity, all of which is mixed up with negative actions, thereby creating negative karma. As a result, both mind and body are trapped in an inescapable prison of unrelieved suffering.

Until the day we die there is no end to this suffering and the grueling, burdensome toil of the mind. If it were all to end when we died, that would be wonderful. However, in reality it is only this body of ours that dies and not the mind. And whatever the mind occupies itself with at the moment in this life—all these negative and inauspicious actions—is just what we have to follow in the life after, experiencing consequences that match it exactly.

Therefore, you will find that in this life and the next, positive action and negative action, happiness and suffering, are all dependent on the mind. What we have to do is to turn the mind around and gather it in. For if you look at the mind, you will see that it is as crazy and as devious as a madman; things you would not even imagine you could ever think, you will think nine times over! Then you will realize that it is mind that is responsible for this craziness, too, and that you need to turn the mind round and bring it home. What we have to focus on is activity that calms and *stabilizes* the mind.

Without bringing some kind of calm, ease, and relaxation to the mind, and pursuing ways of bringing about peace and happiness—or at least thinking about doing so—then even though you may have wealth as huge as Mount Sumeru, as vast as the ocean, still you will not be satisfied. For if you have something, there is the suffering of having, and if you do not have something, there is the suffering of not having. If you start something, there is the suffering of not being able to finish it. Even though suffering may appear to us as happiness, the very heart of it is always suffering. So make up your mind and be certain that the root cause of all of this is the mind.

You might ask: what is this mind like, then? If you were to examine it closely, you would find that there is no form there to look at, no sound to hear; it is like the wind. Suddenly a thought arises, and just as suddenly it disappears. There is nothing else apart from that.

Out of this empty mind arises an empty thought, yet instead of leaving it as it is, we try to catch that thought by generating another one. The first thought gives work to another thought so as to catch a thought...and so on, without any end. One thought employing another like this is what creates delusion and distraction, and only makes our heads spin.

So *this* is what we should realize: how we create an endless chain of thoughts and ceaseless activity, all of it totally pointless. If you chase a thought, there will *never* be a time when you catch it. So instead, let the mind itself look into the mind. When mind really watches the mind, you will notice that the consciousness that looks and the mind that is being watched cannot be separated or distinguished at all.

The cause of *all* delusion and deception is arising thoughts, *namtok*, so do not allow your mind to wander after random thoughts. Instead, when a thought arises, look it right in the face and see how it is, and what it looks like. For if you were to go after it, even a hundred years would not be long enough for you to catch it.

So, without chasing after thoughts, just remain in that natural, settled state of meditation. With mind left on its own, undisturbed in its own space, if a thought arises, that's fine; if one does not arise, that's also fine. Indifferent and unmoved by arising thoughts, you can experience a state where there is no memory or thought at all, but where there is a clear, deep, resonant emptiness. This is what is called the "stillness" of meditation, or *nepa*.

If you let your mindfulness release the mind like this, and let it settle of its own accord, then even in your body you will experience a vibrant lightness, and in your mind a deep peace and clear, radiant bliss. Why? Because mind is able to find its own natural state, and rest in its own nature. When you are able to remain, naturally relaxed, in the nature of mind like that, this state of meditation is called *shamata (shi né)* or sometimes *samadhi (tingedzin)*.

It is when you can relax your mind so that it remains calm and sober like this that you will obtain true peace and happiness. When you discover inner peace in this way within your mind, then there is simply no cause for generating aggression toward either external phenomena or others, nor the slightest reason for feelings of jealousy or competitiveness.

Instead, you will be able naturally and automatically to bring about peace and happiness in the world outside. If we are unable to cultivate this peace and well-being of mind inside, then the mind will become entangled in all kinds of thoughts, and it will be extremely difficult to achieve peace and happiness in the world.

Once we are convinced that peace and happiness are dependent entirely on the mind, with that certainty and conviction each one of us should try to cultivate peace of mind within, which will bring happiness and peace both in this life and in the life after. It is in our own hands. And if we can develop it ourselves, we will not have to seek peace or happiness elsewhere, nor can anyone steal it or claim it from us. Please do keep this in mind and practice it.

When we sit, we leave the body in its natural state, unaltered; the speech unaltered, natural to the flow of the breath; and the mind unaltered, in its own resting place.

The wisdom mind of the buddhas is what we call the wisdom of emptiness; it is therefore emptiness from which, as its own self-radiance, arise the five wisdoms and all noble qualities. The nature of our mind, too, is emptiness; from the point of view of emptiness, the nature of our mind and the nature of the buddhas' mind are exactly the same. But for us, when the radiance of emptiness radiates out, we do not recognize it as the five wisdoms as do the buddhas, and so we become deluded, that delusion manifesting as arising thoughts, misleading us and dragging us further into delusion.

Therefore, if we can recognize our own nature, the true state of affairs, we will not need to search for Buddha far away outside of us; in fact we can find Buddha within ourselves.

Since that is the case, keep this in your mind.

15. Shamata, Vipashyana, and the Nature of Mind

Dilgo Khyentse Rinpoche

In the last year of his life, Dilgo Khyentse Rinpoche undertook a final journey to the West, where he visited La Sonnerie in the Dordogne, France, and then Prapoutel, a holiday resort near Grenoble that Sogyal Rinpoche had transformed into a wonderful retreat center. Dilgo Khyentse Rinpoche was originally from Kham province, a region in Tibet inhabited by nomads, and had always loved living in tents. Beside the main teaching tent that had room for over a thousand people, a small tent was put up that contained his sleeping quarters and a living room, and from there he enjoyed the view over the wide alpine valley that reminded him of the Tibetan landscapes of his home. Dilgo Khyentse Rinpoche gave many empowerments and teachings, including the following short teaching.

SHANTIDEVA SAID, "If we don't apply the ascetic practice of training our mind, what is the use of any other so-called ascetic practice?" Mind is the perpetrator of both virtuous and negative actions. As I often say, it is mind that must investigate mind. Over many lifetimes, our activities have forged habitual tendencies in our mind, and though we may examine our mind, many thoughts and emotions will still pass through it. It is this constant flow of discursive thoughts that prevents us from seeing the nature of mind properly.

Therefore, as a first step it is necessary to calm and pacify the movements of the mind, and this is achieved through shamata practice. The practice of inner calm has many levels and aspects. Shamata practice is taught according to both the sutra and mantra tradition, and although there are many techniques for practicing it, here we will look at one that is simple, easy, and very beneficial.

To begin, we assume a proper, well-balanced physical posture by sitting straight. Then, we visualize a white *Ah*—the symbol of the unborn, absolute nature—on the tip of our nose. As we exhale, the letter *Ah* flies out far away from us, up into the sky, and at the same time we utter the syllable *Ah*. When we inhale, the white *Ah* returns to the tip of our nose, thus completing one cycle of the practice. We count each cycle of breath on a mala until we have practiced it, say, 1,000 times or so.

During our practice we try not to let our mind wander toward any other objects, look to the left or right, or intersperse our recitation with ordinary conversation. We remain in one-pointed concentration and focus our attention on the letter *Ah,* as vividly as if we were seeing something real, directly in front of us.

Practicing in this way allows our mind to become more peaceful. When our thoughts have calmed down, we can look at the nature of our mind. While we are alive the mind is supported by the body, and body and mind together create the conditions for speech. Without the mind, however, neither body nor speech can exist. Since mind is the strongest and most powerful of the three, it is the one that we should examine most carefully.

The rulers of a country are the ones with the power to start a war or to drop atom bombs on another country. In the same manner, it is the mind, through strong hatred or anger, that leads the body and speech into violent and negative actions. If we turn our attention inward and look at our anger, which can seem so strong, we quickly realize that anger has no weapons at hand; nor is it a powerful general with a huge army under its command. Not only that, it has no shape, location, or color. So anger is empty. If we can recognize anger's empty essence, anger's influence over us will be diminished.

The same is true of attachment and desire. We all have a strong attachment to our families and children, and we may also experience powerful desire for an individual, so strong that we are prepared to spend a small fortune getting to know this person. And yet, just like anger, desire is not a powerful commander of an army that can force us to carry out its orders. Desire is merely a product of the mind. If we examine our desire again, we can see that it also has no color, shape, or location. It is just like a rainbow shining in the sky. There is nothing to catch hold of, no substance or entity; desire is simply empty.

Once we have recognized the empty aspect of the mind, we look directly at our empty nature and remain in that state, not falling under the power of our thoughts. But this does not mean that we should block our thoughts from rising. We might think that the best meditation is one in which no thoughts occur at all, one that allows us to remain free of thoughts, but it is a mistake to prevent thoughts from rising. If we are driving a train at high speed and we brake abruptly, we could cause a major accident. Instead, we need to be aware of thoughts as they arise, recognizing them, for example, as thoughts of anger, desire, faith, or compassion. When we stare into a monkey's eyes, the monkey feels shy and looks away. If we stare at our thoughts, they too will lose their power.

When thoughts lose their strength we slowly come to realize their empty nature. In the Wisdom chapter of Shantideva's *Bodhicharyavatara,* it says that thoughts arise in the same way in the mind of an ordinary person as they do in that of a yogi. The difference is that an ordinary person falls under the power of the thoughts, while the yogi does not, as he is the master of his mind. A realized yogi who has reached the level at which all phenomena are exhausted into the absolute nature of *dharmata* sees all forms and hears all sounds. It is not that the phenomenal world disappears; it is simply that a yogi does not fall under the influence of rising thoughts. As it is said, "When the movement of thoughts is left in its own nature, thoughts are freed into the dharmakaya."

When thoughts arise in the mind of a worldly person, like a slave he or she immediately chases after them and completely loses any recognition of that thought as a manifestation of the nature of mind. Then, like a capricious monkey, the mind becomes extremely powerful and utterly uncontrollable, leading beings to take rebirth in one of the three lower realms of samsara.

We often talk about the self, or the ego, but any notion of the self is itself nothing more than a thought. There is no such thing as a separate and distinct self that can be isolated and seen as existing on its own terms. The concept of the ego, of an individual self, is attached to three things: our body, our speech, and our mind. For example, we think that this individual, the "I," is somehow attached to the body, but is it attached to the skin or to any particular organ? And if it is really connected to the body, is it like a bird perching on a pole, or does it permeate the body as water does mud? The more we look, the less we find, and the same conclusion will be reached when we examine whether the "I" is attached to the speech: speech is just like a wind moving through space and cannot serve as a support for the concept of ego.

Now, only the mind remains to be examined. If we think that the self exists within the mind, we should look at this so-called "I" and ask whether it has any definable shape, color, or characteristic. As we discover that there is no such thing as an "I," our clinging to a sense of self, our fixation on the existence of ego, will cease. Our craving for friendship, our attachment to those we like, and our repulsion for people we dislike will also fall away. Even if someone anoints one side of a great bodhisattva's face with sandalwood oil and someone else on the other side threatens to strike him with an axe, the bodhisattva will feel no attraction for the person with the sandalwood perfume and no hatred for the person who is going to attack him.

This is illustrated by one of the former lives of the Buddha, when he was a bodhisattva called Rishi, which means "the teacher of passions." At one point the king was so angry with him that he decided to cut off Rishi's head and limbs. The great bodhisattva was able to change the mind of the infuriated king, but not through feeling an even stronger hatred for the king than the king had for him. Rishi's mind was so infused with compassion that the king's mind was graced and transformed by compassion.

Once our attachment to the concept of ego has vanished, attraction and repulsion can no longer manifest in our mind. Strong attraction for our self, for that concept of "I," also can no longer arise. The idea of reacting toward others with indifference or contempt, with a desire to rid ourselves of others, can never arise in us again.

In this way we should investigate the nature of mind. If our thoughts become very strong again and distract us, we should resume the practice of sending out and recalling back the white letter *Ah* on the medium of the breath until the mind regains its composure.

When the mind is calm, we look at its nature, but we should know that simply calming the mind through shamata practice is not enough to bring us to buddhahood. As Jetsun Milarepa said,

> In the ground of *shamata,* inner calm,
> Grow the flowers of *vipashyana,* greater vision.

Unless our body is like a dome-shaped glass case, simply trying to meditate by remaining inside ourselves will not help us. At the other extreme, if we light a butter lamp and leave it outside in the wind, it will soon be extinguished. Therefore, we need the glass case of the inner calm of shamata practice to protect the burning butter lamp of the broader perspective and insight of vipashyana.

If we unite the practices of inner calm and insight, we bring our understanding of the nature of mind to a point of stability.

Once we have gained an unshakeable understanding of the essence of mind, we will understand that the techniques of inner calm and insight are no more than techniques. For example, when we meditate on the white letter *Ah,* are we actually rising into the sky when we breathe out and returning to the tip of our nose when we breathe in? When we visualize the letter *Ah* rising into the sky as we breathe out, it is not that an *Ah* walks away from us on its legs; it is simply a skillful means to calm our mind, to make the mind tranquil so that we can investigate its nature.

If we fail in our application, we won't ever reach a point of inner calm. Once we arrive at a point of calm, we then apply the insight of vipashyana. So the authentic way to practice is to unite shamata and vipashyana. With the insight of vipashyana we cut through any attachment to inner calm, and, with the help of inner calm we prevent distracting thoughts from interrupting the recognition of the nature of mind, which arises as a result of insight meditation. This is the way we should try to practice.

It is important to know that the letter *Ah* symbolizes unborn, absolute nature. *Ah* is one with our root teacher and of the same nature as our teacher, so we should constantly let our mind be permeated with devotion. *Ah* is the seed from which the 84,000 collections of the

Dharma manifest. It is the symbol of universal, supreme emptiness, the nature of mind of all the buddhas. *Ah* is the absolute expanse, it is absolute nature arising in the shape of a syllable. This practice of shamata can be found in the Great Mother, the Perfection of Wisdom, so please keep these instructions in mind.

We need to experience this practice gradually. If we want to tame a wild horse or elephant, we don't use a drastic or wrathful method. At first, we approach a wild horse slowly, gently; otherwise, it becomes nervous and angry and runs away. Likewise, we may be strongly inclined toward the practices of mahamudra and dzogchen, but if we do not first tame, control, and transform the mind, we will never achieve a genuine understanding of such profound teachings. It is only through continuous and sustained effort that our inner experience can develop. And only through constant and fervent devotion for our teacher, and through the strength of our meditation, can the realization of primordial wisdom blossom within us.

This is what we call *mind teaching,* a teaching that we have to integrate with our experience. Even if we don't have the good fortune to stay in a mountain hermitage because we are so busy with many activities, we can find a gap, an hour or so here or there, in which we can turn our mind to practice and watch the nature of mind. We should practice in a room where there is not so much noise or movement. If, once we have calmed our mind and thoughts are fewer, we attempt to discover how the mind really is and what its characteristics are, we will slowly come to understand the inherent nature of our mind.

16. AWARENESS — THE MIRROR OF MIND

Nyoshul Khen Rinpoche

Homage to the sole master: self-arising awareness.
I am the vajra of awareness—
behold, vajra friends!
If you see me, I maintain unblemished awareness.
I am the mirror of awareness.
I show you clearly: attentive awareness.
Look undistractedly on the essence of mind.
Awareness is the root of the Dharma.
Awareness is the central point of the path.
Awareness is the citadel of the mind.
Awareness is the friend of self-cognizing wisdom.
Awareness is the support of mahamudra, maha ati, and
    madhyamaka.
Without awareness you are subject to evil forces.
Without awareness you are carried off by laziness.
Non-awareness is the cause of all faults.
Non-awareness lets all go to ruin.
Non-awareness is like a rubbish heap.
Non-awareness is like sleeping in a sea of piss.
Non-awareness is like a corpse without a heart.
Friends, I entreat you: maintain awareness.
By the compassionate intention of the jetsun lamas,
may you come face to face with awareness.

*This admonishment to awareness is spread among his friends with an
eye for the Dharma by the bad monk Jamyang Dorje,[17] a buffalo with
sharp teeth.*

17. HEART ADVICE IN A NUTSHELL

Jamyang Khyentse Chökyi Lodrö

In Tibet, Buddhist masters gave their disciples much advice for their practice, including personal advice if they were expressly asked for it. The following was given to Ani Pelu, a close relative of Sogyal Rinpoche, and it is a masterpiece. In its final lines it gives the essence of Buddhadharma, and in earlier sections offers advice on the practice of dzogchen and of various levels of tantra, wherein devotion to the master or to Guru Rinpoche performs a key function. It is said that a single essential practice advice of this quality is sufficient to bring its reader to enlightenment. No other texts or instructions are necessary—if, that is, we are truly able to take it to heart.

Homage to Guru Rinpoche, the Lord of Orgyen,[18] the incomparable object of refuge!

This unique, free, and well-favored human form is so difficult
   to obtain.
Since we have actually attained it this time,
let us endeavor to unfold the realization of its full potential
and not leave it to rot.

The root of all dharmas is one's mind.
If unexamined, it rushes after experiences and is ingenious in
   the game of deception.

If you look right into it, it is free of any ground or origin,
in essence free of any coming, staying, or going.

All the dharmas of samsara and nirvana are one's own mind,
only determined by its display—pure or impure;
in reality, neither exist.

Pure from the beginning, free and empty,
not falling into the concept of an "empty" emptiness.
Instead, in the luminosity of its self-existing energy, it is fully
    accomplished.

This is the very ground for the manifestation of compassion's
    rigpa.
Rigpa is beyond designation and verbalization.
Out of it arises, as its display, the variety of appearances of
    samsara and nirvana.

Manifestation and manifester are not two.
In this state of oneness naturally remain.

BODY	free of walking, sitting, movements	REMAIN
SPEECH	natural to the flow of breath	REMAIN
MIND	free of "afterthoughts"	REMAIN

In the totally free state of mind   open   spacious
restfully   content   carefree   REMAIN

This unborn dharmakaya's rigpa,
uncreated by cause and circumstances, naturally arose,
raw   fresh   nakedly   naked,
unstained by thoughts of "I" and "mine," "this" and "that,"
unspoiled by understanding (mental fabrication),
in the silence of its natural simplicity *(samadhi)*   REMAIN.

"Remain" is only an expression;
in reality it is totally free of that which remains and remaining
    itself.

This rigpa emptiness is the dharmakaya's actual face;

Abide at all times, in this recognition, undistracted.

There is no end to the activity and delusions of samsara—
the more you do, the more they increase.
Animosity and attachment just grow more and more,
gradually working toward your own downfall.

Turn your mind instead toward the Dharma.
If you are able to make the Dharma one with your body,
    speech, and mind,
you will find the first glimpse of enlightenment and liberation;
you won't be ashamed at the moment of death,
and in this life and others you will go from happiness to hap-
    piness, there is no doubt.

The one who has been most gracious to you,
your lama inseparable from Orgyen Chenpo,
visualize atop your head
and offer your "heart and soul" in fervent and one-pointed
    devotion.

Whatever arises, good or bad, happiness or sorrow,
rely only on your father lama and pray to him.
Make your mind one with his.

At the moment of death, abandon thoughts of attachment and
    aversion,
visualize Orgyen Guru, your lama, on your head.
Your consciousness in the form of light symbolized by *Hrih,*
transfer it into the wisdom mind of the lama, Orgyen Chenpo.

If you meditate and practice in this manner always,
at the moment of death, it will come easier.
Recite the prayer of Zangdok Palri.[19]

In conclusion, Dharma practice is:
to cut attachment to samsara,
to generate love and compassion for all beings of the six
    realms,
to tame this mind of ours again and again.
This, I plead, take to heart and practice all the time—please do!

COLOPHON
Even though I have no practice in myself,
this short advice, the words of the noble ones of the past,
was written by the one who has no Dharma,
the stubborn parasite,
the so-called Chökyi Lodrö,
for the fortunate woman-practitioner Pelu
merely to avoid rejecting her request.

The Fresh Mind of Dzogchen

Phenomena are the radiance of the inborn absolute.
The nature of mind is the wisdom of the inborn absolute.
The ultimate teacher—phenomena and mind united in one
taste—abides quite naturally within me. Ah ho! What joy!
Dilgo Khyentse Rinpoche[20]

"The origins of dzogchen go back to the primordial buddha
Samantabhadra, from whom they have been transmitted in
an unbroken lineage of great masters down to the present
day."[21] *These teachings, kept secret for centuries in Tibet, in*
the last few years have been taught openly in the West to
some extent. Sogyal Rinpoche explains this development in
the following way:

> *Some of my masters have told me that this is the time*
> *for Dzogchen to spread....Human beings have come*
> *to a critical place in their evolution, and this age of*
> *extreme confusion demands a teaching of comparably*
> *extreme power and clarity. I have also found that*
> *modern people want a path shorn of dogma, funda-*
> *mentalism, exclusivity, complex metaphysics, and cul-*
> *turally exotic paraphernalia, a path at once simple and*
> *profound, a path that does not need to be practiced in*
> *ashrams or monasteries but one that can be integrated*
> *with ordinary life and practiced anywhere.*
>
> *So what, then, is Dzogchen? Dzogchen is not sim-*
> *ply a teaching, not another philosophy, not another*

elaborate system, not a seductive clutch of techniques. Dzogchen is a state, the primordial state, that state of total awakening that is the heart-essence of all the buddhas and all spiritual paths, and the summit of an individual's spiritual evolution. Dzogchen is often translated as "Great Perfection." I prefer to leave it untranslated, for Great Perfection carries a sense of a perfectness we need to strive to attain, a goal that lies at the end of a long and grueling journey. Nothing could be further from the true meaning of Dzogchen: the already self-perfected state of our primordial nature, which needs no "perfecting," for it has always been perfect from the very beginning, just like the sky.[22]

One final remark, aimed especially at readers who are still new to these profound teachings: even though the dzogchen teachings promise us total freedom from constraints, this never means that the practitioner may ignore the foundations of Buddhist practice, particularly the practice of ethics and discipline. From the beginning, Padmasambhava, the founder of Buddhism in Tibet, explained: "Though my View is as spacious as the sky, my actions and respect for cause and effect are as fine as grains of flour."[23]

18. The Benefits of Dzogpachenpo

Nyoshul Khen Rinpoche

THE GREAT DZOGCHEN MASTER LONGCHEN RABJAM once said that practicing in a place with a beautiful and commanding landscape, full of flowers and blossoming trees, helps our *rigpa*, the innermost essence of our mind, to manifest more clearly. A favorable, natural outer environment also causes the elements of our body to be more responsive to realization. To gather together in such a place, and to practice and receive teachings together, is truly a cause for joy and celebration.

For someone who has actualized and gained complete stability in the realization of *dharmata*, the intrinsic nature of all phenomena, the outer environment has no effect. Wherever such a person may be, he or she is perfectly in command and at ease. For beginners, however, since the point of meditation practice is to realize the nature of mind, and since the nature of mind is related to the mind and the mind is related to the body, an environment where both mind and body are at ease brings about conditions more favorable for practice. Longchen Rabjam describes the types of places that are suitable for practice in his *Ngalso* trilogy, *Finding Comfort and Ease,* in the volume entitled *Samten Ngalso, Finding Comfort and Ease in Meditation.*

The Tibetan word for Dharma, or spiritual teachings, is *chö.* There are many different religions, spiritual systems, and disciplines, and even in the Buddhadharma itself we find the shravaka path, the pratyekabuddha path, and the Mahayana path. The Mahayana path contains both the Middle Way and the Mind Only schools, and not only that, the Tibetan tradition has different schools, such as Nyingma, Sakya, Kagyü, and Gelug, and the paths of instruction of mahamudra, dzogpachenpo, and madhyamaka.

Many instructions exist, but the main purpose of them all is the realization of the nature of mind. Gaining liberation is entirely dependent on the mind, as is rebirth in the lower realms. For example, when we are happy it is the mind that experiences the sensation of happiness. A good question to ask ourselves is, if we had no mind, what would we be like? Without a mind, what kind of situation would we be in, and how would we be? What are the special qualities of the mind? What benefit does mind bring, and what harm is there in it? It is very important for each of us to reflect on these questions for ourselves.

Dharma is not a custom or a tradition, and it is not merely a culture. Dharma is about discovering the true nature of things and examining the nature of mind. Once we have understood what the nature of mind is, we go on to attaining the unaltered realization of our intrinsic nature, the attainment of enlightenment.

If, by mistake, we confuse ourselves and fail to recognize our inherent nature, we are in a state of delusion. To take an ordinary example, if we mistake fire for water and try to wash our hands in the fire, we will burn ourselves. And if we do not know what fire is, and we are indifferent toward it—a condition that is called *lungmaten* in Tibetan—then we are not able to benefit from what fire can bring us. If we fully understand the true nature of fire, then we can use it for cooking, heating, for all kinds of things, even for going to the moon.

In the same manner, if we fully understand the nature of mind, we can use it to its utmost benefit. It is easy to show the nature of fire, because fire exists on the relative or conventional level, the level of delusion and confusion. Since fire exists within the realm of the relative and visible, we can perceive it with our senses. We too are in the realm of delusion and therefore experience things through our senses. Since we are confused, and since the nature of mind is beyond the understanding of our senses—and beyond confusion—it is far from easy for us to appreciate it fully.

The two ways in which we might realize the nature of mind are through the experiential pith instructions of the masters—the heart advice known as *mengak*—and through direct experience.

Mengaks were transmitted by the first buddhas who realized the absolute, unaltered state of dharmata out of their great compassion for us. The first of these buddhas was the primordial buddha, known as Samantabhadra in Sanskrit and as Kuntuzangpo in Tibetan. From the dharmakaya he transmitted the realization of dharmata to the five buddha families of the sambhogakaya, and to the nirmanakaya Buddha Shakyamuni and Padmasambhava. It is through these transmissions that the mengaks are still available to us today to help us to realize the nature of mind.

The experiential mengaks of the wisdom mind of the primordial buddha, Samantabhadra, are recorded in the 6,400,000 tantras of dzogpachenpo. These tantras are divided into three categories. The outer category is *semde,* the category of mind; the inner is *longde,* the category of space; and the secret is *mengakde,* the category of instruction, which is known as *upadesha* in Sanskrit. The *mengakde* is further clarified in the teachings known as *Yeshe Lama* or *Lama Yangtik,* and these experiential instructions are still available to us through the unbroken transmission of the dzogchen lineage masters.

Even now, in the present century, it is still possible for us to gain the realization of the unaltered state of the wisdom mind. This is no myth; we can actually realize it. The realization of the nature of mind is the teaching of dzogpachenpo.

Could we possibly discover the nature of mind on our own? Scientists and psychologists have been trying to discover it for decades, and they are still carrying out research and conducting experiments. They even put machines on people's heads, but they still have not realized what the nature of mind is. However much we might try, it is extremely unlikely that we would ever attain the nature of mind without the guidance of a teacher. Even when we simply try to examine the nature of mind, let alone realize it, it is very hard for us to arrive at any definitive conclusion about what the mind is. Although the mind we examine is our own, and no one is hiding the nature of mind from us, our inherent nature remains a secret to us. This is why the teaching of dzogpachenpo is so precious.

If we were to fill the whole world with gold, we would still not be able to find a teaching as valuable as dzogpachenpo. There have been times when people have not been able to receive teachings like this for generations, so we should appreciate what a great opportunity it is to encounter these teachings. Our good fortune should bring about such a sense of urgency in us that, given the choice between discovering these teachings in the morning or in the evening, we should immediately rush without any hesitation to meet them in the morning.

The Sanskrit word *shunyata* and the Tibetan word *tongpanyi* are often translated as emptiness. The teachings on emptiness in the Buddhadharma in general and those in the dzogchen teachings are fundamentally the same, but simply explaining emptiness is not sufficient for us to realize the true quality, benefit, and meaning of emptiness. Seeing an empty room doesn't bring us much benefit, and neither can looking into an empty cup help us much. The true meaning of emptiness or of dzogpachenpo must be realized directly.

Merely saying that everything is empty, and that therefore there is ultimately no karma, no cause, and no effect, is not enough; we must fully realize the benefit of these statements. If we say that there is no karma, cause, or effect, it is also a sign that we have not realized the true meaning of emptiness, because it is our conditioned mind that is deciding for us. In these circumstances, to say that karma is empty is no better than saying it is not empty.

The great master Guru Padmasambhava, on realizing the true meaning of dzogpachenpo, was able there and then to dissolve his physical body of flesh and blood into the rainbow body. In the same manner, Vimalamitra was able to dissolve his ordinary body into the limitless rainbow body, which is sometimes known as the wisdom or vajra body.

A rainbow in itself is not very special. Whenever there is rain and the sun is visible at a certain angle, a rainbow appears in the sky. Sometimes we can even see a rainbow when we water the garden or look at a fountain. What *rainbow body* means is that the physical body has become completely free of harm and no longer obstructs the elements; it has complete independence. Realizing the rainbow body means becoming free of all suffering, as suffering is connected with our physical body. Attaining rainbow body is a sign and benefit of realizing the true nature of dzogpachenpo.

The ruler of Tibet at the time of Padmasambhava was King Trisong Detsen. When he recognized the innermost nature of mind, such a tremendous sense of compassion arose in him that he dedicated his entire kingdom, his wealth and power, everything, to the service of the teachings. This selfless act ensured that the dzogchen teachings could be brought to future generations. That these teachings still exist is in many ways due to the efforts of this one man and the tremendous compassion, strength, and dedication that arose in him on realizing the true meaning of dzogpachenpo.

When the great dzogchen master Longchen Rabjam recognized the inherent nature of mind, the wisdom nature of all the teachings spontaneously arose out of the state of his realization, without him even having to think about it. He wrote thirty volumes on the meaning of the single word *dzogpachenpo*. This was not something that he achieved through study alone; the wisdom nature of the teachings flowed naturally from him, like spring water bubbling out of the ground.

The realization of the true meaning of *dharmata* can release an unceasing and effortless compassion for all beings who have not realized the nature of mind. If crying could express this limitless compassion, our tears would flow endlessly, never stopping. To someone who sees the absolute nature of phenomena, beings who have not realized the nature of mind can seem like madmen, making a complete mess of everything.

When we realize the true meaning of dzogpachenpo, tremendous skillful means arise in us. Through the power of these skillful means, we are able to expound without any effort on the 84,000 dharmas that comprise the teachings of the Buddha, and we know each of them within an instant.

Direct recognition of the nature of mind also liberates us from all suffering, from all fear of eventualities such as birth and death. We are also liberated from all fear of the bardos. Our suffering is self-liberated since we recognize the illusory nature of the bardos.

If we want to attain wisdom and compassion, to realize the dreamlike quality of suffering, and to put an end to that suffering, we need to realize the root of all dharmas. That fundamental essence, and the heart of all, is dzogpachenpo. The buddhas say that if you could gather all the glory, enjoyment, pleasures, and happiness from every world system throughout existence, you would still not be able to touch one pore of the hair of the bliss that is experienced upon realizing the nature of mind.

At the time of Buddha Shakyamuni, there was a tradition of ringing a gong at certain times of the night. After six years of penance, Buddha Shakyamuni gained realization under the Bodhi tree at the sound of the first gong, which would have been about 3:30 in the morning. He was filled with an uncontainable joy, and he proclaimed this tremendous realization as "profound peace, free of complexity, luminous, uncompounded" and remained without moving from that state of realization for seven days.

The mahasiddha Saraha was a great teacher and scholar at Nalanda University, one of the greatest centers of learning in the ancient world. He was from a high Brahmin caste, yet upon recognizing the nature of mind, he abandoned worldly cares and concerns and became a yogi. He is always depicted in paintings wearing a simple cloth, rather like a skirt, and holding an arrow. From out of the state of his tremendous realization emerged wonderful songs known as *dohas*. These *dohas* and his attainment of the rainbow body are the signs of Saraha's realization of the true meaning of dzogpachenpo.

The story of Saraha does not imply that upon hearing the teachings of dzogpachenpo, we will become instantly enlightened like him. We won't suddenly find ourselves naked and holding an arrow. Enlightenment depends on our past karma and the maturation of the aspirations and prayers we have made in the past. Only when all the right conditions come together will we see the true meaning of dzogchen.

A story about the great master Vairochana illustrates this. An old man of eighty years who had previously received many teachings requested Vairochana to introduce him to the nature of mind, and Vairochana did so. There and then the old man became realized. The revelation was so astounding for him that he hugged Vairochana and refused let go of him for a whole day. The old man went on to live to the age of 112, and when he died he dissolved into a rainbow body. Now, many other people received the introduction to the nature of mind from Vairochana at the same time, but the old man was the only one to recognize it, due to his past karma and previous aspirations. Every one of us has a unique mind and unique karma, and they both contribute to our ultimate fruition.

When we receive the teaching of dzogpachenpo, we realize just how precious this life is. So many people do not know how precious their lives are and completely waste their time in idle pursuits. There are also those who, having received the teachings, do recognize how precious this life is yet lack diligence. Such people stay the same from year to year; the only ways in which they change is due to getting older. If we do not have the right conditions, even if we receive dzogchen teachings, we will not be able to realize them. Creating the right conditions, appreciating the preciousness of these teachings, and diligent practice are all of crucial importance to our ultimate realization. We don't need to innovate the methods and instructions for realizing the nature of mind because they have already been discovered. Thousands and thousands of beings have become completely realized through this teaching, which is proof of its validity.

I am presenting the benefits that flow from recognizing the true meaning of dzogpachenpo. We must not see dzogchen as just a tradition, as just another system or spiritual approach. Dzogchen can only benefit us and allow us to benefit others if we realize its essence for ourselves. Here is the essence of the benefits of practice.

Ngöndro, the preliminary practices of the Vajrayana path, is not primarily an accumulation of mantras and prostrations (although that is of course important) but rather a method for gaining a basic understanding of the Dharma. The real benefit and purpose of ngöndro is that, having purified our mind through the outer teachings and understood the basic teachings, we can then enter and understand the higher teachings.

Chegom and *yogom* are two types of meditation. I have here been explaining *chegom*—*reflective* or contemplative meditation. We should reflect deeply on this teaching; it is not something we should discard or fail to value properly, thinking something like, "Oh, how amazing! An old man from Tibet, a lama called Khenpo, says all these things; how marvelous!" It is not enough to consider these teachings interesting; we must reflect on this teaching over many years and genuinely see what benefit is gained in practicing this approach.

The sole method for realizing the innermost nature of our mind is through the blessing of the lama. It is said that the dzogchen teachings are the true meaning of the realization of the wisdom mind of the primordial buddha, and that this realization is transmitted from mind to mind, from master to disciple. The teachings we have received are not discourses for our eyes, hands, body, or speech; they are all concerned with the realm of mind, particularly the nature of mind. Therefore the wisdom mind of a master must be transmitted to the mind of the student.

Ultimately, when the minds and hearts of a master and student fully meet, the unaltered recognition of the nature of mind can be transmitted. But for that to happen, the student's mind must be clear and pure, utterly free of all confusion, doubt, and negativity. It is only with a pure and open mind that we can see our inherent nature. There is of course great benefit in taking refuge, for example, since it creates good karma and habits, but that alone will not bring about realization in one lifetime.

As the examples of Guru Rinpoche and Vairochana demonstrate, realization within our lifetime only ever takes place when a disciple with an open heart meets a master who then transmits his wisdom mind. The teachings state that *samaya,* or purity, is a crucial factor. *Samaya* is pure perception. The student should see the teacher as the Buddha, and the teacher should see the student as a buddha; each recognizes the other as a buddha.

All practices are ultimately based upon guru yoga practice. Refuge and mandala offering are forms of guru yoga, as is Vajrasattva practice, because when we start the practice, we consider the lama as inseparable from the nature of Vajrasattva. *Yidam* (deity) practice, *kyerim* (generation stage), and *dzogrim* (completion stage) are all practices of guru yoga, as is considering the lama in our heart during *tsa lung tiglé* practice. All these practices are founded upon the principle of receiving blessing. The true meaning of dzogpachenpo can only be transmitted through the blessing of the master and the practice of guru yoga.

The primordial buddha Samantabhadra is still here, and even though he has passed away in the physical sense, Buddha Shakyamuni is present in the state of dharmata. But we ourselves cannot reach out and touch the primordial buddha; it is the master who creates the bridge to the buddhas for us. The master is this profound link, and this is why only guru yoga practice can confer the true blessing of dzog-pachenpo. Devotion and purity of perception for our teacher as well as for our vajra brothers and sisters, our Dharma friends, are therefore of paramount importance.

Even though everyone has buddha nature, it is obscured, and inevitably people will have faults as a result. Sometimes we seek out the faults in others, and we can find many, but it is far better to look for the good qualities in others and to focus on those. Practicing purity of perception means not dwelling on the negative qualities we observe in others. We should wipe them from our mind and generate good feelings toward one another. To receive these teachings, our mind must be pure, and in such a state the transmission of dzogpachenpo definitely can be attained. One day we could even realize the great body of transference, just like Guru Rinpoche and Vimalamitra.

19. TOWARD THE NATURE OF MIND

Khetsun Sangpo Rinpoche

Of the three key elements of our existence—body, speech, and mind—it is mind from which everything emerges. Khetsun Sangpo Rinpoche takes us on a journey to find the mind's origin and its place of abiding. At first we find nothing, but in the end we find something beyond existence and nonexistence. As in the teaching from Nyoshul Khen Rinpoche above, we discover wondrous things: the dissolution of the material world, of dream worlds, and of the dreamlike everyday world, to be led back to the most wondrous place of all: the here and now.

FIRST OF ALL, IT IS VERY IMPORTANT to develop the compassionate attitude explained by Patrul Rinpoche in *The Words of My Perfect Teacher (Kunzang Lama'i Shelung)*. Cultivating this attitude is the essence of sutra and tantra, for whatever we do should be for the benefit of all beings throughout space, without any exceptions. With the wish to bring them to the ultimate state of buddhahood, we develop the correct attitude with our mind and support that with our actions of body and speech.

Today I have the great opportunity to speak about the nature of mind. I have been very fortunate in having many great masters for teachers. All my teachers are fully awakened; every single one is like Buddha in a human form. So, with the prayer that the blessings of my teachers will benefit you, and with great joy at having such an opportunity, I will share a few words.

The nature of mind can be introduced in two different ways. According to the tradition of the learned pandits, if we study in detail the teachings of the Tripitaka (the three collections of Buddha's teachings) and go through the various analyses using the three types of logic, we will realize the nature of mind. The second way to realize the nature of mind is with the method of the great accomplished ones, the yogis. Those who have practiced a great deal can guide us and introduce us to the nature of mind through their own realization, guiding us with experience and with the crucial pith instructions.

If we apply ourselves to the gradual approach, we will find that there have been many great and learned scholars, all of whom have different philosophies of understanding the nature of mind. By going through the various levels of study, we gather the knowledge of the great masters, philosophers, and scholars, and we become able to explain the views of the great teachers of our own tradition.

This gradual method must be based on the teachings of the Buddha, and especially the Tripitaka—the *vinaya collection,* which is related to discipline, the *sutra collection,* which is related to wisdom, and the *abhidharma collection,* which is related to meditation. All possible ways of misunderstanding that need to be avoided are identified, and the correct view is established.

There were as many different philosophical traditions in India as there were philosophers. When the Madhyamaka teachings came to Tibet, distinct schools evolved, such as *shentong* and *rangtong,* that correspond to the different opinions that were upheld. Every great scholar wrote long commentaries; you can find commentaries of over four and five hundred pages in length. And this is why the Dharma is often described as vast.

Let us take the less complicated route: that of talking about the nature of mind based on the experience of the great yogis. This tradition is called *nyongtri. Nyong* means "experience," and *tri* is "guiding with personal experience." In this tradition, neither the teacher nor the student uses a text; the basis for the investigation is one's personal experience of how the mind functions. Of course, in this method we also progress using stages of logic, for if we did not use a framework, it would be impossible to understand what I am saying.

We all possess a body, speech, and a mind. The first thing we should analyze is which is most important. According to tradition, we should reflect on this question carefully for at least one week, in the solitude of a quiet place. Then we should inform our teacher what we have found and what conviction we have arrived at. If we are correct, the teacher agrees and tells us to go to the next step. If we are wrong, he gives us advice, and we go away again to try to find the right answer.

Say we have found that, of the body, speech, and mind, our mind is the most important. As it says in the Buddha's tantric teachings, the body is like a servant who carries out all kinds of positive and negative actions, and speech is like a minister who coordinates. But mind is like a king who gives the body orders about what it should and should not do. Therefore mind is the most important of the three. On the basis of the Buddha's teachings then, let us consider the mind to be the most important.

When we talk about *mind* in Tibetan, two of the words we use are *sem* and *yi*. *Sem* can be translated as "mind" and *yi* can be translated as "thought." Our next step is to determine whether mind or thought is the more important.

Mind and thought are inseparable in nature but manifest differently. We should take great care in finding out from where mind originates and where it dwells. Let us imagine that we have understood the nature of mind. According to tradition, we would arrive at the conviction that there is no place from which mind has manifested, no place where it dwells, and no place to which it goes.

Three elements are important here: *ye, gak,* and *me*. *Ye* means "from where it has manifested," *gak* means "where it dwells or remains," and *me* means "to where it has ceased or disappeared." Regarding *ye*, if we examine and trace the mind's origins, we might say that mind began at the very moment of conception with the union of the essences of our father and mother. However, we cannot prove that the mind begins solely as the result of the uniting of these two essences; many other factors have to be taken into consideration. Let's look at this more closely.

If mind is the product of two substances, then the resultant mind should itself have a form. If mind has a form or a shape, then mind must also have a color. Does the mind have any particular color, shape, size, or location? If mind has no material form, it can have no color, shape, or location, and is therefore very difficult to find. Therefore, we conclude that we cannot say that the mind has a particular color or shape, and we cannot say that mind is located in a particular place.

If mind has neither color nor shape, then perhaps this so-called mind does not exist. But we cannot conclude that there is no mind, because we do experience sensation, and we can say things like "I am feeling well," or "I am feeling awful." We have all kinds of sensations, and when we check carefully, we find something inside us that is intelligent and at the same time mischievous, like a playful monkey. We cannot say that there is no such thing as mind, as we would have to conclude that mind has no intelligence and is insensate, like a stone or a clod of earth. This is clearly not the case. We know something exists because we have senses and feelings.

However, if mind exists, we should be able to find it. It cannot be outside our body, so it must be inside. So let us examine our body thoroughly, from the hairs of our head down to the nails of our toes, taking all the different aggregates apart. Even if we were to conduct surgery and cut our body into pieces, we would still find nothing that we can call the mind. Our lungs are not the mind, and neither are our intestines or our skin. Let us presume we have determined that the mind cannot be found in an analysis of the body. Finally, if mind has no origin and location, we must also conclude that there is no place where it ceases or dissolves.

When we look for the nature of mind, we cannot find where it has come from, we cannot find where it dwells, and we cannot find where it ceases. Therefore we have to conclude that there *is* a mind but that this mind is totally beyond beginning, dwelling, and ceasing.

Since it is hard to say that mind exists and hard to say that it is nonexistent, we conclude that mind is beyond logical analysis and examination but that there is nonetheless a state of mind. We might arrive at the notion that there is something called *mind* that is free of the two extremes of existence and nonexistence. Still, we hold strongly onto the concept that mind exists.

When we try to trace mind back to its origins one step after another, finding that neither does it exist nor does it not exist, we arrive at a difficult point. We have to conclude that mind has two aspects: one deluded and one free of delusion. Throughout a beginningless series of lives, we have followed the deluded state of mind, which in Tibetan is called *trulpé sem,* "the mind that falls into delusion."

My present explanations are made on the basis of the deluded state of mind, and you are reading this with your deluded state of mind. Those who have studied deeply would try to differentiate between these two aspects of mind. We would call the deluded state of mind *relative* and the nondeluded state of mind *absolute.* In this way we differentiate between the two truths, relative and absolute.

What has actually happened is that the intrinsic nature of our mind has been totally obscured by the deluded state of mind, the *trulpé sem.* It is as if we wrapped somebody in many layers of cloth until we could no longer tell whether anyone was inside the cloth. In the same manner, we have completely obscured the intrinsic nature of our mind with delusions and habits.

Recognizing our deluded mind is quite easy. If we criticize someone, calling them a thief or a liar, for instance, strong anger may erupt in that person. This manifestation of anger is *trulpé sem.* The deluded mind also takes recollections of past events at face value, just accepting them without examination or analysis. Similarly, when somebody tells us "this is earth" or "this is water," we generally accept it, without examination. And yet within this mind is a more subtle state.

There are no so-called external phenomena that exist as concrete and solid entities. Milarepa proved this by passing through hard rocks without difficulty. He could sit in fire without being burned, and he could be thrown into a river and not be carried away by its currents. The five elements could not obstruct him because he had realized the empty nature of mind; he was free of all concepts and all gross clinging onto phenomena. By realizing the nature of mind, we can prove that all phenomena, which we believe to be concrete, have no real truth or essence.

When the great master Solchungpa was giving teachings, another philosopher sent some learned scholars to debate with him, and Solchungpa introduced the different aspects of emptiness of the nature of mind to them. The philosophers asked Solchungpa, "Is this earth something that can obstruct us, or is obstruction space?" And Solchungpa said, "For me space is beyond solidity or emptiness." And he got up and just sat in space. Then the philosophers asked, "Does this pillar exist or not?" Solchungpa replied, "For a great yogi, phenomena are beyond obstruction and nonobstruction." As he said this, he moved his hand through the pillar as if he were moving it through the sky, without hindrance. The scholars could not argue with Solchungpa and were very impressed when they saw what he had accomplished through his practice. They eventually became some of his most important disciples.

How is it possible for great masters like Solchungpa and Milarepa not to be burned by fire or carried away by a river? How could they do things beyond the explanation of ordinary logic? Generally, we say that they had some supernatural power and just leave it at that, not examining how such a thing is possible. Such masters demonstrate their abilities in order to introduce us to our inherent nature as it is. Things in their ultimate nature do not manifest in accordance with our ordinary perception because our perception is deluded. We perceive things falsely. This is what Milarepa and Solchungpa are trying to show us so that we can come to see our true nature.

How have we come to believe things that are not true? If what we believe were the ultimate truth, we would have no problems, but unfortunately this is not the case. Our worldview contradicts the true nature of things. This true nature can manifest as the result of practice, however, or through the experience of great masters.

What causes us to believe in things that do not exist, or to think something is true when it is not? This is due to ego-centered habits we have formed over the course of our present and previous lives. We know these habits by many terms, such as "I" or "my," and we form concepts and give names to things that do not in reality exist. If "I" or "mine" really existed, we would be able to find them through reasoning and logic, or with the aid of the teachings of enlightened beings. But when we examine these things thoroughly, we have to conclude that our ordinary perception has no basis in truth.

We perceive things differently from how they are in their true nature. If we see a striped rope at the same time as someone is saying, "Watch out, there's a poisonous snake over there!" we get really scared and move quickly away from the snake. The instant we hear a poisonous snake is in the vicinity, we are afraid, and there is no difference between the fear we feel on seeing a real snake and the fear that arises when we see something that merely looks like a snake.

Every phenomenon we come across over the course of our life is like this. As with our fear on mistaking a rope for a snake, we frequently believe in things that are not true. When teachers explain the writings of Shantideva, they often tell the following story about how the things we ordinarily believe in are false.

There was once a man who was very fond of horses. One afternoon as his wife was taking care of the animals—milking them and making butter and yogurt—he fell asleep. He had a long dream that began when a man came to sell him a wild horse. He bought it, and gradually he tamed the horse. After finally breaking the horse in, he went out for a long ride, and together he and the horse covered many miles.

Time went by and it became dark. Suddenly, the horse threw him off and ran away, leaving him stranded. It was too far from home for him to get back that night, and he had no hope of catching the horse, so he started walking. After a while he saw a house in the distance, so he went toward it. When he got there, he found that a woman lived alone in the house. In his dream, he married her, and they had three children together.

One day a huge storm arose. The family's livestock was on the far side of the river and was in some danger. The wife, carrying the youngest child and with the other two children following her, went to bring them to safety. As they reached the middle of the rising river, the powerful current overwhelmed them and carried them all away.

The man was now alone. He became distraught and depressed and spent his days weeping over his misfortune. When he had bought the beautiful wild horse, he had been excited, but it had all ended in him losing his wife, his children, and seemingly everything.

But all this happened as he slept; it was all a dream. When his wife saw that he was having a nightmare, she woke him up. She had been busy with her work, and as far as she was concerned nothing else had happened. On seeing his wife, the husband was so grateful and relieved that he leapt up and hugged her. "What's wrong with you? What happened?" she cried. He told her the whole story. Even though he had woken up, he couldn't bring himself to believe that nothing had actually happened. He had one opinion about the validity of his dream, while his wife had another.

To an enlightened being, the way in which we go about our lives is similar to this man and his dream. Everything we do is mistaken. We believe in things as they appear to us, and even if someone tries to explain that we are mistaken, it is hard for us to accept. This is the extent of the difference between nondeluded and deluded mind.

The most compassionate Buddha taught that all experiences of the relative mind are examples of illusion. All the dreamlike, illusory perceptions that we experience have no basis in absolute truth. We feel that there is a distinct difference between what we experience in our dreams and what we experience while we are awake. Because our delusion is so intense, we have great difficulty accepting that our daytime experiences are very much like dreams.

In the absolute state, there has been no change throughout beginningless time; the essence of our mind has always been perfectly pure; it is pure at this very moment, and it always will be pure. But we cannot recognize our true nature because of the intensity of our delusion. We believe our deluded mind because of the strength with which we hold onto our habits, and we are constantly carried away by the afflictive emotions, such as ego-clinging, desire, hatred, jealousy, and ignorance. These afflictive emotions prepare a nest in our five aggregates. We hold onto them so strongly and believe in them so much.

If we tell a mentally disturbed person to stop what he is doing because it is really crazy, he will more than likely say that we are the crazy ones and refuse to accept that he has a problem. In the same manner, we hold on to our delusion so strongly that we cannot accept it if someone tells us that our perception is deluded and dreamlike. We can't accept it because of the force of our habits.

When we practice Dharma, our teacher introduces us to our deluded state of mind and corrects us. All the various types of experience or perception we come across in the wheel of existence known as *samsara*—the experiences of the hell beings, the hungry ghosts, the animals, gods, and demi-gods, as well as humans—are perceived in a particular way as a result of habits and delusion.

In our absolute nature, we understand all these perceptions as false; nothing we experience with our relative mind exists in reality. Only enlightened beings, the buddhas and the bodhisattvas, are able to show us our deluded perception and introduce us to the reality of our true nature. Throughout beginningless time we were never separate from our empty nature, but somehow our emotions were so strong that they completely overpowered us, such that we have had no chance to recognize and realize the essential nature of mind.

We can be introduced to the intrinsic nature of mind and be shown that we have fallen into delusion, but what is most important is that we learn the ways to free ourselves of delusion. We achieve this through *semtri özer:* being guided to our essential nature of mind, and becoming free of the deluded state of mind.

What is it like to be free of delusion and the influence of our negative actions and afflictive emotions? Let's snap our fingers. In this instant, neither follow past thoughts nor think about the future; simply leaving mind "as it is." Just looking at the face of mind here and now, see how your mind is. In this instant is a state not influenced by past and future thoughts. There is a gap, a recognition of total freedom. This is the luminous, nondeluded, and unfabricated intrinsic nature of mind, which is completely free, unspoiled, tranquil, vivid, and radiant.

The nature of mind is introduced in this very naked and natural state of mind. Then, having received the introduction, we should be able to develop great confidence in the recognition of our essential nature. It is said by the great bodhisattva Shantideva that absolute mind is completely free and fresh. I bow down and pay homage to the nature of mind that is embodied by all the buddhas of the past, present, and future.

Gradually and naturally, gaining total confidence, we find freedom in our true nature, and there is no longer any fear or expectation and no doubt. After being introduced to our true nature, not only should we gain confidence in it, we should continue to abide by that freedom and freshness, and integrate and maintain it throughout our lives. If we can do this, we will have no regrets at the moment of death.

And so I ask that you please try to recognize the nature of your mind. Develop confidence in it, and maintain its freshness and clarity in every situation and experience of your life. This is my request and my prayer.

20. THE UNITY OF MAHAMUDRA AND DZOGCHEN

Kalu Rinpoche

> *Kalu Rinpoche discusses the deep similarities and historical connections between the Dzogchen and Mahamudra lineages, and touches on a subject often remarked on in this book: the importance of the master, whose guidance enables us to make progress on the path leading to realization of the nature of mind. But this teaching, for all the exalted views and profound insights of dzogchen that it offers, ends with the wonderful words of Shakyamuni Buddha that point to the fundamental task of any practitioner.*

SOGYAL RINPOCHE REQUESTED ME to teach on mahamudra and dzogchen, yet as we have little time, I will only speak briefly by way of creating a connection. Sogyal Rinpoche is someone who in Tibet received the teachings of both the Ancient *(Nyingma)* and New *(Sarma)* traditions, and in whom are gathered the eight traditions of Tibet.[24] All these eight traditions are identical in essence, the only differences being in details and the particular terminology used.

In Tibet, the Nyingma tradition originated with the Dharma king Trisong Detsen, the great master Padmasambhava, and the khenpo bodhisattva Shantarakshita. The teachings of this tradition, which came down through the so-called *King and twenty-five disciples* contain both the words of the Buddha and the *termas* of Padmasambhava. Then, from the time of the translator Rinchen Zangpo and the great pandit Atisha, came the New, or Sarma, tradition.

According to the Ancient or Nyingma tradition, the ultimate teaching is called *dzogpachenpo,* and according to the New traditions, *mahamudra,* but essentially dzogchen and mahamudra are one and the same, as if two names had been given to one person. The word *mahamu-dra,* or *chaggya chenpo* in Tibetan, can be explained in this way: *chag* refers to the wisdom that understands deep emptiness, and *gya,* which means "vast," signifies that nothing is beyond this emptiness. In fact, all phenomena originate from this empty mind. The only difference between phenomena as we experience them, and phenomena from the point of view of enlightenment, is whether mind is pure or impure.

Mind is not only empty; it is also luminous, intelligent, primordial wisdom. All phenomena are contained in this mind, this fundamentally intelligent wisdom that is the awakened mind. The *chenpo* in *chaggya chenpo* means "great" and signifies that there is no higher realization. So *chaggya chenpo* refers both to emptiness and to the all-encompassing wisdom.

The progressive path of mahamudra has four main phases, namely,

1. one-pointedness,
2. simplicity, or nonconceptualization,
3. one taste, and
4. nonmeditation, or beyond meditation,

each of which contain three substages or degrees of intensity, making twelve subdivisions in all.

The first three degrees of *one-pointedness* are important elements of both mahamudra and dzogchen. They deal with the training in perfect pacification of mind *(shi né).* All beings of the medium and lesser capacities must go through this training, but for beings of superior capacity these stages are not necessary. The minds of beings of medium or lesser capacity are akin to choppy water in which the moon cannot reflect clearly. For the reflection of the moon to become clear, the water must first become still. For people of superior capacity, however, this is not necessary; it is as if they owned a camera that gives a clear picture straight away. One need only introduce them to the nature of mind and they understand immediately.

What is the nature of mind? It is said that mind is clarity, emptiness, and intelligence, without obstruction. Once introduced to the nature of mind, we have to observe what mind is. Yet mind is not an object that mind itself can look at; therefore, there is nothing to see. Nevertheless, if we do *not* observe mind, we'll never see it either. Therefore it is said, "How wonderful—this is something that must be seen but can't be seen!"

What does "to observe without seeing" mean? Gampopa said, "When mind is not contrived, it is spontaneously blissful, just as water, when not agitated, is by nature transparent and clear." This means that there is no other thing to observe but mind. The mind to observe is mind in itself, without mental fabrication, resting in its own nature.

The mahasiddha Tilopa said: "If mind is left without any reference, that is mahamudra; if we meditate continually in this, we reach buddhahood." When we leave mind to rest in itself, in its own nature, without any mental fabrication, it thereby rests in its own emptiness, in its own clarity; that is mahamudra. This mahamudra is also called "ordinary wisdom," or "ordinary awareness," *(tamal gyi shépa), ordinary* in the sense that mind has no need to produce or fabricate anything, but simply rests by itself in its own mode of existence.

What is the result of being able to meditate or remain well in that state? Buddhahood itself is the result. Why? Because the emptiness of mind is the dharmakaya itself, the absolute body of a buddha. The clarity of mind is the *sambhogakaya*—the luminous body of a buddha— and the indivisible union of these two is the *nirmanakaya*—the manifest body of a buddha.

To be ready to be introduced to the mind's ultimate nature requires an extensive accumulation of merit and purification. A person of superior capacity has already completed this in the past. But persons of medium or inferior capacity must first carry out the accumulation of merit and purification. Above all, great devotion to one's lama is essential. Kagyü lamas of the past used to say that to realize the ultimate, inherent primordial wisdom, there is no other way than through purification, accumulation of merit, and most important of all, thorough devotion to the lama.

As our realization of this develops a certain spontaneity, it is said that we have arrived at the lower degree of intensity of the phase of *simplicity,* or *nonconceptualization*. Then we gradually progress through the medium and higher degrees of this phase.

As we progress further, we arrive at that stage of realization where samsara and nirvana, all aspects of phenomenal experience—forms, sounds, smells, tastes, textures, thoughts, and states of awareness—are no longer perceived as different from the mind that perceives them. That phase is called *one taste.*

After attaining the third degree of intensity of this realization of one taste, we come to a state where we no longer need to meditate to preserve this realization. There is neither meditation nor distraction, and our realization is totally stable. We have reached the stage of *non-meditation,* or *beyond meditation.* This phase, too, has three degrees of intensity, and when we arrive at the third, that is buddhahood. It is said in the New tradition, particularly in the Kagyü tradition, that this instantaneous knowledge of the present is what is called the "ordinary wisdom," or "ordinary awareness" *(tamal gyi shépa).*

When, through the introduction to the nature of mind, meditation, and realization, we arrive at the second phase, that of nonconceptualization, this is equivalent to obtaining the first ground *(bhumi)* of the bodhisattvas known as "supremely joyful." This first stage of realization and activity of a bodhisattva is called the *supremely joyful* because until that moment we have not recognized the true nature of our mind, we are not conscious of the illusory projections of the mind, and we are therefore subject to all sorts of sufferings and difficulties. Realization of the true nature of mind is like pouring cold water into a pot of boiling water—instantly, the boiling stops. Likewise, through this realization, the mind immediately knows a great peace and a great happiness. Hence, it is called the *supremely joyful.*

The Nyingma tradition uses another expression to describe this introduction of the student to the knowledge of his or her true nature: "introducing directly the face of *rigpa* itself." Once we have discovered the true face of our mind through this process, we develop an absolute certainty. Then even if the buddhas themselves were to come and say, "That's not the way to meditate!" we would reply, "I know that this is the way to go." In the method of dzogchen this is called "decision complete and direct in certainty." Once we have established this, our meditation practice goes on to become deeper and deeper, and very rapidly, from one instant to the next, we cross the stages and paths toward buddhahood and attain enlightenment.

Whereas mahamudra has the three stages of nonconceptualization, one taste, and nonmeditation, dzogchen has the three equivalent stages of *introduction directly in the face of rigpa itself, decision complete and direct in certainty,* and *direct confidence in the dissolution of arising thoughts.*

In the Kagyü tradition, the ground is mahamudra, and in the Nyingma dzogchen tradition, the ground is *trekchö.* This basis of mahamudra or trekchö is comparable to a plane that can fly very fast. A plane may be fast as a means of reaching buddhahood, but a rocket would be even faster. In the Kagyü tradition, this rocket corresponds to the Six Yogas of Naropa, the Six Yogas of Niguma, the Six Yogas of Sukhasiddhi, or the six yogas of the Kalachakra system.

In the Nyingma dzogchen tradition, what corresponds to this extremely rapid vehicle to buddhahood is *tögal.* The practice of *tögal* contains instructions on physical posture and on ways of placing the mind and working with energies. According to the individual's particular capacity, a student can use the light of the sun and moon, or even sometimes total darkness. With this practice, one develops progressive visions of rainbow lightrays, discs of light, forms of deities, buddhafields, and so on, and proceeds through four stages:

1. manifest dharmata,
2. increased experience,
3. rigpa reaching fullness, and
4. the exhaustion of concepts and of phenomena; the wearing out of dharmata.

On reaching this final stage—the exhaustion of the ultimate nature of phenomena—through the total purificaton of the energies and elements of the body, one attains the rainbow body. Upon leaving the body, nothing material is left behind. You might say, "That means that one can obtain the rainbow body through dzogchen but not through mahamudra." Don't believe any such thing. Milarepa's life story recounts how seven of his closest disciples, four female and three male, obtained the rainbow body.

The different lineages of mahamudra and dzogchen contain a lot of great masters with extraordinary qualities. It is according to the karmic links established in the past that we follow one teacher or another. When we follow a teacher, we should think that this teacher shows us more kindness than all the buddhas together because he is the one who directly introduces us to the true nature of our mind. Whether these lamas who teach us are buddhas or ordinary beings is not that important as long as they give us unerring instructions that will allow us to progress toward the realization of the true nature of our mind. Therefore, we should think that their qualities are like those of the buddhas, and the gratitude we have toward them should be the same as that we would have for the Buddha.

If we are without devotion, then even were a great number of buddhas to stand before us, it would be in vain; they would be unable to help us. There is a saying, "What can the shoot of a burnt seed be? If a seed has been put into a fire, though it is planted, no shoot will ever sprout from it." Likewise, if one has no confidence or devotion, no spiritual progress is possible. It is said in the tantras, "If you consider your lama as a buddha, you will receive the blessing of a buddha; if you consider him as a bodhisattva, you will receive the blessing of a bodhisattva; if you consider him as a good, ordinary member of the Sangha, you will receive the blessing of a good, ordinary member of the Sangha, and if you have no faith in him at all, you will receive no blessing."

Because of connections made in past lives, we have now found a lama again. For some of you, this lama teaches dzogchen, for others, mahamudra. There is no difference. What matters is that you practice. Through the instructions you have received, you have everything that you need to practice; you need not look for anything else. But if you have no faith or devotion, even if an actual buddha tried, through every kind of means, to explain the Dharma to you, the most you might ever think would be, "This sounds intelligent." His efforts would be fruitless.

Therefore, practice with confidence and devotion the instructions you have been given. If you do not practice at all, you will end up like those who have passed lots of exams and have many degrees but make nothing of their lives and are no benefit to others. As Buddha himself said: "I have shown the path toward liberation; whether you take it is entirely up to you."

III. BRINGING THE TRANSCENDENT INTO EVERYDAY LIFE

Finding Inspiration for the Practice

If your mind is pure,
everyone you meet is a buddha.
If your mind is impure,
everyone you meet is just an ordinary person.
Trulshik Rinpoche

For the third part of this book the key theme is inspiration, that quality necessary to translate the teachings into practice so that hard-won understanding doesn't remain mere theory. Sogyal Rinpoche speaks of the need to develop enthusiasm for the path, and how this might arise from an understanding of impermanence. Impermanence is taught in a variety of ways by Buddhist teachers, and insight into it seems the crucial factor in developing inspiration on the path. A deep understanding of impermanence—one that doesn't veer off into a nihilism bereft of meaning—brings almost of itself a letting go, an open attitude toward the world, and an awareness of what is most important in life.

Dzigar Kongtrul Rinpoche takes a different approach to inspiration. He first investigates our motivation: just as a selfish motivation for practice can lead us astray, so the right motivation can keep us on the right path. He then analyzes the various kinds of laziness and offers antidotes to them so that we can revitalize our practice with fresh inspiration.

In his second teaching in this section, Sogyal Rinpoche encourages us in our hectic lives to orient ourselves toward three essential things, which Dudjom Rinpoche called the three most important qualities of a Buddhist practitioner: a good heart, inner stability or reliability combined with spaciousness, and, finally, an ability to be at ease with ourselves. Here we encounter once more the familiar themes of letting go of hope and fear, perseverance on the path, and the integration of the Dharma with our daily lives so that it becomes one with our very being.

22. Losing the Clouds, Gaining the Sky

Sogyal Rinpoche

A passion for the path

When we try to follow a spiritual path, I feel that we often don't have enough desire for the spiritual teachings. We don't have enough patience, or enough interest. Think about when we really want something in everyday life: we're willing to go through anything and be as patient as we need to be. But when it comes to spiritual life, that kind of patience is lacking. Of course, we know—to some extent—that we need spiritual things, and we feel somehow that our life is not quite right. Yet even though we suffer, unfortunately suffering doesn't teach us what it could. Because if we really understood suffering, then it would show us, at the very least, how vital the teachings are.

This is also why people are not so stable on the spiritual path: that sense of *want* is lacking. Say you come to a talk on Buddhism, for example. You're sitting there expectantly, but then you feel there's something wrong with the microphone, or the sound system isn't working properly, and because for you the talk does not get off to a good start, you get up and walk out. It means that your desire for the teachings is not strong enough. And it shows that you've not understood suffering.

The terrible thing is that we do suffer, but we don't know how to learn from it. That's why the frustration and pain go on and on, and we suffer continuously. If we really knew suffering, if we really knew pain, then it would give us a real determination. That desire, that drive, that passion—we need it. Look at the lives of the mystics, in all the traditions: they were consumed by a tremendous passion and desire, a determination to continue, whatever the difficulties.

Without this passion, we'll never last on the spiritual path. What also happens is that we're all over the place, dabbling a bit here, a bit there, discussing philosophy, reading a few pages of a book, a bit of yoga, some meditation, a few mantras, now a Tibetan teacher, then a Zen master...the whole thing's like a buffet. Our minds are perpetually restless and fidgety, hesitant and nervous; they just cannot stay still. Yet what we don't see all along is that it's only the restlessness of our mind. Instead we interpret whatever we experience, and we project: "The situation isn't right" or "This is not for me." Instantly, we see a problem, problems galore. And we don't have the slightest patience; immediately we jump to our ready-made conclusion. It's like a scene from an action movie: someone's fishing in his pocket for his lighter, but you think he's going for his gun and shoot him dead.

We need the passion and the desire to follow the path right up until the end. This is not the kind of passion that is related to the destructive emotions, the *kleshas*. It's a spiritual fervor. It's true discipline, and it's crucial. It might be aroused in us because of what we are going through in our lives, experiences that deepen our understanding of suffering. Or it might be through the teachings. Whichever it is, without it we'll never actually stay around long enough to taste anything, or to find anything. We'll always be jumping from one thing to another, like a dog sniffing around. And even if we tell ourselves we're on the spiritual path, we never really go deeply into it. Our path is always superficial. That's because there's no real passion; we haven't really suffered, or even if we have, we haven't gone through suffering and truly understood it. It means that our character is weak, and we're easily distracted. The slightest problem and we're lost.

We need that kind of passion in whatever we do. To get a job, to make a career, to be an artist—to accomplish anything in life, we need it. Otherwise we simply won't succeed. We need the drive, the will, the focus, the character, and the patience. And we need the stamina and energy to keep on going for a long time, so that nothing can make us waver or give up.

Our interest in the spiritual teachings needs to be profound. We need to taste life, to taste suffering, and to know what suffering is, in order to discover renunciation. We need to reflect deeply, but that doesn't mean too seriously. If we become too serious, we become obsessive, and that is counterproductive. It's such a delicate balance. That's why we need so much guidance on how to follow the teachings, and, even more important, on how to work with ourselves.

In this day and age, following a spiritual path is not easy, especially when you haven't had a spiritual education and you don't have the culture or the support for your spiritual quest. As much as you want to, you don't know how. You don't yet have the qualities to follow the spiritual path, which are something we have to acquire. They are potentially there, but we have to know how to bring them out. What we need to do is to look at life, to understand it, and to understand ourselves—what's actually going on—to understand and to change, not to go into some spiritual bubble. Frequently, people follow the spiritual path conceptually, far removed from reality. How often are we convinced that some difficulty is not our problem, that it must be something else? We can go on endlessly inventing all kinds of stories in our minds without ever recognizing the one simple problem in front of our face. Say, for example, your microphone isn't switched on, but you make up your mind that there's something wrong with the amplifier or that it's the sound technician's fault. All the while, it's actually just a tiny switch on the microphone lead that you can fix yourself. Basically, we need to be able to recognize one simple problem—the real one, like that little switch.

The message in the mustard seed

Sometimes we need to grieve something before we can bring ourselves to let it go. Unless, that is, we are one of those great practitioners who have no grasping at all. For someone without grasping, there is no real attachment to speak of, but that doesn't mean there's no love. There can be a love without attachment, and, if we have it, we'll go through less grief. Grieving seems to become necessary as soon as we've formed an attachment. Once we're attached to someone or some thing, then to lose them feels like losing a part of ourselves. This is something that almost all of us have to come to terms with.

The question that comes up then is: "How can we overcome this inclination to grasp, which often brings us more grief?" We all want to love and be loved fully, but we don't want attachment and grasping; or in other words, to end up getting hurt. What's interesting is that for us humans, here in samsara, something is never totally delicious unless there's some hurt or suffering. Passion is intimately connected with suffering. The trouble is, we've led this samsaric kind of existence for so long that we are used to it, and, in a way, we've been spoiled.

But remember, there is a love which is without attachment, and it's one we can learn.

We all know that things change, that they're impermanent, but whenever it happens to us, we take it personally and get hurt. Yet the teaching on impermanence is quite clear: it shows us that impermanence is the very nature of life, and it tells us to look and see for ourselves how everyone suffers at the hands of death, including us. As soon as the universality of impermanence dawns on us, and we accept it, then with that acceptance comes a natural letting go.

In the heart and mind of an experienced practitioner, that acceptance of impermanence is always there, in the background. Yes, there is love, but no attachment. It's almost automatic: as soon as a tendency toward attachment awakens, it triggers a recollection: "Oh, but this is impermanent." Of course, when we begin this kind of training, it may sometimes be painful, because we have not actually realized what it means to say that everything is impermanent. We will inevitably have attachment. After all, the reason we become so fiercely attached to things—from our emotions, ideas, and opinions to our possessions and other people—is because we have not taken impermanence to heart. So the extent to which we can avoid being attached is directly related to how completely we have realized the impermanent nature of things. Once we have, then that realization brings with it nonattachment. They are identical, like a mathematical equation:

realization of impermanence = nonattachment

So when we first go through this training, it may not be so easy because we are obliged to let go. That's why I think it's important, when we come to contemplate death and impermanence, not to start by reflecting on personal issues—on the loss of someone close to us, or some grief we are right now struggling to resolve. It's all too raw, too fresh, and we are not ready. Instead, we need to look around us and reflect on something more universal, more general.

You may know the story of Krisha Gotami, the young woman whose only child fell sick and died when he was almost a year old. Buddha could not teach her simply to let go, there and then, because she was too grief-stricken. She was too attached to the child, cradled dead in her arms. Buddha sent her to every house in the village to ask for a mustard seed from any that had never known death. He did not tell her to find a house that had never experienced death. He just asked her to bring a mustard seed, something so small and neutral.

Krisha Gotami's realization came gradually, and in the same way we too can slowly make our own discovery. We need that space; we need that time, to allow ourselves to realize, to see how others experience death, and to catch sight of our experience reflected in theirs.

Little by little, perhaps each time Krisha Gotami turned away from a house where somebody had died, her attachment was loosened, and it gradually peeled away. When she realized that she could not find a mustard seed from a home that had never experienced death, then she realized the universality of death. There is nobody that does not die. That's the reality. It is not a conspiracy, nothing personal, it's just a fact of life.

Realizing this brings our own experience home to us, because now we have a perspective. Impermanence now appears as a kind of consolation. It shows us how futile it is to grasp. And so the more we have that realization of impermanence strongly in our minds, the less attachment we'll have. What was once sadness at the impermanence around us now becomes compassion. If we cry at loss and death, we will not just be crying for ourselves alone but for the grief of the world, that grief that attachment gives us. We'll cry because we'll know that if everyone were to realize the truth of impermanence, then even in the thick of change and death and bereavement, they would not feel any unbearable sense of loss.

Our tears then would not be because death and impermanence were facts of life, but because of something much deeper. We would weep with compassion, because we'd know that all the pain and hurt and suffering we go through do not need to be there. They are only there because we fail to understand that everything, absolutely everything, is transient.

We often ask ourselves, "When someone dies, is there still hope? Is there really anything after death?" If we truly follow the spiritual teachings, then even when the worst happens to us, even the end of the world, we can still be happy, because we know of somewhere to go to. Difficulties may come, but instead of withdrawing into depression, we can take refuge in the innermost nature of our mind. Even though we see tragedy, suffering, and pain all around us, still there is hope, still there is something that nothing can destroy or take from us.

As long as we do not realize the truth of impermanence, there is something for us to let go of: our view of permanence and the grasping that comes with it. It's as though we have to let go of grasping in order to realize that the very nature of impermanence is nongrasping. In other words, impermanence itself is the letting go. To take this one step further: if we realize deeply the truth of impermanence, we see there is not even anything to let go of. When light shines, no darkness remains.

The point here is subtle, simple, yet profound. As we have seen, when we realize the truth of impermanence, there is no longer a sense of loss, and there is no longer grasping. At that point, what has happened is that the mind that is grasping—the dualistic mind, the ego mind, the same mind that is afraid of dying—has already dissolved. This is a state that cannot be described in words because it is beyond thought, beyond words, beyond description. The famous verse in praise of transcendent wisdom says:

> Beyond words, beyond thought, beyond description,
>   prajñaparamita:
> Unborn, unceasing, with a nature like the sky.

Once we realize this limitless nature of impermanence, then in the place of loss and sadness, we experience happiness and love. We discover peace, confidence, and fearlessness, because there is finding, not losing. I always say, it's as if you lose the clouds, but gain the sky.

Our usual limited perception of impermanence or change is always associated with losing, isn't it? But looking in a limitless way and realizing the profound nature of impermanence, then we see there is no loss. Because there is no losing, there is no loser—no one to lose—and there is nothing, anyway, to lose. This is called paramita, the "transcendent" understanding that shines through the bodhisattvas' entire way of life.

A love divine

Of course, when we lose something, almost always a little sadness comes over us. Sometimes realization brings with it a tinge of sadness, too, but part of that sadness is compassion and another part is renunciation. It is not the sadness of loss.

What if someone you love very much dies? If you've been through this process of deep reflection, then when you lose somebody, you'll realize that it's the nature of life. At that moment, you can feel that the person you've lost is still there; you're not separated, and it's as if you are with that person who's gone, and able to communicate with him or her. At that moment then, in that realization, just give your love. In that moment, you will also see that you are not at a loss as to what to do. If your love is limitless, there is nothing that can limit *you*.

As Dr. Elisabeth Kübler-Ross and others have said, the most important thing we can do for the dying is to give our love, and of all the love we can give, the most important is unconditional love. We may have heard of unconditional love, but perhaps not many of us know what it really is. When an experienced spiritual practitioner, one who has realized the view of the nature of mind, gives his or her love in a powerful moment of practice, then it's not just ordinary, conditional love. It's unlimited. It has a special quality of freedom. This kind of love is beyond all attachment; it's like divine love. You could almost say it's the love of the buddhas, the love of all the masters, the love of Christ, or of God. You could call it the love of, and for, the truth. And it is extraordinarily powerful.

In the moment of realization, that love springs from your innermost being, from your own enlightened nature. When you touch the absolute, you realize this to be its radiance.

Love that springs truly from the nature of mind is so blessed that it has the power to dispel the fear of the unknown, to give refuge from anxiety, to grant serenity and peace, and to bring inspiration in death and beyond.

At the same time, in that state you also feel, without contriving, that Christ, Buddha, all the buddhas, and all the masters are present. The love you are giving is the love of the buddhas, the love of Christ, and they too are actually there.

So when you think of your loved ones who have died, you can feel in such moments that the love of the buddhas and enlightened beings is there with them, surrounding and blessing them.

23. MOTIVATION:
LAZINESS AND ITS ANTIDOTES

Dzigar Kongtrul Rinpoche

How to enter the Buddhist path

Buddha said, "I have shown you the path of liberation, but whether you attain liberation is up to you." The most important thing that we could accomplish in this lifetime is enlightenment. We are not dependent on external factors to achieve enlightenment; it depends entirely on our own attitude toward study, contemplation, and meditation.

First of all, we must be quite certain about the nature of our attraction to Buddhism. Perhaps our inspiration for study and practice, and for being a student of a teacher, is very genuine. On the other hand, we may simply be looking for therapeutic help.

The former type of motivation—that of genuine inspiration—has much more depth to it than the latter kind, because for genuine motivation to arise we need to realize what lies at the root of our problems. Our real problem is not so much our superficial difficulties but the harm caused to us by our own ego and egocentric *kleshas*—our intellectual, emotional, habitual, and karmic obscurations. We should feel a sense of renunciation toward our ego and kleshas, and motivate ourselves to eliminate them through the application of *prajña*, or wisdom.

The second kind of motivation is based upon our experience of gross human emotions, or some tremendous difficulty that we cannot cope with single-handedly. Unexpected circumstances and unwanted suffering have befallen us, our capacity to deal with them is inadequate, so we look for help. For as long as we are faced with those conditions, we will have some sense of renunciation toward our suffering and existence. However, when those conditions are no longer present, our motivation to continue with our practice and to attain realization might well waver.

During times of suffering, we might make the big mistake of approaching a teacher in the same way a client would approach a therapy that strengthens his or her ego and encourages a desire to be happy that is mistakenly based on the interests of the ego. At first we may be quite open to what our teacher says, because it could be very healing for us. But as time goes by, we could allow our interest to dwindle. We might perceive a conflict between our own interests and the advice of our teacher, and find that our teacher's words no longer touch our hearts in quite the same way.

The Buddhist approach is to diminish the strength of our ego and conflicting emotions. When a teacher speaks from this point of view, students who have approached him for some kind of therapy might become critical of what he says, and there is a real danger of that criticism turning into cynicism. These students have in the meantime received many teachings and initiations and have formed a karmic connection to their teacher.

A cynical attitude toward our teacher can cause us to remain stuck on the path for years. Even people who have been practicing Buddhism for fifteen or twenty years can slowly come to realize that nothing has really changed for the better within their mental continuum. In all probability they have become more cynical, not only about their own teacher and other teachers, but also about everybody else. They are no longer appreciative of anything and are reduced to complaining about whatever happens to them.

These signs indicate we have turned our mind inwardly for the sake of our ego rather than to discover the nature of our mind, that whatever meditation practice we have done has been for the sole benefit of the ego. This is why it is so important at the very beginning to see just what our inspiration for studying, contemplating, and practicing Buddhism is. If our motivation is that we are not clear about how to deal with our egocentric problems, and how to remove our ignorance, then we are on the right track. If it is not, we need to cultivate the correct motivation by becoming aware of how our mental continuum functions.

We suffer from our egocentric problems every second of every minute of every day. Every moment of consciousness, even this very moment, is based upon hope and fear. But it doesn't always have to be like this, because hope and fear have no reference point other than the ego.

Our mental continuum is profound and imbued with magnificent qualities such as love. All beings, from humans down to the tiniest ants, love and feel kindness for their own children. We also rejoice when our own child, or someone we love, attains some measure of happiness. But as long as our perception is governed by the ego's limited perspective, we can only love and be kind to those close to us—our children, relatives, and friends.

The problem is that our precious, inherently present qualities are bound and imprisoned by our egocentric mind. *Ego* means perceiving things in terms of how they belong or relate to us. The concepts *me* and *mine* bind our profound inherent nature to our emotions. Our motivation for following the Buddhist path should be to remove all the ideas of I and mine, which currently influence our mental continuum and daily activity so strongly. When our motivation is to remove the I, we follow the bodhisattva path quite naturally.

Three types of laziness and their antidotes

Before rushing into a teacher's life, it is vital we examine the teacher. When a heart connection beyond the limitations of the ego is formed, and a sense of how the teacher helps people to benefit themselves and others has been established, empowerments and instructions on how to simplify our lives can be received. Then, we need to let this advice take root in our heart and life—which is not going to be that easy, because we have been conditioned by our habitual patterns of laziness for a long time. Overcoming laziness requires diligence. If we are already diligent we can rejoice, but if we are not, then we need to determine how we are going to become so.

Shantideva defines *diligence* as "delight in virtue," and enumerates three kinds of laziness. The first is simply that we are attracted to mundane activities like keeping our house and garden tidy, making tea even when we don't want any more tea, going for a walk when we are already tired, or trying to sleep when we are not tired. We have a strong attraction for these ordinary, worldly things. But our attraction is not the result of a genuine inspiration to engage in these activities; it is just to keep us from being still and quiet.

Generally we are attracted to dull, ordinary activities and lazy in relation to things that are actually beneficial. When we realize that we have to do something important, pressure builds in our mind. As we have always been lazy, we cannot deal with the pressure. So, in order to avoid the pressure, we do something else to distract ourselves from being still and to avoid our responsibilities.

The second type of laziness is our tendency to undermine ourselves. We see that Buddhism is a wonderful path, but then our next thought is that we won't be able to accomplish it. We think that meditation is a truly beneficial practice but worry that we may never be able to do it properly. Without ever seriously examining whether we can do it or not, we undermine ourselves by assuming we are incapable.

Thirdly, the more we sleep, the more sleep we need. Sleep is like salty water—the more we drink, the thirstier we get. This is the case with every kind of desire, but it is particularly true of sleep. The more we sleep, the less we accomplish. Of the three types of laziness, lethargy is the biggest harm and obstacle to us accomplishing anything with our lives, both on the spiritual path and in worldly activity.

The antidote to feeling attachment for mundane activity is to reflect upon our motivation for meditating, and then to actually do the practice without any preconceptions about how we are going to go about it. The Kadampa tradition recommends that a beginner practice like an enraged madman who acts without any reference or plan. When we get up in the morning we should not think about brushing our teeth, taking a shower, or making some coffee before we meditate. If we postpone our meditation, we might never do it. So as soon as we get up, we should charge into the practice without giving laziness the slightest chance to assert itself.

The antidote to the second kind of laziness, our tendency to undermine ourselves, is as Shantideva says in the *Bodhicharyavatara*: developing the determination to accomplish something with our lives, and the most important thing we *can* attain is enlightenment. And we can attain enlightenment. It is not the case that we cannot become enlightened while others can. The buddhas and the bodhisattvas who have attained realization didn't just fall out of the sky; neither did they grow out of the earth. They were ordinary beings like us, but they were diligent and attained enlightenment. We have exactly the same opportunities and all the right materials to work with, so if we apply ourselves diligently, we will become just like them.

Khenpo Rinchen, who was a student of Jamyang Khyentse Wangpo, was my philosophy teacher. Once he compared himself with Milarepa, saying that if their respective karmic debts as they both began on the path had been weighed, his would be lighter than Milarepa's, for Milarepa had killed eight people but he had not killed anybody. Yet it was Milarepa who realized the purpose of life, applied himself diligently, and attained enlightenment in one lifetime.

We have to determine for ourselves that we can conquer the ego and the kleshas. Such confidence has nothing to do with the klesha of pride. The difference is in the effect. Confident pride has a positive effect, so it is not one of the five kleshas, whereas if pride has a negative effect, then it is a klesha. We should be confident that, if we apply ourselves diligently to the Buddha's teachings, follow the instructions of our guru, and realize the Buddha's teachings, we will weaken our ego and the kleshas.

Because of the strength of our habitual patterns, it feels like the ego and the kleshas are an inherent part of our being. In reality, though, they are as temporary as a cloud, totally unlike our buddha nature, the *tathagatagarbha*. Clouds sometimes appear to be very thick, but a strong wind can remove them with ease. In the same manner, egocentric kleshas are seemingly eternal, but if we apply antidotes from the Buddha's teachings, they will not last forever. When we gain confidence in this fact and diligently apply ourselves to practice, we will be able to conquer our kleshas. This is the antidote to the second kind of laziness.

The antidote to the third kind of laziness is knowing your highest priority. If it is practice, then you actually give meditation top priority. You won't achieve this by abruptly adding long practice sessions to your daily schedule, and long-term solitary retreat may not be ideal for your current circumstances. Instead double the duration of your daily practice gradually. To accomplish that, let go of anything that would cause you to miss your practice. For example, you might decide to do an hour's practice at 8:00 every morning. If you then schedule a dental appointment at 8:30 and only wake up at 8:00, then you must choose between the appointment and practice. Many people would just skip practice and go to the dentist. Situations like this give us an insight into how highly we prioritize our meditation. We might think we give it the highest priority but in reality, deep down inside, we do not.

If this is how we practice, then we have no real depth of trust in meditation. We fail to attach much importance to becoming a genuine practitioner, and our belief in what we are doing remains conceptual and superficial. To deepen our conviction, we need to understand why we should give our practice the highest priority.

Whatever our occupation—artist, businessperson, philosopher—as we draw closer and closer to the end of this life, all our experience, skill, and knowledge slowly fades away. And when we make the transition from this life to the next, no ring or hook can secure our skills and abilities and allow us to take them with us. Just as every single experience from our previous lives has evaporated, so will those from our present life. The only experience that we can keep is our realization of the Buddha's teachings.

How is this possible? Just as a shower removes the dirt from our body, when we journey from this life to the next, it is the essence of our mind that continues. The nature of mind is not going to fade away, because there is nothing in it that ceases to exist. This is why we should give the highest priority to daily study, contemplation, and practice, and strive to realize the nature of mind. If we do, we will slowly be inspired to sleep less, not because of external pressure but because of inner conviction. Not only that, our sleep will be lighter. As it says in the dzogchen tradition, our sleep at night would be no different from that of the day. This is the antidote to the third kind of laziness.

Ideally, the length of our daily meditation session increases gradually. If we begin by sitting for half an hour, after six months we should be practicing for forty minutes. Within a year we can extend our practice to an hour, and in two years, two hours. After ten years we will be able to do three hours meditation every day without ever thinking for a single moment that it is too much. If we continue like this throughout our lives, we can progress to five or six hours of meditation daily and come to view postmeditation as a dreamlike, illusory phenomenon. If we do not, our meditation would be a mere conceptual fabrication; and whether someone is tied with a chain of metal or gold makes no difference, because they are still bound.

If we gradually double and redouble the duration of our practice and overcome every kind of ignorant conceptual contrivance, we will eventually become buddhas.

24. FINDING THE THREAD

Sogyal Rinpoche

How can individuals embracing spiritual values, and trying to follow the spiritual path, avoid the many pitfalls on the way, and strengthen and stabilize their understanding and practice? This is one of the topics Sogyal Rinpoche addressed during teachings given in Montreal and Paris:

SOMETIMES IT CAN BE FRIGHTENING to look at how we live today. Everything is accelerating, and we are going so fast. Too fast. We need to stop for a moment, to look into ourselves, and ask, "What am I doing? And why?" And what we'll find is that there seems to be a contradiction: extraordinarily brilliant minds coupled with such weakness. We are so fragmented; it's as if we're all in pieces, and we have no idea how to thread it all together.

Imagine a string of beads. We're just like the beads, a collection of bits. We go through so many different things in life. But we need something to thread us together, to stop us from falling apart. There's a basic value, a fundamental goodness, that we need—and this is what the Dharma can give us.

Sometimes, even those who follow the Dharma have difficulty finding the thread; instead they just find confusion and difficulties. When problems arise, they don't know how to cope with them because they let them become so important. But actually the difficulties are not the issue; *what happens* to us in life is not the point, however much it seems to be. The point, actually, is *how we deal with it*. So everything, in a way, is a teaching, or a test. That's the basic understanding. And if you have that thread running through your life, then you have understood the Dharma; the Dharma is in you.

We need that thread, so that we don't fall apart. If you look at a string of beads, you'll see that although it's very flexible, the beads don't fly all over the place. The trouble with us is that we do, because we don't have that thread—call it sanity, call it basic human values, fundamental goodness, call it trust—to keep our lives together. Isn't life often completely unpredictable? Yet we have to manage. And if we have the thread, which is what the Dharma can hand us, then we can cope with anything; we can hold everything. And if we progress still further, not only can we manage and cope with things, but we can actually transform every circumstance into a blessing.

Go all out at the beginning

These days, many people are very enthusiastic about the Dharma, the teaching of the buddhas. What is so important, I feel, is that at the initial stage, when you're really in love with the Dharma, when you feel inspired and enthusiastic, that's the time to go all out and get a good basis in the Dharma and stabilize it then.

You mustn't lose that opportunity, when everything is auspicious and things are going well. That's when you need to find a good understanding; that's the time you should really study and practice, so it becomes integrated into you, and you and the Dharma get married. If you don't, then what'll happen? After a while, when difficulties and obstacles come, just as they usually do in life, your initial enthusiasm can be marred by them; and if the Dharma is not strong in you, they can sweep you away.

What the Dharma brings us, what it teaches us, very essentially, is to be pure, authentic, and natural. The first and most important thing is pure motivation. There's a famous story, about a hermit long ago in Tibet, called Geshe Ben. He was in retreat, and one day he heard that his sponsors, who were financing his retreat, were coming to visit him. So he cleaned his room, arranged the shrine very neatly, set out all the offerings perfectly, and then sat and waited for his sponsors to arrive. Suddenly, just before they arrived, he reflected on his motivation and said to himself, "What am I doing? This is all fake. I'm just hoping to create a good impression, that's all!" He snatched a handful of ash from the stove by his side and flung it all over the shrine and the offerings. A great master called Padampa Sangyé who heard about this called it "the greatest offering in the whole of Tibet."

Pure motivation and a good heart are fundamental. I remember how Dudjom Rinpoche always used to say that a person needs three qualities. The first, he said, is *sampa zangpo*—a good heart.

The second is *tenpo*—to be stable and reliable. One of our greatest problems is that we lack stability. However much we want to be stable and reliable, everything is so impermanent that things are always in a state of flux. Then, if our mind is not strong, we can be swept away by circumstances and changes. When everything is so impermanent, we become unreliable.

It seems that many people are all too stable when it comes to being negative—stable in their wrong views. Sadly, often that's not the case in terms of the teachings; the teachings have not become a part of us, so we don't have that stability.

For example, a string of beads has a thread running through all the beads, keeping them together. What we need is a thread too: of sanity and stability. Because when you have a thread, even though each bead is separate, they hang together. We are all different individuals, with our emotions, our likes and dislikes, but it's all right, because we've got a thread. At the end of the story—because life is a little bit like the cinema—we just come back, and our thread is always there. We're not scattered everywhere, all over the floor. It's when we have the teachings in us, stabilizing us, that there's a thread to keep our life together, and prevents us from falling apart.

And when you have this string, you have flexibility, too. That's how you can have the freedom to be unique and special and individual, and still have stability as well, and humor. This kind of character is what we need to develop; this character is the thread.

Without discipline, it's very difficult to develop stability; that's why we have a practice. And when we live according to the Dharma, when we follow a teacher, when we follow the Buddha, the Dharma, and the Sangha, what it really does is to bring us stability within ourselves. So, for example, when we have taken refuge, we find a refuge in ourselves; when we need ourselves, we are there for us. So often when we need ourselves, we're not there.

Then the third quality Dudjom Rinpoche spoke of is *lhöpo*—to be spacious, at ease with ourselves. Most important is to be at ease with ourselves. If we are at ease with ourselves, we are at ease with others. If we are not at ease with ourselves, then we will be uncomfortable, especially in company. And especially at parties—imagine you find yourself at a smart party in Paris. All kinds of people are there, from different backgrounds, slightly different from you, and one very suave and successful person turns round to greet you. Even the way he says "bonjour" has a supercilious air about it, as he looks down his nose at you condescendingly. If you're at ease with yourself, there's no problem. He can drawl "bonjour" and look down on you, and you feel completely fine, because for you it is actually a *bon jour,* since you are well with yourself.

When we are well with ourselves, then whatever happens, it really doesn't matter because we have equilibrium and stability. We don't feel any lack of confidence. If not, we're always on edge, waiting to see how someone reacts to us, what people say to us or think about us. Our confidence hangs on what people tell us about how we are, how we look, how we behave. When we are really in touch with ourselves, we know ourselves beyond what others may tell us.

So these three qualities—a good heart, stability, and spaciousness— these are really what you could call basic human virtues.

Beyond hope and fear

How can we ever arrive at a state beyond hope and fear? In our lives, we go through so many stories, we're taught to believe in so many things, and when we grow up we find that many of them are simply wrong. We live under all kinds of confinement, all kinds of imprisonment, which place so many limits on us, and so many rules.

In one way, of course, rules can be good, if used well. As a great Zen master says, "Rules are to free us." But then, when we don't know how to follow rules, they become a limitation. When we know how to follow them, they are a way of freeing us. There are endless things that condition us, endless standards and norms that we measure ourselves by. If we have a good look at ourselves, we'll see how we're all affected by our conditioning. Because of that, we have so much hope, and so many fears. And all of them are something we've learned.

Sometimes in life, we realize that the things we're most afraid of are not even there; and we don't have to fear them at all, because it was all just a myth. Hope is a myth. Fear is a myth. That doesn't mean we say to ourselves, "In that case we don't need to care about anything." Rather, when we become wiser and realize more, we see that the whole thing is a process.

At the moment, our ordinary conditioned self is held in this prison of ignorance. The more we realize how things truly are, the less ignorance there is, and gradually we come to understand that even the prison is an illusion. There is no prison, and there's no one holding us back.

As you go through the teachings and as you practice, what happens is that slowly you become lighter and lighter. You have less worry. Maybe you can let yourself worry a little bit, on a relative level, but actually there's no real anxiety inside. There's a space between you and things, a humor. It's as if things are not happening—even when they are.

Even though things *are* happening, and *to you,* yet in some extraordinary way, you're free. Then, each time something happens, whatever it may be, you begin to realize why. And so every time you go through something, your understanding becomes deeper and deeper. Everything brings you a gift of understanding, and everything brings you back to yourself, to your wisdom nature. Everything, absolutely everything, becomes a teaching. The whole universe becomes your master. The whole of life is your master, constantly showing you. This is called "the universality of the teacher." Your life itself has turned into a teaching.

Gradually you'll find that you don't have to let go; things let go by themselves. It's almost as if everything happens naturally. You don't have to force anything, you don't have to let go heavily; it just happens. Actually letting go happens anyway, because life is always changing. So if you are in step with life, and you can let go while things are happening, then nothing could be more natural.

When you've learned to let go like this, you grow, you blossom, you discover yourself, and then there's tremendous joy. There's hope as well, but not the hope of "hope and fear." Not that small-minded kind of hope that expects a good experience in meditation and worries if you have a bad experience, which immediately wants to classify your dreams into good and bad, and that agonizes over whether you look all right when you meet people, or what they're going to think of you.

Learning how to be

Basically, the essence of the Dharma is to learn how to be—with your mind. How to be comfortable. If you don't separate from your mind, you are completely *with* your mind and comfortable, then you can have all sorts of thoughts and it's fine. Each time you have negative emotions, you just accept them completely. It's normal: emotions are normal. But you don't take them seriously, and you don't fall apart, because you have the basic thread that holds everything together. And because you have that thread, then you too are able to hold together.

There will come a time when all you can see is the contrast. This is the pain of a spiritual practitioner: to see where they are lacking. When you begin to know your wisdom mind just a little, then you begin to see, in a way unlike before, just how confused your mind is, how petty it can be. It's as if you had been a regular smoker, and you didn't really know what smoke was because you'd been surrounded by it for so long. But once you stop smoking, and you go into a room and someone lights up, you can hardly stand it. You realize what smoke is.

So when you begin to see what your mind is like, sometimes, instead of giving you confidence, it gives you lack of confidence, because you see the contrast. You see the disparity between how the teachings are—how you've experienced your true nature—on the one hand, and how you are in your everyday life on the other. You feel there is such a gap, and then you can lose heart and even despair.

If that happens, don't get sucked into that either, for if you think it's a problem, it is a problem. It's not a problem: that's *why* it isn't!

Whenever you're depressed and you start to say to yourself, "How wonderful the teachings are and how terrible I am," stop and ask yourself, "Who is making this separation?" You are. What you have to remember is just the teachings. Find a recording of the teaching that works for you and listen to it again and again. And as you begin to feel well and connected again, your confidence will return.

But you'll need to do that again and again. When you lose it, you need to find it again. You lose it, you find it. Like when you're distracted, you come back to the breath. Like when you forget the teachings, you remember the teachings. So, listen again and again.

In the Tibetan tradition, we are supposed to do many of the practices 100,000 times. What is the point of that? Of course there is a tremendous merit when you do it many times, but the real point is to find yourself again and again. Because when you find yourself again and again, things become a little better. The disparity is a bit less, the fear is a little bit less.

So don't get stuck in the contrast. That is why it is so important to have a teacher or a regular teaching: both to educate you, and, on a deeper level, to bring understanding, to bring balance. It is a kind of processing, an inner processing. Slowly, the teachings and the practice become more integrated and become part of you. After a while, the teachings are so much a part of you that you almost become the Dharma, translating every circumstance. When you have a translator, everything you say is translated. Now, everything you see is translated by the Dharma. You can understand what other people are saying. When you translate everything into Dharma, you begin to understand everything. At the beginning, you need a translator all the time, but after some time you get to the point where you don't even need translation. You simply realize. And as you progress, you come to a level where Dharma is just part of your being.

Healing and Transformation in Life and Death

The way to prepare for death, whether we are approaching our own or caring for someone who is dying, is to train the mind. On one level this means cultivating a sincere compassionate motivation and performing positive actions, serving other sentient beings. At another level it means calming and controlling the mind, which is a more profound way of preparing for the future. Identifying negative states of mind like anger, hatred, jealousy, and pride, we can work to eliminate them. At the same time we can cultivate positive attitudes like compassion and love, tolerance and contentment. Training the mind in this way is both useful and realistic. Love and kindness are not a luxury, but a source of health and happiness for ourselves and others.
His Holiness the Dalai Lama[25]

The Buddhist approach to death is not yet so familiar to us in the West. From the Buddhist perspective, sickness belongs to the suffering nature of life and is accepted as a fundamental part of life. It is even welcomed by practitioners as an opportunity to dissolve and get rid of bad karma. The understanding of healing, however, goes deeper than the mere cessation of pain or of illness; rather, it is related to the transformation of the mind. The pacification of emotional turmoil can be accomplished in deep states of meditation and contemplation, and from this arises another possibility: Even physical conditions can be transformed from within.

The suffering we experience during the dying process, and death itself, can be used as a preparation for the transition from gross levels of being to more refined realms. The moment of death offers a supreme opportunity for our mind to recognize its own original nature, because in death our body and all our delusions and obscurations cease for a few moments, and the pure nature of our mind manifests spontaneously. For this reason Buddhism is quite positive about death. The focus rests on the experience of the "immortality" of that which lies beyond the material dimension, in full recognition of the limitation and impermanence of the body.

This section offers just a few ways into this crucial area. Frank Ostaseski looks at this moment of passage from the carer's perspective, and shows how to offer spiritual care to others during their final days with an attitude of genuine compassion. This enables the carer and the person cared for to meet on equal ground, where personal agendas cannot undermine the healing process. Christine Longaker offers us the Buddhist understanding of suffering and the end of suffering based on the four noble truths. The meditations she introduces show us how training our minds leads to a deconditioning that permits a permanent transformation.

Finally, Sogyal Rinpoche shows how coming to terms with impermanence and death offers us deep consolation, and that a spiritually based care during our final moments can enable confidence and trust to arise—"a sense of hope and meaning."

25. Learning How to Serve

Frank Ostaseski

Two of the most important considerations in caring for the dying are taking good care of ourselves and learning how to listen, and neither takes much effort. The Indian poet Rabindranath Tagore wrote:

I slept and dreamt that life was joy.
I woke and found that life was service.
I acted, and behold, service was joy.

There can be no genuine service unless both the server and the served benefit. At an installation ceremony for the new abbot of a Zen center, a student asked, "What can the Dharma teach me about serving others?" The abbot replied, "What others? Serve yourself!" The student persisted: "How can I serve myself?" "Take care of others," said the abbot.

My work is with people who are dying, and some of them are very tough individuals: they might have been living on the streets and are angry about their loss of control; they might have lost faith in humanity, or turned toward the wall and withdrawn into themselves. Most of them don't give a fig about Buddhism. These people don't trust anyone easily, and if I am going to be of any use to them at all, I have to be especially clear and honest about my intention. If I am not, they will sniff out my insincerity and sentimentality in seconds.

Some of the individuals that I work with blossom, and the way they die is a great gift to everybody else in the center. They reconcile with long-lost family members and find the kindness and acceptance for which they have been searching the whole of their lives. It can be quite wonderful to be in the presence of such a transformation.

However, my motivation for doing this work cannot be that it sometimes works out well. Chasing such rewards causes exhaustion and ultimately leads to manipulation. I would be so busy trying to create the conditions that produce a reward that I would miss what is actually happening. I do this work because I love it, and because it serves me. I try to see myself in each person that I serve, and I try to see them in me. Those that I work with know and trust that, and come to rely on it. They understand that we are in the same soup.

At the very heart of service lies the understanding that the act of caring is always of mutual benefit. By nurturing others we care for ourselves, and this understanding fundamentally shifts the way in which we provide care for others. We are no longer heroes galloping to the rescue on white horses; we are compassionate companions.

Compassion literally means "suffering with others," and "with" is the most important word in this definition. *With* implies belonging. *Companion* means "one who travels with another." No one takes the role of leader and guide in this relationship. There is no healer and no person to be healed; we simply accompany one another. And as my friend Reb Anderson says, "We are walking through birth and death, holding hands."

When we enter a room in which someone is dying, if we are paying attention we will immediately see just how precarious life is, and we will also understand how precious life is. When we keep an awareness of death close at hand, we become less compulsive about our desires. We can take ourselves and our ideas a little less seriously, and we can let go of them more easily. We are more open to generosity, and to love.

It may sound like a paradox, but working with the dying makes us a bit kinder with each other. In the face of death, all of the ways in which we have created our identity will either be given up gracefully, or be methodically stripped away by illness. Ideas that have been the bedrock of our identity, such as "I'm a father," "I'm a mother," "I'm a hospice worker," or, "I don't fit in this society," will all evaporate.

One of the wonderful things about the people I work with, who are mostly indigent, is that while their lives might appear on the surface to be very different from mine, we often discover that we belong together. They might be black while I am white, they might shoot heroin and have AIDS and might be homeless and alone, while I pay a ridiculous amount of rent and have four teenage children. It would be easy to convince myself that I am separate and fundamentally different from these people. After all, a few months ago we might have walked past each other on the streets, each oblivious to the other's presence. In the hospice we are thrown together in the most intimate of circumstances, but in the midst of the details of activity and service, we find a meeting place where we all belong.

The helper's disease

Prior to any action, thought, or spoken word comes a moment of intention. We need to be aware of this very subtle fact, since clarity about the nature of our intention allows us to choose how we are going to proceed. A moment of contact with our intention can break our habitual patterns, or stop us from operating on automatic pilot.

In Zen Buddhism, there is a practice called *dokusan,* an interview with the teacher. The student is instructed to wait outside the teacher's door and gather him- or herself completely into the moment. The student has no idea what lies on the other side of the door, no idea what the teacher will ask, so he or she has to be ready, flexible, and open.

Entering a dying patient's room is just like *dokusan.* Ideally, our bodies and minds should enter the room at the same time. Sometimes that is not the case. We can easily leave our minds a long way behind, or enter the room hours before we actually arrive.

A patient once said to a hospice volunteer, "Oh, I'm so glad you're here. Finally I have someone to talk to about my death." The volunteer got very excited and said, "Yes, I'll get some books by Elisabeth Kübler-Ross and Steven Levine. I'll be back next week and we can talk all about it then." The next week he came back with piles of books, and the patient said, "Hi, we're watching the football game on TV. Come in. Watch the game with us."

All too often in caregiving, we are not so much looking to see how we can serve as to confirm some idea that we have about ourselves. We want to be somebody, to be able to say, "I work with the dying," with the emphasis firmly on "I." Consequently, we invest in the role and not in the function of caregiving. I sometimes call this "helper's disease," and it is even more virulent than AIDS or cancer. Through pity, fear, professional warmth, and even through our acts of charity, we can distance ourselves from other people's suffering.

Working with the dying has nothing to do with charity. A few years ago a woman in our hospice, who was just a few days away from death, was quite sad and depressed. This seemed natural enough—after all, she was dying. A nurse saw her condition and suggested that we start her on a medication used to enhance people's moods and that usually takes about three weeks to start working. I asked her why, and the nurse said, "Well, she's suffering, and it's so hard to watch her suffer." I suggested that maybe she should take the medicine instead.

Helping, fixing, and serving

Attachment to the role of the helper is well established in most of us. Helping others can provide us with the compensation of power and respectability; it's like a paycheck that we can collect at the end of the week. Unfortunately, if we are not careful this identity will not only imprison us; it will imprison those we serve. If we are going to be helpers, somebody else has to be helpless. Rachel Raymond, who runs the Common Wheel Cancer Center, speaks very beautifully about this:

> Service is not the same as helping. Helping is based on inequality; it's not a relationship between equals. When you help, you use your own strength to help someone of lesser strength. It's a one up, one down relationship, and people feel this inequality.

When we help, we diminish people's self-esteem and may inadvertently take away from them more than we actually give. When we help, we are made very aware of our own strength. But we don't serve with our strength; we serve through our whole being.

In order to serve, we must draw on the entire experience of our lives—even our wounds, limitations, and darkness can help us to serve. The wholeness in us serves the wholeness in others, while helping incurs debt. When we help someone, they owe us something, whereas service is mutual and debt free. Helping might be satisfying, but it is only when we serve someone that we experience gratitude.

Serving is not the same as fixing. We might be able to fix broken pipes, but we can't fix people. When we decide to fix another person, we automatically see that person as broken. Fixing is a form of judgment that separates us from one another, and it will always create distance between people. When we help, we see life as weak; when we fix, we see life as broken; and when we serve, we see life as whole and complete. Serving brings us the understanding that somebody else's suffering is also my suffering; that his joy is my joy. Understanding inspires us to service, and our natural wisdom and compassion arise naturally and effortlessly.

A server not only realizes that he or she is being used; he or she is willing to be used in the service of something greater than the self. We may help in many situations and fix many things in our lives, but when we serve, we act exclusively in the service of wholeness. Caring for those who are suffering, whether they are dying or not, is not the point; serving wakes us up and opens our hearts and minds to the experience of wholeness.

Unfortunately, we are usually stuck in our idea of ourselves and our habitual roles, and this separates us from other people. Lost in a reactive state of mind, busy protecting our self-image, we isolate ourselves from that which would truly serve our efforts and inform our work. To help others, we have to be prepared to bring our full selves—our passions, our wounds, and our fears—to the bedside. It is our personal understanding of the nature of suffering that builds the bridge between ourselves and the person we are serving.

Let me give an example of how this works. A few years ago, a dear old friend of mine named John was quite sick with AIDS. In the course of just one afternoon, he found that he could no longer speak, hold a fork, stand, or form a comprehensible sentence. It just so happened that this particular afternoon was my turn to take care of him. It scared the hell out of me—"Mr. Hospice" was terrified.

I spent the whole afternoon trying everything I had ever learned to do. John had enormous fistulas, constant diarrhea, and anal tumors, so we moved in a constant circle from the toilet to the bathtub, and back again to the toilet. I was exhausted; all I wanted to do was to go back to bed. I tried every trick I knew: I was cajoling, manipulative, and paternalistic. I changed wardrobes more often than Madonna. And then, in the middle of one of these moves from the bathtub to the toilet, from far inside his garbled mind, John said, "You're trying too hard."

Indeed I was, and I stopped right there, sat down beside the toilet and started to cry. I have to tell you that this was the most exquisite meeting of our whole relationship. There we were, completely helpless together, inseparable, without a trace of professional warmth.

If we are not willing to explore our own suffering, we will only be guessing when we tell a patient that we understand them. It is the exploration of our own suffering that allows us to serve others, that allows us to touch another person's pain with compassion rather than with fear and pity. Not only do we have to be willing to listen to the patient; we also have to be prepared to listen to ourselves. We must pay careful attention to what is immediately in front of us.

A year ago I got a call to come to the hospice because one of our patients, a tough old Jewish woman from Russia, was dying. By the time I arrived she was gasping for air. Her attendant said to her, "Don't be frightened, I'm right here with you," to which she said, "Believe me, if this was happening to you, you'd be frightened too." A short while later the attendant said that she looked a little cold, and asked whether she would like a blanket. "Of course I'm cold," she said. "I'm almost dead."

If we were going to help her we had to pay attention to what she was telling us. She was struggling with her breath, and she wanted to be dealt with very honestly, without any bullshit. I went to her and said, "Adele, would you like to struggle and suffer a little less?" She said she would like that, so I explained that between her in-breath and her out-breath there was a little space where I had seen her resting. I suggested that she put her attention there, just for a moment. She was a very rough old woman, with no interest in Buddhism or meditation whatsoever, but she did want to struggle a little less. As she tried it, the fear in her face began to recede. She took a few more breaths, and died quite calmly.

To be of service to someone, we have to pay attention to what is immediately in front of us, act with minimal intervention, and bring to the situation the same attention and equanimity that we might cultivate on our meditation cushion. The degree to which we are willing and able to live in this ever-fresh moment is the measure of our ability to be of real service. When the heart is open and the mind is still, when our attention is fully in this moment, there is no division between us and the world, and we know instinctively how to act appropriately. Everybody is capable of this; there is no need to have done years of Buddhist practice. We can all embrace another person's suffering as our own; we have merely forgotten how.

One evening, one of our volunteers was helping a patient move from his bed to the commode. Unfortunately, with his pants down around his ankles, the patient fell over, and there was a small Hiroshima—this is what caregiving is really like. The volunteer fumbled through, got the patient back into bed, and called me for some advice. He wanted to review the techniques for positioning people in bed. I told him, "Okay, let's just do this: The next time you go to move the patient, before you start, just check your belly and see if it is soft. If your belly is not soft, don't do anything."

"Don't give me that Buddhist stuff. I just want to know what to do with his knees."

"Just check your belly and call me back later." It was a bit like saying, "Take two aspirin and call me in the morning," but he did call back a bit later.

"Frank, it was the most amazing thing. I went to move the patient and my belly was hard as a rock, so I stopped. I took a few breaths, my belly softened, and the next thing I knew, the patient was in my arms, like a lover or a small child. It was no trouble at all."

The experience of unity

Buddhism holds the view that we have all been born many times before, that we have all been each other's mothers, fathers, and children, and so we should treat everyone with the same great love and respect. In relation to service we can witness a common pattern: all habits that hinder our work engender a sense of separation. Common to all actions that truly serve is the experience of unity. Albert Einstein wrote:

A human being is part of a whole called by us the universe, a part limited in time and space. He experiences himself, his thoughts, and his feelings as something sometimes separate from the rest, a kind of optical illusion of consciousness. This delusion is a kind of prison for us, restricting us to personal desires and affection for the few people nearest to us. Our task must be to free ourselves from this prison, by widening our circle of understanding and compassion to embrace all living creatures, and the whole of nature in its beauty.[26]

When the heart is not divided from the world, everything we encounter is an expression of our practice. Service becomes a sacred exchange, just like quietly breathing in and out. We receive a physical and spiritual sustenance from the world, which is like breathing in. And then, because each of us is born with certain gifts, part of our happiness in the world comes from giving the gift back, which is like breathing out.

A friend of mine calls this way of working "simple human kindness." Our work obliges us to get out of the way of our own innate wisdom and compassion, our inborn ability to see what another needs. We should embrace the entirety of our lives because it is with wholeness that we serve both the dying and the living. Don't push anything away; meet everything with tenderness, and offer it gracefully to those you serve.

QUESTION: *I understand compassion to be both suffering with the other and feeling with the other. However, I cannot die with the patient. What limits are there to compassion?*

FRANK OSTASESKI: Compassion is not only about suffering with others; it is also being joyous with others. Although it is important in this work to make boundaries, we should understand that they are like scaffolding on the outside of a building: boundaries are put up to serve a purpose, and when the purpose is served we can take them down again.

In the relative world of caregiving, we have to understand that the caregiver and the patient are separate individuals. However, if this is our only perspective, our serving will be limited and will ultimately isolate ourselves and the person in the bed from one another. A sacred Indian text asks what, in all worlds, is most astonishing? The answer it gives is that the most astonishing thing in the world is that none of us, even though we see people dying all around, believes that death will happen to us. If we haven't explored our own relationship to death, we can't serve other human beings.

QUESTION: *I work with dying people, and I also take care of their bodies after they have died. Recently, I have felt a strong fear when a body becomes cold. What should I do?*

FRANK OSTASESKI: John, the good friend I was describing earlier, was a Buddhist practitioner, and he had requested to be laid out at home in his bed for three days following his death. At one point I reached over to touch him, just to express my love for him, and a cold feeling shot through my arm, like intravenous fluid. It touched me in a cold, dark place that I had previously been unwilling to look at, and I was really scared. I sat there feeling lonely, and my whole body became infused with a sense of isolation. I began to realize how common it is for someone to feel lonely, and saw that there was no separation between me and all the other people who felt equally isolated. This is what grief is like. We first experience it as isolation, but later understand that grief is common to everybody. This understanding connects us all with each other. The doorway that leads to grief, loneliness, and fear can also be the doorway to joy. We must, however, go through the doorway; we can't just walk around it. Therefore, I would encourage you to feel your fear.

QUESTION: *You said that we can only serve through the wholeness of our life. Could you say a little bit more about this?*

FRANK OSTASESKI: Imagine a puzzle, and that this particular puzzle is a picture of our own face, of our body, of our entire self. If this puzzle is dropped on the floor, it breaks into a thousand pieces and needs reassembling. On a whim, we decide that we don't like our anger; that we've been taught that lust is no good; and that we shouldn't need to feel grief ever again—so we remove these pieces from the puzzle. The result is that we can no longer recognize ourselves because we are looking at a fragmented picture. To be whole, we have to welcome everything and use it all as a bridge that allows us to meet others with compassion.

QUESTION: *I would like to help dying people because I myself face death. I don't know if it's okay for me to do this, because I'm not free of my own problems with illness and dying.*
FRANK OSTASESKI: We all have a great need to express our generosity. Sometimes the need can be so strong that it frightens us. When we come across a homeless person our first response is one of generosity, but the next is often one of fear, which makes us question our motivation and creates doubt. We can trust in our own innate wisdom and compassion, and believe that we will know what to do. It is important to discover for ourselves when the right moment to serve has arrived, and we shouldn't let anyone else make that decision for us.

QUESTION: *There is truth, which, if one has cancer and could die in a year or two, means facing death; and there is hope. Hope is very powerful, so how much hope can we give others? My father has cancer and, without lying, I would like to give him hope and make his death easier; but I would also like to help him face death.*
FRANK OSTASESKI: I don't know if we can actually give hope to someone else. Where can we buy hope? A while ago, a man in the hospice wanted to kill himself because he was very sick with cancer and he could no longer find any pleasure in living. He asked for books that would help him to end his own life. We got them for him and even read them to him. He stayed with us for three months, and I got to love him very much. His struggle didn't go away, but after living in a loving and compassionate environment, at the end of his life he said, "I want to thank you all, because I'm happier now than I've ever been in my entire life." I said that what he'd just said was bullshit, and reminded him that only a few weeks ago he had wanted to kill himself because he couldn't walk in the park. "Oh, that," he replied. "That was just chasing desire. It's not the activity that brings me joy, it's the attention I pay to the activity. Now my pleasure comes from the coolness of the breeze or the softness of the sheets."

We don't have to give hope; we only have to turn our attention to what is in front of us. In daily life we all practice distraction, so help your father to pay attention by paying very careful attention to him and to the details of his life. Listen to every detail, and believe every detail.

26. Transforming Suffering
Through Compassion

Christine Longaker

H ERE IS A SIMPLE IMAGE that might help you glimpse the potential of meditation. Our mind has two aspects. The first one we are very familiar with: our distracted mind—our thinking, dualistic mind. That mind is constantly commenting on and reacting to things, making plans, projecting, dreaming about the past, and fantasizing about the future. It is as if we take a glass of muddy water and constantly shake it, making the water turbulent and cloudy. That is the way our distracted thinking-ego mind normally functions. We are busy chasing one thought after another, and we are all over the place, leaving no one at home.

So what happens when we sit quietly? Imagine taking this turbulent glass of muddy water we have been constantly shaking and just setting it down. What happens? The mud settles. But before it settles it still swirls for a while. So, even when you are sitting quietly, bringing all these scattered aspects of your mind and energy home, for a while you will be aware of many thoughts and emotions, like the swirling momentum in the cloudy water.

Gradually, though, if you don't chase after the thoughts, react to them, or create new chatter in your mind, the distracted mind will slowly settle. The mind's natural clarity, which was always there, and is in fact the mind's true nature, will naturally and spontaneously manifest. What a relief to experience our mind's turbulence settling down! The result—that we become more at home in ourselves, more present, and more aware—is very useful for every aspect of life. And the presence and clarity that meditation brings is invaluable for helping us support friends, family, or patients who are suffering.

I directly experienced the benefit of this kind of presence in 1977, the year that my husband Lyttle was ill with acute leukemia. Lyttle was cared for at the Medical Center of the University of California at Los Angeles (UCLA), which had a unit especially for leukemia patients. The nurses played an important role in designing the ward, which was similar to a modern palliative care unit, with a higher ratio of nurses to patients. The nurses were able to spend time with and get to know their patients, and they supported the family members as well. Many of the hospital rules were relaxed in this ward, making it more friendly to loved ones, allowing overnight stays and free use of the kitchen.

One nurse on this ward had made a special connection with my husband. Lyttle felt he could really confide in her. In the first few months after he was diagnosed with acute leukemia, Lyttle was hospitalized repeatedly for life-threatening complications to his illness. He spent three weeks out of every four in the hospital. On this admission, his fourth, the symptoms that had necessitated his admission were finally resolved, and he was looking forward to going home. But in the morning he had new, potentially dangerous symptoms, and the doctors recommended he stay in the hospital for an indeterminate period. As a result, on this bright and sunny morning, Lyttle was feeling very depressed and hopeless.

There was a young man in the room next to my husband's who was also in isolation for leukemia. He had a very boisterous, outgoing personality, constantly talking and laughing and carrying on with people in his room. It sounded like he was always in the middle of a party. And when there were no visitors, he was on the phone talking loudly and having fun. He drank lots of soft drinks, and when he was done he would crush the can and try to make a basket into the trash. We knew whenever he missed, because we could hear the can as it crashed against the wall!

Just after my husband received the depressing news from his doctor, I was in the bathroom that adjoins both of the patients' rooms. I heard the nurse come into the other man's room and heard them joking, laughing, and playfully teasing each other. In the first moment I felt very happy for him, but then I felt sad, thinking, "Oh, that's too bad.

If the nurse is feeling so happy today, she won't be able to support my husband in his depressed mood."

After a few minutes I was back in my husband's room, and I saw the same nurse open the door to come in. I saw her body and her face, and I observed that she was completely "present." Gazing toward my husband, she sensed his mood, and coming to his side, she made a deep, caring connection in a very short time. Although she couldn't remove the source of his suffering, her ability simply to be with him this way brought him great comfort.

I understood something that morning. Our ability to be fully present, open, and clear, as we are just after meditation, can have a very powerful, healing effect on others. Of course, when she was between these two patients' rooms, the nurse didn't go somewhere and sit quietly in meditation. However, once we develop a consistent daily practice of meditation, we can learn to integrate the presence of the meditation into every moment of our daily life and work, and this is the main objective of the trainings we offer medical professionals in Rigpa's Spiritual Care Program.

Actually, to help any of us cope with life's myriad stresses, changes, and disappointments, it is vital to train in meditation so that we become more centered, more present, and more aware. Meditation helps us drop the leftover emotional baggage of the previous moment so that we can be clear, present, and aware in the present. Once we have established a daily meditation practice, then even in little gaps during the day, when we are on hold on the phone or walking down the hall between two patients' rooms, we can simply "bring our mind home" to its true nature once again.

This way of integrating spiritual practice with medical care not only helps us be present and supportive of patients, like the nurse at UCLA, but it also prevents burnout. Imagine going through the day without accumulating stress or emotional baggage. When you let go of the mind's cloudy, reactive aspect and take refuge instead in the clear, open, peaceful aspect, you also leave behind all the suffering you might have felt as a result of disappointments, harsh words, or attachment. Bringing your mind home again and again while letting go of troublesome memories, emotions, or fantasies, you become clearer and more peaceful throughout your day. By the time you arrive home, you are free of most, if not all, of the day's emotional baggage, and more present and relaxed in the remainder of your day.

"How we are" is what helps

Over the years I have observed that, more than anything we say or do, what helps people who are suffering is "how we are." What are the qualities of how we are that we can develop that will enable us to give more effective and compassionate support to people who are suffering or dying? There are three qualities: presence, authenticity, and confidence. I have introduced the quality of presence and awareness above. However, this quality of presence is also connected to how we view our patients or friends when they experience suffering. We must learn how to break out of our narrow conditioning and begin nurturing a vast perspective. A common mistake we make, which also contributes to burnout, is to view the person we are caring for as a helpless victim of his or her problem—be it serious illness, emotional pain, or some other difficult circumstance.

With this limited perspective, we end up feeling even more responsible to relieve his or her suffering and make everything all right, which is usually impossible. We disempower the other person, and ourselves, when we view him or her this way. Reflecting on the spiritual dimension of life and death enables us to expand our perspective and learn to see the other as a whole person, worthy of our respect, no matter how painful the circumstances he or she may be going through. We can train ourselves to view the suffering the person has as a temporary layer, like a thin mist on a mirror. Yes, the person has suffering, but that is not who that person is; it is not his or her identity. We look beyond the suffering to see the person's essence, or true nature, which is pure, complete, and untarnished. Some call that indestructible essence the divine within, or buddha nature, but whatever name we give it, we are pointing toward the absolute truth or fundamental goodness that is inherent within each being.

It helps to recognize that we cannot always relieve another person's suffering; nor should we take his or her suffering personally, or try to shoulder his or her burden ourselves. We learn to develop a profound compassion while maintaining a "vast perspective" on the whole of life.

The second quality we can develop is *authenticity*. Sometimes we might say a person with a terminal illness should get over his denial and face the facts squarely. He should get his affairs in order, heal any unfinished business, make his peace with God, and prepare for his coming death. You might be thinking, however, "I don't have to do that myself; I'm fine."

Your seriously ill patient sees right through your game. He knows that there is no certainty about who is going to die first, he or you. So who is in denial? Both of you are in your own little boat going down a river headed toward that unexpected waterfall called "the moment of death." There is no saying who is closer to the waterfall right now. Authenticity comes from realizing that both you and the dying person are in fact on a journey toward death. You must get beyond your denial, face and overcome your own fears, and get your life in order so that you are fully prepared for your own death. Once you do so, then you will have more understanding, insight, and genuine compassion for the people in your care—because you genuinely know how hard it is.

Imagine that you are going to die in a year. What do you need to do to prepare and feel ready? You might apply yourself to the "four tasks of living and dying," which I expand on in the section below:

- Understanding and transforming suffering
- Healing relationships, making a connection, and letting go
- Preparing spiritually for death
- Finding meaning in life

One by one, you could begin working with these tasks to help you prepare for death. You might be surprised to find that doing so also helps you begin enjoying your life more fully! You can free up a lot of energy and discover a deeper meaning to your life. And preparing for your own death with humility and courage prepares you for all of life's vicissitudes. Finally, working deeply with yourself and your life prepares you to support with authenticity others who are suffering.

You can never apply a "patch" of philosophy to another person's problem because, sooner or later, the patch falls off. The other person doesn't even want your truth. You have to be right in there with her, facing her suffering, her grief, her uncertainties and pain, remembering all the time that both of you are on a journey of evolution through life and death. When you can look in a dying person's eyes with this authenticity, she knows you understand and you are not judging her. Perhaps you have something to offer, and just as likely, you have something to learn from her.

Allow the dying to give you their last gifts of life wisdom. The dying hate to feel that they are reduced to being a burden on others, that their lives have no more meaning. When we genuinely listen to them and are interested to learn from them about life, coping with illness, or what it is like to face death, this can give meaning to the last part of their life.

The third quality we can develop is *confidence*. How much confidence do we have in our own spiritual path? Spiritual care does not mean giving our beliefs to someone else in order to save them. Spiritual care is a deepening of confidence, as a result of daily spiritual practice, until we come to embody the deepest truths of our own spiritual path. Then, when we are with others, without even speaking about it, our presence radiates that confidence and goodness and lends strength to those who are suffering or dying.

The more we are able to inspire ourselves, the more our confidence inspires others and brings them peace. In his inaugural speech, President Nelson Mandela said,

> Our deepest fear is not that we are inadequate; our deepest fear is that we are powerful beyond measure. It is our light, not our darkness that most frightens us…We are made to manifest the glory of God within us. It is not in just some of us; it is in everyone. As we let our own light shine, we unconsciously give other people permission to do the same. As we are liberated from our own fears, our presence automatically liberates others.

That is the key to really helping people to die with peace of mind, with trust, with a sense of inspiration and even fulfillment. Without sharing what we believe, but simply embodying it, our presence can liberate. Once we have trained in our own spiritual path, we are able to hear and appreciate the inherent spirituality or life-wisdom in another. We can ask what he believes in, or what gives his life meaning, and help him reconnect to that trust or spiritual tradition in a way that is meaningful.

The four tasks of living and dying

In my trainings for hospice and palliative care professionals, I used to describe the principal sources of pain or difficulty a dying person and his or her family experience. Gradually, though, I realized that these were not simply the pains of dying; they were in fact the tasks of dying. Very few people I have met want to passively give up and accept death. When we realize that there are actually tasks in dying, and that there is something we can do, then we have a chance to develop and grow, and to complete our life well.

However, we don't have to wait until we are dying to work with these tasks; and if we do wait, we only make things harder on ourselves. These are the tasks of living as well. They are the developmental tasks we face when we go through major losses or change, bereavement or serious illness. The four tasks apply to all of us, and they are especially important for those who care for people facing death.

The first task is the need to understand suffering and to find ways to transform our suffering. We don't just suffer when we are dying. In fact, we die a thousand deaths before we die. The immense changes and losses we experience in life can feel a lot like dying. Most of us are very ill equipped to go through those changes and the suffering they bring. We don't know how to work with them ourselves, nor how to support others. I will expand on this task in the remainder of this chapter.

The second task is to heal our relationships, make a connection, and let go.

The third task is to understand what death is and to prepare spiritually for death throughout our lives.

The fourth task is the need to find meaning in our lives. This task is especially important when a person has no spiritual tradition or belief. To enable someone to die with a peaceful mind and heart, the bottom line is to make sure they don't die feeling empty handed. We can help them remember they have accomplished something in their lives, that their lives have had meaning for others. Or we can help them feel that even while dying their lives are meaningful. This is key in supporting others, because it is easier to let go if you feel your life has been conducted well. The second, third, and fourth tasks are described in more detail in my book *Facing Death and Finding Hope: A Guide for the Emotional and Spiritual Care of the Dying.*

The role of compassion in suffering

What do we mean when we say "compassion?" In Buddhism, profound compassion is considered to be one aspect of our wisdom nature. The skylike openness and clarity of our true nature has a quality of infinite compassion—compassion that is limitless and unbiased, like the rays of the sun that shine equally on all. Our essence is a fundamental goodness, or the good heart.

Ordinarily, what we call *compassion* is seeing someone suffer and feeling sorry for him or her. Because they have more difficulties than we do, we may look down on them with a mixture of fear or pity. Yet if the person suffering happens to be our wealthy neighbor who seems to have everything we don't, we may not feel "compassion" when he loses his wealth or his home. Or, if someone has hurt us, or rejects our offer of help, our "compassion" evaporates, because it is limited and biased.

Real compassion is without any limits or judgments. Real compassion is a profound state of love that is pure and boundless; it is an altruistic wish that each and every being, without exception, be completely free of suffering and even its causes. It is the ability to see all beings, whether rich or poor, happy or unhappy, as completely equal to us, and equally worthy of reverence. We may not honestly feel it is possible to have that depth of compassion just now. Buddhism offers a number of meditations that help us tame our selfish, stubborn, conditioned mind and train in profound compassion, so that we might connect authentically with others as well as ourselves. And these practices for training the mind in compassion give us tools for transforming our own suffering.

Generating profound compassion in your heart can give meaning to your suffering. When you go through a period of very deep suffering, if you open your eyes and look around, you will see that many other people are going through the exact same problem or worse. When you get a sense of the universality of suffering, the compassion in your heart is aroused, and you feel more connected to humanity. You generate a strong intention that all beings everywhere might be free of suffering, just as you wish to be free of your suffering. By purifying your heart and mind, this altruistic intention brings apparently meaningless suffering on to your spiritual path.

There are many different ways of practicing compassion, and one such method that is described in every major spiritual tradition is *dedication*. Dedicating is a positive and empowering way to direct your mind and heart when you experience unwanted pain and suffering. Even those who have no spiritual beliefs welcome the idea that they can dedicate their suffering. Dedicating your deep experiences of pain and suffering can help you transcend the cause of suffering—your grasping ego—because you are no longer just thinking of yourself.

We can dedicate for one person we know, generating a strong wish or aspiration such as: "May this suffering I am going through relieve the suffering of my friend." Or we can dedicate for all beings, with the thought: "May I take on the suffering of everyone who has this same difficulty; may they be free of all suffering and pain and even its causes." Dedicating doesn't change your external circumstances, but it will change the way you feel about them.

People approaching death try to find meaning in their life. Some may feel regret, realizing that they withheld their love, or harmed others, or lived in a very selfish way. If they are weak and bedridden, they might wonder, "Now what can I do?" We can dedicate to atone for any harm we may have brought others, with the thought, "Through the suffering and pain of my dying, may I take on myself any harm that I brought to others. May their suffering be relieved, and may they have healing, and enjoy every happiness in life."

A close friend of mine, Jean, told me she was going to visit her dying father-in-law, Ed, who was comatose. Jean wouldn't be able to have a normal conversation with him, so it would be difficult to communicate. In addition, her feelings about Ed were mixed—she knew it would be good if she could help him let go and die peacefully, yet because of his alcoholism Ed had brought considerable suffering to his entire family, including Jean's husband, and she was angry with him. After being part of the family for twenty-five years, she observed that the family members were distant, uncommunicative, and not the least supportive due to Ed's past behavior.

Together we acknowledged that Jean's anger was normal. It was all right if she wanted to communicate her frustration and anger to him, as long as she had the intention to completely let it go. I proposed that, before communicating with Ed, she could meditate quietly by his side, reflecting on how much she would have liked to have known the real man and not the alcoholic.

She asked, "Can he hear me?" I told her that there are many anecdotal accounts of people who were comatose who, after coming back to consciousness, described that they understood everything that was going on in the room, even what people were thinking.

"Yes," I said, "I think he can hear you."

The Buddhist tradition reminds us that the essence of every person is a pure awareness that is never harmed or diminished, even if the cognitive functions of the brain are impaired. This pure awareness is always present and aware of what is happening in the room. That is why you can still communicate, and trust that what you say is being received.

But how could Jean view the situation from a different perspective? We reflected on how much Ed must have suffered in his own childhood to come to recreate this same anguish in his own family. I also described to Jean that after his death, Ed would undergo a comprehensive review of his entire life. As the near-death experiences reveal, he would be acutely aware at that time of all the pain he brought onto his loved ones, and he would personally experience all of their suffering together with his painfully strong remorse.

As Jean reflected on Ed's past, present, and possible future suffering, a sense of understanding and compassion began to replace her anger. "Is there anything I can do to help him now?" she asked.

"When you are with him," I suggested, "remember that although Ed appears to be comatose and unresponsive, the pure awareness of his true nature is still there, and this aspect of him can always hear you. Let him know that if he feels any regret for how he has lived, he can dedicate his suffering and death for his family. In the moment of death he can radiate his love and blessings with a strong prayer that they be healed of any hurt or pain he might have caused them."

When Jean later visited her father-in-law, she meditated by his side, sending him her understanding and compassion, and sensing that it was gratefully received by the unconscious man. Jean told Ed of her years of frustration and anger, but went on to suggest to him that if he felt regret for his actions, he could dedicate the moment of his death and generate a strong aspiration for healing for his entire family. Then Jean said goodbye to him.

Later that evening, she was driving home while her husband slept in the passenger seat. Suddenly he woke with a start, saying, "This is so much easier now. The bitterness I felt earlier is simply gone." Later they learned that this had been the moment of Ed's death. Jean wondered if Ed had in fact dedicated his death to atone for his life. A different kind of confirmation came the next day, when, after the funeral, she observed that the family members, who for twenty-five years had never said two kind words to each other, were now very loving and affectionate and supportive.

The power of compassion can give meaning to what seems like a meaningless situation, and this can transform our suffering. In some states of extreme suffering or pain, compassion might be the only thing we can focus on.

Lama Yeshe was a Tibetan master who lived in Nepal and traveled extensively, and he had many students in the West. He was hospitalized once with a very serious heart condition. In a letter to his spiritual friend, he described how his illness, and the treatments he was receiving, made it extremely difficult to focus on the spiritual practices he was committed to doing daily.

First there were unending injections throughout the day and night. Second, because the capacity for my heart to pump oxygen was impaired, in order to breathe I needed oxygen for which a rubber tube ran to my nose from a tank. This was never disconnected and caused me great discomfort. Third, I had to constantly take medicine day and night, sometimes more than ten pills at a time. Due to this medication my mind was power- lessly overcome with pain every two hours. My memory degen- erated. Food lost its taste. I was given only saltless bland food. I had no appetite and whatever food I ate, I threw up, and I suf- fered. Some days I could not do my commitments. Often in my mind's confusion my speech would become garbled. I would laugh at myself and then become sad. I experienced and under- stood the confused mind even in regard to merely this. It is extremely difficult to maintain control without becoming con- fused during the stages of death when the four inner elements are being absorbed. It was at this time that I felt the power of my mind degenerating. When I tried to think about different things and ideas, my mind became confused.

Lama Yeshe's friend reminded him to rely on "mind training" in the midst of his terrible illness. Mind training is a specific set of teach- ings and practices that helps us tame our stubborn, egoistic mind and retrain ourselves to identify with the open, pure, compassionate essence of our being, all the while focusing on the suffering of others and generating a deep desire to free them of suffering. Lama Yeshe responded:

Through reading your series of advices, I developed immeasur- able joy and happiness in my mind. The strength of my mind increased, and my problems lessened and ceased. I will write here in verse the essence of the series of advices of my heart jewel, spiritual brother:

Practice and meditate mind training,
The sole remedy alleviating unwanted sufferings,
The main object of cultivation of really awe-inspiring
    retreaters.
You need a happy mind, a conscientious mind, an open mind.
Especially you must cultivate the precept of transforming bad
    circumstances—

The experience of unwanted suffering—into the path.
Take into your heart the sufferings of mother sentient beings.
Again and again give away your merit and happiness to them.
Transform the ripening results within the beings and the
    environment.
And transform unfavorable circumstances into the pathway
    leading to enlightenment.
Live contemplating just this—mind training.

Mind training includes the compassion practice of *tonglen*, a Tibetan word that means "giving and receiving." It is described fully in chapter 12 of *The Tibetan Book of Living and Dying*, by Sogyal Rinpoche. In the tonglen practice, with each in-breath, we take in with compassion the suffering of others. And with each out-breath, we give with love all of our happiness, joy, and well-being to others.

Tonglen is not easy to do at first because it is just the opposite of our ego's strategies. The selfish ego wants to build a little protective wall, keeping suffering on the outside and every happiness and good circumstance we may have on the inside. However, suffering is not caused by the painful circumstances we experience but by our aversion to pain and loss. Our fear and aversion only make things worse. That is why this practice of mind training is so meaningful and brings such great benefit—because it invites us to do just the opposite of what our ego wants us to do. By developing a more profound and courageous compassion in the midst of our pain, we slowly become free.

Understanding the universality of suffering

This is how we begin "taking difficulties on to the path." Rather than taking life's difficulties personally, regarding them as a punishment or failure, we realize that the sufferings of pain, loss, illness, or death happen to everyone. Suffering is universal.

The universality of suffering is one of the very first teachings the Buddha gave after his enlightenment 2,500 years ago. Buddha explained that the very nature of existence is suffering. If we think that the purpose of life is to get everything we desire and keep it with us forever, we are bound to suffer needlessly. We nurture an illusion that most people are happy and do get everything they want, so we conclude that, "There must be something wrong with me, because I've missed it."

But if you look more deeply at the lives of those you think are happy, you will see that their apparent happiness is superficial and temporary. Buddha asked us to look deeply to determine whether or not it is true that suffering pervades our life. He described three kinds of suffering.

The first kind is *pervasive suffering*. The Pali word *dukkha* doesn't translate exactly into suffering. *Pervasive suffering* means that the fundamental nature of everything in life is frustrating, imperfect, and unsatisfactory. You might want to examine your daily experience with this question in mind: Is it true or not that everything I experience has some element of imperfection, frustration, or unreliability?

You might notice that when you finally manage to get one thing working right, something else disintegrates or breaks down. This is the second type, the *suffering of change*: Even if we find ourselves in good circumstances, our satisfaction cannot last, because sooner or later something changes. Everything in the external world that we grasp onto for happiness will eventually disappoint us, because absolutely everything is subject to change, disintegration, dissolution, or death. This could sound depressing, but if you finally realize and accept that everything is by its nature impermanent, this is the greatest protection. Once you fully understand that this is how things are, you stop believing that grasping on to things or people can make you happy, and you stop creating unrealistic expectations that only lead to loss and disappointment. To become free of this constant cycle of suffering, the first step is to understand that nothing is permanent, nothing belongs to you, and everything is subject to change.

In the third kind, the *suffering of suffering*, you experience the inevitable pains of birth, aging, illness, and death. This is the most obvious kind of suffering, similar to the conventional notion. The suffering of suffering includes getting all the things that you really do not want, and not getting all the things or circumstances that you do want.

Buddha taught that our present relation to life is like being caught in a prison of our own making, where things only go from bad to worse. But we are not stuck with suffering: there is a way out. The first step to being free is to become aware of the true cause of our suffering.

When we experience difficulties, we usually blame our suffering on external circumstances or other people. But if we look deeply to see where the suffering comes from, we find our insecure mind is constantly cycling through states of hope and fear, grasping and aversion. We grasp on to external things—"mine"—and we grasp tightly onto our self—"me."

The source of this grasping is unawareness of our true nature, which is pure, perfect, and complete. Our true nature is unborn and undying, clear and open, boundless and unchanging, like the sky. Like the radiant sun, our nature is the profound luminous radiance of compassion and love, a fundamental connectedness with all creation. This deathless essence of our being is never harmed or diminished by anything we do, or by any changes we experience. The skylike essence of our mind is a natural deep peace and joy. Whether or not we are aware of it, our essence is always there at the core of our being.

That is the truth the Buddha offered. It is possible, if we want, to become free once and for all of this constant cycle of hope and fear and resultant suffering; the cycle that leads us from birth to death in lifetime after lifetime. Every spiritual tradition offers a similar hope that ultimately we can become free of our burdens and suffering. There are many different ways of describing this hope. It is never based on finding lasting happiness in the things of this world but in turning toward and realizing an ultimate goodness, truth, or God. This is the promise of enlightenment.

Finally, Buddha taught that to attain the unbroken freedom and happiness of enlightenment, we must apply ourselves on a spiritual path. The path helps us evolve on two levels: through meditation we come in contact with our absolute nature, and through training the mind in compassion, we develop a more loving and skillful way of being in the relative world.

Our ordinary, conditioned mind is so tough and negative and causes so much harm. Most of the time we are not even aware of all that we do that brings harm to others or to ourselves. Our unkind and harmful actions eventually lead to suffering, so if we truly want to be free of suffering, we must begin to work with the mind itself.

We train our mind and heart in compassion in order to reconnect with our fundamental goodness and tenderness toward all beings.

When we truly feel compassion for others, our suffering diminishes. As the mind training texts explain, "All the happiness in this world comes from thinking of others. All the suffering in this world comes from thinking of oneself."

The spiritual path shows us that in every moment we have a choice. We can relate and identify with our ordinary mind, which often feels like a prison, or we can identify with the boundless skylike essence of our being. Thus, by training our mind and heart, we re-orient ourselves, moving away from our conditioned egoistic attitudes and behaviors toward a more vast and compassionate way of being.

A practice for deepening understanding and compassion

There are many practices that awaken a profound sense of compassion and love for others. For example, sometimes we have a problem understanding someone and therefore have difficulty communicating with him or her. Maybe the person irritates us or pushes our buttons; or perhaps it is a patient who has become demented and we don't know how to make a connection. There is a very simple meditation you can do to help you understand someone, and it has two parts.

First, instead of seeing this person in their usual role—parent, sibling, colleague, or patient—see him or her in your mind's eye as "just another you," as just the same as you.

Reflect for a moment and realize that, just like you, this person yearns to be free of suffering and pain and misunderstanding. And, just like you, he or she wishes for good circumstances, happiness, love, and peace.

Spend a few moments reflecting, seeing this person as just another you.

Once you have established this feeling, then imagine that you have become the other person. Now you are in his or her life, standing in his or her shoes.

Considering yourself as this person, think that you have his or her history, including possible past experiences of rejection, pain, disappointment, or loss.

Consider that you have whatever constitutes the person's present suffering as well: feelings of being misunderstood and unfairly judged, deep experiences of pain or fear, or hidden insecurities and frustrations that give rise to constant feelings of unhappiness.

Consider as well the fears this person may have about the future: a fear of poverty, fears about the physical deterioration and pain of aging or illness, the grief of losses to come, the loneliness of dying or being abandoned.

Second, from this perspective of seeing the world through the other person's eyes, now imagine seeing the former "you" enter the room to have a talk. Ask yourself, "What would I most want from this person coming to see me? How do I wish him or her to see me and connect with me?"

When you conclude the formal part of the meditation, be aware that you have a choice in this moment. If the meditation has brought you a deeper understanding or sense of compassion, then resolve to sustain this presence and awareness in your next activity and your way of being.

When you imagine being the person that you normally don't understand, you have broken out of your ordinary pattern; you have dissolved the prison walls, momentarily. Hopefully, it has helped you feel more open and connected.

The real source of compassion is making the effort to truly understand another person and see what life is like from his or her point of view. With this deep understanding as the basis, you have a more authentic compassion. The training in compassion is fundamentally healing; besides deepening our understanding and compassion for others, we also gain more confidence in the infinite wisdom, compassion, and love that is our true nature.

The training works on two levels: On the relative level, the practices transform our way of being in daily life so that we become more open and connected, more understanding of others, and therefore more skillful in our way of relating and connecting.

On the absolute level, the training helps us connect with our *bodhichitta*, the heart of our enlightened mind. The more we train in bodhichitta, the more we find a radiant sun at the core of our being. And we wish, more than anything, to bring all others to this state of lasting happiness and peace that is enlightenment. Throughout our spiritual path we may catch glimpses of this potential, but through sustained study and practice, we can eventually realize our true nature. This is how we finally bring an end to suffering; this is how we dissolve the prison walls and become free.

27. THE ART OF DYING

Sogyal Rinpoche

"LEARN TO DIE and thou shalt learn how to live. There shall none learn how to live that hath not learned to die." These words, written hundreds of years ago in the medieval Book of the Craft of Dying, often come into my mind when I think about our understanding of death and its relationship to life. Because if we can only learn how to face death, then we'll have learned the most important lesson of life: how to face *ourselves* and so come to terms with ourselves, in the deepest possible sense, as human beings.

Yet all too often, it seems, we only start to think about death just before we die. Even those fortunate enough to receive hospice care only do so shortly before the end of their lives. Then again, the different religions, and the near-death experiencers, speak of a life review at the moment of death. But isn't that a bit too late? Shouldn't the knowledge and wisdom we need to negotiate death, and life, be available to us earlier on? Shouldn't our whole lives be devoted to such an education?

There can be few areas of life in which we need to make such a radical shift in our perspective as in our care for the dying. Amazing work has been done in the area of death and dying over the past few decades, and now more and more people appreciate that every attention must be given to the emotional and practical needs of the dying, so that they can die with dignity, without too much pain, and surrounded by love. Yet we are still lacking in our ability to offer spiritual help and care to the dying and to answer to their deeper needs. In a world like ours, fascinated by short-term goals and quick solutions, it's all too easy to assume that once someone has died, it's the end of the story. What characterizes spiritual care is a long-term vision, one that embraces

the complete picture of the dying person and his or her future, and recognizes that we can help someone long before they die, at the moment
of death, and even after they are dead.

What is the most important thing when we come to help a dying
person—or a living one, for that matter? To give our love. With all our
heart, without any conditions, and as free as possible from attachment.
For a dying person, that love can be the key to creating a special environment in which he or she can let go of everything that holds him or
her back. And yet our love can so often be entangled in all kinds of
complicated stories, our history of suffering and pain, and what we
take for love may in fact only be attachment. If we really want to know
what love is, we have to learn to let go, again and again. The tragedy
is that we grasp.

Our task is to find that pure love, and curiously it is death, or rather
impermanence, that can help us. The reason we become so fiercely
attached to things, from our emotions, ideas, and opinions to our possessions and other people, is that we have not taken impermanence to
heart. Once we can accept that impermanence is the very nature of life,
and that everyone suffers, including ourselves, at the hands of changes
and death, then letting go becomes quite natural. Our attachment to
our grief is loosened, and impermanence becomes a consolation, bringing us peace, confidence, and fearlessness. Most important of all, we
come to see clearly how futile it is to grasp at something that is simply
ungraspable.

With impermanence securely in our hearts, we'll see that if everyone
were to realize its truth, then even in the thick of change and death and
bereavement, we would not feel any great sense of loss. Our tears then
would not be because death and impermanence are facts of life, but
because of something much deeper: we would weep with compassion,
because we'd know that all the pain and hurt and suffering we go
through do not need to be there. They are only there in fact because we
fail to understand that everything, absolutely everything, is transient.

What the teachings of all spiritual traditions offer us is the knowledge that even when the worst tragedy and suffering befalls us, there is
still hope; there is something that nothing can destroy or take away
from us. Until we have realized the message of impermanence, our

deeply ingrained desire to make everything permanent will always be something we struggle against and try to get rid of. But once we have truly taken the truth of impermanence to heart, we discover there *is* nothing to let go, because impermanence and freedom from attachment and grasping are identical. Already the mind that grasps, the mind that fears death, the thinking ego mind, has dissolved, and we find ourselves touching the limitless, gazing into the innermost essence of our mind. A famous Buddhist prayer describes it:

Beyond words, beyond thought, beyond description,
Wisdom gone beyond:
Unborn, unceasing, its nature like the sky...

What a mysterious irony it is that through exploring our mortality we come to see our immortal nature! Often I imagine it like this: the clouds of thoughts and emotions part and dissolve, to reveal the skylike nature of our mind and the brilliant shining sun of our true, enlightened nature. Just like the sun, with its light and warmth, our buddha nature pours out wisdom and compassion and a limitless stream of love.

All of us need to give our love to a dying person, but if we have come in touch with the nature of our mind, stabilized it through our practice of meditation, and integrated it into our lives, then the love we have to give can only be deeper, because it comes from a different source: from our innermost being, the heart of our enlightened nature. It has a special quality of freedom. This kind of love, beyond all attachment, is like divine love. It is the love of all the buddhas, the love of Christ, of God. In that state, without contriving, and even without thinking, we can feel the presence of the Buddha or of Christ. It's as if we become their ambassador, their representative, our love backed by their love, and infused with their blessing. Love that springs truly from the nature of the mind is so blessed that it has the power to dispel the fear of the unknown, to give refuge from anxiety, to grant serenity and peace, and to bring inspiration in death and beyond.

As we will discover for ourselves, the more we can *embody* the spiritual teachings, the more natural and more effective we will be in giving spiritual care to a dying person. *How we are* is so much more important that what we say or do. If we are following a spiritual path, we ought to bring to the bedside of the dying our pure self, inspired as much as possible by our practice, and without all our history and baggage: a dying person deserves nothing less. Then our presence, by itself, can reassure our dying friend and evoke in him or her a fundamental confidence and trust, a sense of hope and meaning.

What does a master in the Tibetan Buddhist tradition do when he helps a dying person? He enters into meditation and with all his strength he invokes the buddhas and masters and their blessings. Then he directs to the dying person the power of the wisdom and compassion he has come to realize through knowing the nature of his mind. I know that when I come to die, I could do nothing more than that. I will invoke all the buddhas and my masters, unite my mind with them, rest in the nature of mind, and send that love and compassion out to all beings everywhere. I will pray that when I die, my death may benefit all; that I may die successfully and, in the future, be reborn to help millions and millions of beings.

I believe that the ancient Buddhist teachings on death and dying have a tremendous gift to offer, to people of any faith or of none; one that is offered, in the spirit of Buddhism, quite freely and with no notion of conversion or exclusivity. Anyone should feel free to try them out. It is one of my deepest hopes that teachings such as these should be made available to people everywhere and at all levels of education. To know that when we die we will be surrounded by the very best in spiritual care should be, I believe, one of our basic human rights. The kind of death we have is so important; death is the most vital moment of our lives, and all of us should be able to die in peace and fulfillment. I hope that in the years to come we can see a continuing revolution in our approach to caring for the dying, one that carries the deepest spiritual values at its heart, and that will give birth to different environments and places where people at all stages of living and dying can come to draw benefit.

Let me conclude with a prayer: For all who are engaged in the noble and often heart-rending work of caring for the dying—may all their aspirations be fulfilled! May all those who are dying find a peaceful death, and may all who are struggling in life find happiness and a true spiritual path! May the blessings of the buddhas and all enlightened beings shine upon us, transforming our hearts and minds!

Integrating Buddhist Practice
in the Twenty-First Century

It is important that we connect every practice we learn to
our behavior. As Buddhists we must try to implement the
teachings we receive—only then can we experience their
true value. When starting out on practice we should not
expect too much. Inner development is not simple; every-
thing depends completely on oneself, and it takes time.
Therefore it is particularly important to develop patience,
which means not to slacken in one's efforts and resolution.
His Holiness the Dalai Lama[27]

In his short teaching, Orgyen Tobgyal Rinpoche echoes the
words of His Holiness above in advising beginners not to
expect too much and to develop patience. He puts under the
microscope the Western mentality of needing quick results,
done to perfection, and recommends a way of small but
steady steps, which keeps closer to the Middle Way than an
over-keen striving for inflated goals.

Sakya Jetsun Chimey, one of the greatest women teachers
of Tibetan Buddhism, also makes it clear that Dharma prac-
tice requires a lot of self-discipline and that many small steps
are needed. In her teaching here she engages, among other
things, with the challenges that face a mother with growing
children.

The future of the Buddhadharma in the West depends
on each individual's integration of it in ways appropriate to
his or her life, and this lies with each individual to decide.

The integration of Buddhist philosophy and its translation into meditation practice—and further out into daily life—is a long and complex process, and each practitioner has a unique set of challenges to overcome. Only through these concrete individual attempts to apply the teachings, these many individual small steps, will Buddhism's possible contribution to our society be realized. "The future of the Buddhadharma lies in the hands of the sangha, of individual practitioners. As much as students can immerse themselves in the teachings and practice, what they are actually doing is safeguarding the future of the Dharma—in themselves. It means that integration is the future, and out of that will come all kinds of appropriate applications."[28]

That the books ends with dialogues, in dialogue, seems fitting: the future forms of Buddhadharma will only come about through communication between East and West, old and young, experienced and beginner, as an ongoing engagement with the unfamiliar. The book ends with a call from His Holiness the Dalai Lama, who reminds us of the Tibetans' ongoing struggle to preserve their threatened culture, one of the oldest on the earth, and with it one of the most complete forms of Buddhadharma.

28. Women on the Spiritual Path

Sakya Jetsun Chimey

QUESTION: *Why are there so few women teachers?*
JETSUN CHIMEY: I think the two primary reasons are karmic and cultural. Karma is a factor in deciding our gender; and differences in gender roles—what men and women do in a society—are also products of karma. On the cultural side, in Asia there were more men than women who wished to put their effort into spiritual practice. I am not aware of any other reasons. Certainly there are no arguments for this in the teachings themselves.

QUESTION: *Could you explain the karma of being born a woman?*
JETSUN CHIMEY: I really don't know what the karmic causes are to be reborn as a woman; I have never seen any explanation of the karma of being born a woman in the scriptures. But personally, I think individuals have a special karmic connection to their first life of spiritual practice; so if a person was a woman in their first life of practice, they might choose to take rebirth as a woman.

I know there are prayers in which we pray not to be reborn as a woman but as a man. Most of these were written at a time when the life of a woman was very hard, and I think that is the reason people prayed for rebirth as a man.

QUESTION: *In terms of the spiritual path and the ability to attain enlightenment, is being a woman an inferior birth? I believe that the teachings of the Theravada tradition say that it is more difficult for a woman to attain enlightenment than for a man.*

JETSUN CHIMEY: Yes, and in the Mahayana teachings, too, but the Vajrayana doesn't say that.

QUESTION: *Why is it more difficult according to Theravada and Mahayana?*
JETSUN CHIMEY: Women are said to have more desires, all sorts of wild thoughts, and are also very prone to doubt. Buddha said that doubts and desire are unhelpful for religious practice, and in the Theravada and Mahayana teachings he pointed to them as obstacles.

QUESTION: *So, women were said to be at a disadvantage on the spiritual path because they have so many emotions, and emotions are seen as defilements?*
JETSUN CHIMEY: That's right.

QUESTION: *Yet in the Vajrayana almost the opposite is true, and women are seen as a symbol of wisdom.*
JETSUN CHIMEY: Fundamentally, men and women are the same—they are both human beings. However, the masters have found that there is a difference between their minds. Women have very sharp minds; they are actually sharper than men, which is why in the Vajrayana—the path that works directly with the mind—women represent wisdom and men represent method. Often a woman will have thought through an idea many times, long before the idea has even struck a man. This is something I have noticed when comparing my husband and myself.

In the Theravada and Mahayana, on the other hand, there are many examples where women are shown to be bad, and this view is also sometimes reflected within the culture. In India, for example, women have a lower status than men.

As most of Buddha's disciples were male, he used the example of beautiful women to demonstrate impermanence. Monks were trained to consider that a woman's beauty is only skin deep, and, however beautiful she may be when she is young, one day she will grow old and ugly. This is a method for reducing sexual desire and was taught by Buddha because he felt that sexual desire was not helpful for spiritual practice.

He also taught another method, called "sealing the doors of the senses," in which the beautiful woman's body is skinned mentally, and monks consider how ugly and repulsive it is inside as they "look" at the pus, blood, intestines, and so on. Using these examples, Hinayana and Mahayana monks who had taken the vow to lead a life of renunciation would purify their minds.

The point here is not that women themselves are ugly and impure—if Buddha were to teach a group of nuns, he would use the same example in reverse and tell them to scan the body of the man they desired. Men and women are both human, they both come from the mother's womb, there is no fundamental difference between them. This is my view, it is not something I've been told. Buddha taught all sentient beings. There is nothing in the scriptures to tell us that he taught men rather than women.

QUESTION: *So, to summarize, from the Theravada and Mahayana points of view, both men and women are basically the same—they have emotional and intellectual defilements that need to be purified, and the difference between them is one of degree; but from the perspective of the Vajrayana, there is a subtle difference between the minds.*
JETSUN CHIMEY: That's right. In the Vajrayana, especially in the Sakya and Nyingma traditions, there are dakinis who are considered to be spiritually more advanced than men. I've heard that at some levels in the Nyingma, you cannot get enlightened unless you have a spiritual consort. A Vajrayana monastic still has to keep all the Mahayana vows; it's only at very high levels that a physical consort might be taken. Normally a physical consort isn't used; instead a mental consort is visualized.

QUESTION: *Let's turn to everyday life. Modern women often feel an enormous conflict between wanting a husband and family and having a career. Even once they have children, many women still feel they want to be independent, have a job, and become somebody in their own right and are not content with being a wife and mother alone.*
JETSUN CHIMEY: The first thing I'd like to say is that virtually all Western women are independent compared to women in the East. I think the conflict you mention depends on the individual's mind. If you have a big

heart, the heart of compassion, you can do anything. If you don't have a big heart, although your mind might want to achieve many things, physically they won't work out. The mind is very tricky, you know; it wants to do all kinds of things. The mind can think up goals that are far beyond the bounds of possibility. So, if you expect too much of yourself you will never achieve anything. What you can manage personally, as an individual, depends on your mind.

I was a nun, then I married and had five children, but I didn't plan it that way—even now I don't make plans. Then, suddenly, although I had never thought of it before, H.H. Sakya Trizin told me to teach, and so I did. For women who have a supportive husband, it's a little easier. My husband is very good—he is not jealous at all, whereas some husbands have a very jealous nature. I am not jealous of him either, and we trust each other completely. This makes it easy for me to travel and teach; if my husband were a jealous person it would be quite difficult. He has many good qualities and supports me completely.

I think that women who want both a career and a family have to find a balance and give equal time to each. It's easier if your husband supports you, and more difficult if you both have a career, because then life becomes rather hectic. And remember that children don't stay small forever; they grow up and don't always wait until they are eighteen years old before they leave home.

Some women become anxious and feel they can't manage, but if you really want to do it, you can. But always keep a balance. For example, I teach and I have a full-time job. I have to work because we bought a house and we have to keep up the mortgage. On top of that, children are quite expensive—especially boy's sports clothes! So I have a full-time job, teach part-time, and spend weekends with the children. As I am a Dharma practitioner, I also do my practice. Practice actually helps you to discipline yourself. A family, a career, and everything else can be exhausting, and to fit it all in—as well as your practice—you might have to skip some sleep once in a while. At first it can be hard to get up early in the morning to practice because you're not used to it, but by the second week it's already a little better, and after a month you'll find it's much easier.

If you find you are too exhausted to do everything you have to do, watch your diet. Eat smaller quantities, eat less meat, and don't drink alcohol.

QUESTION: *Parents may have started a spiritual practice and wish to bring their children up according to spiritual values, yet their practice may not be firmly established, and their understanding may not be mature enough for them to do this well. What advice do you have?*
JETSUN CHIMEY: Start with a very simple teaching and a very simple practice. Doing long practices or retreats is difficult if the children are too young, though if you are rich you can hire a babysitter! So, wait until the children are older before committing yourself to intensive practice. You can bring the children along to simple practices, and they can learn something too. It will give them some understanding as to why their mother or father is part of this religion and they won't think it's so strange. But actually they can't understand until they are four years old anyway. So do a simple practice, not a strict one, and every so often do it with your children.

QUESTION: *I have heard some teachers say that having children can be a distraction from spiritual practice.*
JETSUN CHIMEY: When you look at the world, you will realize that whether you have a child or not, there are plenty of distractions. As I said, you may have to start with a simple practice and wait until your child is older before doing longer retreats. But the important thing is to have the aspiration to follow the spiritual path and to be dedicated to it from the beginning. Then, somehow, you will be able to do it. However, if you just have a vague wish that it will happen, without really pursuing it, then of course nothing will happen.

QUESTION: *Buddha taught that we should regard all beings as equal. As you know, modern women demand equality with men usually in terms of jobs, income, social status, decision making, and so on. How do you view the way we manifest our basic equality with men?*
JETSUN CHIMEY: The equality you are talking about is samsaric equality. In the Dharma it is said that women have eight virtues or qualities: not to be under the sway of desire; the ability to treat all beings

equally and without jealousy, as you would your own children; to have sympathy and motherly kindness; not to chatter; to speak the truth; to have few wrong views; to have appropriate intelligence; and to bear fine children. These qualities don't come so easily to men. But men are often better able to keep things to themselves; this is one of their qualities. For example, a man told something in confidence won't feel compelled to speak about it with others, whereas women tend to want to share it.

QUESTION: *Western women have been brought up very differently from Eastern women, and, as you said, are much more independent. Perhaps as a result of this, some find it difficult to relate to traditional practices such as devotion. How can we relate to such practices, and how could we adapt them so they fit the way we are?*

JETSUN CHIMEY: I think it's important to remember that there are different kinds of teachers, and also that you go through different stages in your spiritual life. When you take spiritual vows and precepts in the Mahayana, you regard the master as a teacher and guide, but when you enter the path of Vajrayana, it's essential to realize that there is much more involved. The Vajrayana master is not simply a teacher, or a person, but is seen to be none other than the true presence of Buddha himself. So, as we find ourselves at different stages along the path, we have different needs and, accordingly, follow different requirements.

What is required to begin the spiritual path in the first place is, above all, a measure of responsibility for ourselves. You can study some of the important texts, such as the *Fifty Stanzas on the Spiritual Teacher* by Aryashura, which explain how to relate to a teacher, but long before you enter the path and accept a teacher as your teacher, and long before you learn to develop devotion, you have to think very carefully about whether you want to enter the path at all. Nobody is asking you to do it or indeed not to do it; it is up to each and every individual to decide where their interests lie and where they wish to put their efforts. If you find that spiritual practice is good for you, then examine very carefully what it entails, and only after that should you decide whether to enter the path.

Once you have entered the path, especially in the Vajrayana, look for a teacher who is worthy of your devotion and respect. Having decided to follow the direction and teaching of a master, you must actually focus on this in a dedicated way; otherwise you will never accomplish the path.

It is important to remember that your interest in a teacher, your dedication to a teacher, and the state of mind in which you feel pleased with a certain teacher, should not be confused with similar experiences in relationships with your parents, friends, or relatives. The nature of the teacher-student relationship is completely different. Normal human relationships are based on a certain attachment and desire, whereas the relationship between student and teacher should be free of attachment, desire, and craving. That's very important. You should learn to cultivate that. If you do, then whatever devotion you develop will be meaningful; but if you don't, and have lots of thoughts about your teacher, then it will be hard to accomplish anything at all. Take the initiative of thoroughly examining the path and the teacher at the outset, and this will help you develop a healthy and beneficial relationship with your teacher.

Heart advice

- Whether you are a man or a woman, you should always keep the Buddha, Dharma, and Sangha (the Triple Refuge of Buddhism) in mind. In this way, you will progress throughout your daily life.

- At the same time, try to learn patience in everyday life. Patience makes everything much smoother.

- When your mind is calm, other people are more relaxed.

- If someone else makes a mistake, we are all likely to blow up. Instead, remember that everyone makes mistakes and that you can make mistakes, too, because you are only human.

- Always be kind to everyone, in every way you can, physically and mentally.

- Whatever you do, it is your motivation that really counts. Without good motivation, even if you do things that are generally considered to be "good" they won't be very beneficial because your motivation is not as good as your action appears to be. So for example, cuffing or scolding a naughty child, because nothing else works, but with the good motivation of wanting the child to have a better life, will actually help him. However, if you speak or act out of anger or hatred, then it won't benefit the child at all. It all comes down to motivation: that's something you should never forget.

29. DILIGENCE AND CONTENTMENT

Orgyen Tobgyal Rinpoche

SINCE I'VE BEEN COMING TO THE WEST, I've noticed that there's a great deal of grasping involved in the way Dharma is practiced by many Westerners. Rather than just trying to do your best, you feel that if you can't practice perfectly there's something wrong with you, and you often get caught up in a self-imposed depression and self-punishment because you are convinced you're not "good enough." This kind of attitude will only make your problems far worse, adding more and more worries to the worries you already have, making your mind tighter and more depressed, until all you can do is sit and cry about how terrible things are. This is not going to work.

All we can ask of anyone is that they are willing to do what they can, as well as they can. Of course, it is said in the teachings that we should be unflagging in our diligence and practice. Yes! But it is not said that you should drive yourself into a catatonic depression in your attempts at being diligent. Instead, it is stated that the more you practice, the more enthusiasm you will have for being more and more diligent.

It's important to feel content with the amount of benefit you accumulate in your practice. Suppose you recite the mantra *Om mani padme hum* a hundred times in one day. At the end of the day, reflect on that and feel good about it. It's great! You recited the mantra a hundred times. Be content and congratulate yourself, thinking, "What I accomplished today is good, and I'll do even more tomorrow."

It's a skillful balancing of inspiration and enthusiasm with a realistic acceptance of your current limitations and how much you can actually do in a day. To punish yourself because you didn't do more, to worry and become more and more depressed, is hardly useful. You don't gain any kind of happiness or contentment that way. Real happiness and spaciousness of mind come about when you do what you can and feel content that you've done your best, while at the same time maintaining inspiration and aspiring constantly to do better. This is a very effective way to proceed.

Nowadays in the modern world, many people find it hard to be content. There's an insatiability about Westerners that causes them enormous problems. The main message of modern culture seems to be that nothing is ever enough: you may be the ruler of the world, but instead of feeling content, you look around for another world to conquer.

Modern people are also very indulgent of their desires, sexual and otherwise. You're always looking for new tricks, anything that has never been tried before: something remarkable, something on the "cutting edge." And it's true that you've accomplished marvels, some might even say miracles, in the technological realm. But to practice with the same fever of insatiability is not the right approach to Dharma. It won't bring you happiness, nor will it bring spiritual results. To achieve any level of spiritual accomplishment, you have to have the right kind of karma, motivation, aspiration, and good fortune. You can't have enlightenment just because you want it so desperately and nothing else is enough.

The Buddha himself said that you should practice the Dharma moderately, according to your own abilities, so that your practice proceeds at a rate you're able to cope with. And this has been my own experience; I do what I can. I practice as well as I can, and whatever I can't do I don't worry about. Instead, I pray to my lineage and my gurus for the ability to do better.

So diligence is not being driven obsessively with a sense of having to be perfect, or doing more than you realistically can. You might be able to sustain it for months or even years, but eventually you'll crack, and you might even give up the Dharma altogether, which is the worst thing that can happen. You'll have spent all that time fooling yourself. Far better to develop some sense of contentment so that, at the end of your life, you'll say, "I accomplished what I could in this life. I didn't waste it." And you'll have no regrets.

30. THE JOURNEY TO LIBERATION

Sogyal Rinpoche

Two things count when we die: how we are, which is the
result of what we have done; and our state of mind. These two
factors are very much connected with each other, because our actions
and habits ultimately create the state of our mind. Habits and actions
have a very strong influence on us; on one hand they can purify our
mind, but on the other they can also obscure it.

Losing touch with a glimpse of the nature of mind

For a practitioner of meditation, and of mahamudra and dzogchen, it
is crucial to understand that one small glimpse or experience of the
nature of mind is not enough. A glimpse does not last very long, and
our habits are so strong that they return swiftly. We may have wonderful experiences, but they can be almost like illusions, and when we
see this we may despair a little.

During an inspiring teaching we might feel that our spirit has been
liberated, only to find that we later return to more mundane states of
mind. If we experience something very powerful, such as a blessing, or
we understand something of great significance, we might believe that
this experience is going to last, and we can be so disappointed when it
fades away that we might even lose faith in the power of the teachings.
At such times, it is helpful to remember that we sometimes expect far
too much of the spiritual path.

Here we have missed a rather small point, which is called practice.
The reason why our experiences don't last is that we haven't practiced
enough. If a master introduces us to the view of dzogchen, we may have
a small glimpse of the nature of mind, but that view must be sustained

through meditation; we need to abide by the view and to remain in that understanding.

A powerful experience can transform the atmosphere of our mind and completely change the way in which we perceive the environment and the context of our emotions. It could even be that we enter the state of bliss and emptiness. There is tremendous clarity in this moment; we sense the authenticity of our experience, and feel and taste that "this is it."

If this happens to us we should try to rest in that state and maintain it. It is the way in which we maintain the view that is crucial. If there is any kind of fabrication, it detracts from the power and strength of the view, and this results in us getting distracted. Although we want to remain in our inherent nature, something happens; we hear a little noise, or somebody disturbs us, and when we return to the view, we find that it is no longer the same; it has changed.

This happens simply because we do not yet know how to maintain a glimpse of the view. In terms of dzogchen and mahamudra, we do not know how to meditate, and we do not know how to practice non-meditation. In the moment that we have a glimpse of the nature of mind, it is a mistake to try and meditate. Instead, we should remain undistracted in the natural and authentic state of nonmeditation and abide by that pure presence.

Again, our glimpse of our true nature is very fragile; it is only an experience and not yet the realization of the nature of mind, and for this reason we need to practice. Suppose we try to maintain a wonderful experience and fail; suppose that experience gets spoiled. In that particular instant, our practice is the attitude we take. If our attitude is, "Oh, that was a wonderful experience, but now it's gone. I had it, but I lost it; how awful!" then we have made a mistake.

Hope and fear

The teachings advise us not to be attached to experiences and, most importantly, not to have too much hope and fear. Hope and fear are dualistic, and duality is the manifestation of ego. The mind, heart, and very being of ego is ignorance. Just as light removes all trace of darkness, when all ignorance has been removed, ego can no longer exist.

Hope and fear, and the manifestation of duality, is often what catches practitioners out; whenever we regret losing a wonderful experience and hope that it might come back, we have been caught out.

There are two kinds of hope: the hope that is the opposite of fear, and the hope that is similar to faith, which is something that we all need. Small-minded hope and fear can weaken our behavior so much that we can seem very ineffective in the eyes of other people, and in a subtler way, hope and fear can weaken our meditation, too.

What's crucial is our attitude. If a wonderful experience dissolves, we should not feel sad. Instead, we should just simply let go and not become attached to the experience. If we have the right response, and remain free of hope and fear, such an attitude toward a powerful experience can instill lasting benefit in us.

I began by saying that the two things that count when we die are our state of mind, and the way in which we have lived. Even though the fundamental nature of mind is always present and we may occasionally experience it, the nature of mind doesn't really have a great impact on us if the way in which we live our lives does not accord with it. We might glimpse our inherent nature, but it will inevitably become obscured again.

We might think that the only thing that matters when we die is the recognition of the nature of mind, but it is not that simple. How we are determines whether we can gain stability in the nature of mind. It is really not that easy to recognize the nature of mind. To arrive at a point of realization, our life must support our practice, and we must be disciplined. Although we may have had a glimpse of the nature of mind, a glimpse will not suffice.

Merit and wisdom

We might also wonder what the use of having such an illusory experience is, but if we use it well, it really is a tremendous blessing and of great use to us. If we fail to use it well, it is almost as if we do not deserve or merit that blessing. In the Buddhist teachings there are two accumulations; the accumulation of merit and the accumulation of wisdom. Merit is the result of practice, and is what makes it possible for us to be worthy of wisdom. What determines whether we deserve wisdom or not is our accumulation of merit.

In ancient Tibet there was a myth about the milk of the snow lion. It was said that no ordinary container could hold it and that it could only be poured into a vessel of pure gold. In Tibet, the snow lion represents the wisdom of the Buddha. What this example shows us is that it is only when we have purified our obscurations and accumulated merit and positive karma that we can hold the precious wisdom of the Buddha, and it also shows us just how important practice is.

This example is also applicable to dzogchen. In some ways, in the ultimate state of dzogpachenpo there is no practice or meditation to do. But even though there is no meditation, there is nonmeditation, the discipline of remaining in the purity of the nature of mind, and this is not so easy to accomplish. It is far easier to pray, visualize, or to recite mantras, because such practices allow us to enter a mental process. It is far more difficult to remain in the purest state of our mind, unobscured by even the hint of a cloud of confusion.

Although, on an absolute level, there is nothing to do, the relative is connected to the absolute, and we are part of the relative world. This relative truth is called practice, and somebody who knows how to do this practice is a realized being. Even though there is nothing to do in the nature of mind, if we *think* that "there is nothing to do," we are making a mistake. Even in relation to dzogchen, there is a need for us to be disciplined.

Remembering to remember

What is the most vital point of the highest teachings of the Tibetan Buddhist tradition? What is it that brings realization, and how can we maintain and integrate it?

The recognition of the nature of mind is made stable within us simply by us remembering it. Dzogchen speaks of the remembering of non-remembering, while the great Indian master Saraha taught on the memory of "no memory." We might think that this is mere wordplay, but it is far more than that. After reaching a certain level of attainment, there is no need to remember, because we *are* the remembrance. We have not yet arrived at this state of perfection; until then, we need to rely on memory.

What is the connection between meditation and nonmeditation?

When we finish meditation, that *is* nonmeditation. What does this mean? Our problem is that we are always distracted, and the antidote to our distraction is mindfulness and remembering. *Mindfulness* is immediate, the initial moment of recognition, and *remembering* is the next moment, the postmeditation. Mindfulness is the practice, and remembering that mindfulness is action.

We usually begin practice by developing mindfulness of the breath or perhaps by reciting a mantra. Whatever method we use, the method is only the vehicle and not the goal.

It is possible to mistake the technique of meditation for the goal, but a method such as mindfulness is only the means through which our mind and emotions are processed and purified. Through practicing the method, we become more present, less stuck, and we carry less and less baggage. It is rather like taking off our shoes before entering a temple: in some ways this simple act reminds us to leave all our mental baggage behind.

Practice gradually purifies our mind and increasingly frees us from our ego. All our confusion, emotions, and thoughts are slowly purified, and we become more and more settled. Something melts away of its own accord, and we are freer, purer, and cleaner. Finally, we become the mindfulness, and we become the breath.

Transcending the conceptual mind

Our initial experience of becoming the breath is not the recognition of the nature of mind; it is *shamata,* or calm abiding, that opens us to the possibility of glimpsing the nature of mind. We might mistake such an experience for the nature of mind itself. Sometimes people think that when they are relatively calm, peaceful, and clear, they have arrived at the nature of mind, but it is simply an experience of shamata.

As we continue to settle, almost as if reality were opening a door for us, something becomes clear. Our eyes are opened, and we see without hindrance, interference, or obscuration. We see things clearly, without any emotion or intimation of ego, and when ego has dissolved, there is no one left to be judgmental; there is only wisdom and compassion. The heart of wisdom is compassion, and the intelligence of compassion is wisdom.

As we open onto our true nature, we no longer see things in isolation from one another; we see with the panoramic and expansive view of *vipashyana,* or insight. Then, knowledge becomes *prajna* (transcendent knowledge) and the door of *shunyata* (emptiness) swings open. It is only prajna that can perceive shunyata; our ordinary conceptual mind is incapable of perceiving emptiness. How can conceptual mind experience something nonconceptual? As the great master Shantideva said, "Absolute is beyond mind; that which is within the realm of mind is called relative."

As we cannot experience the absolute with the ordinary mind, we must transcend conceptual mind. *Prajna* means "wisdom," or "best knowledge," and it is with this wisdom that we see reality. Generally, reality presents itself to us, but we do not see it. As Jesus said, "You have eyes, but you do not see." The third eye is a symbol of wisdom, of the ability to see without duality. As I said earlier, when we no longer have any hope or fear, we have become nondual, and nonduality is the golden container that holds the milk of the snow lions, or the wisdom of the Buddha.

As the door to reality opens, we see with the eye of nondual, transcendent wisdom. What we see is called *shunyata,* and that which realizes shunyata is the nature of mind. There are many stages to this realization. We begin by understanding shunyata, and then we experience it. While experience is not the same as realization, if our attitude is right, it is the material out of which realization can arise. Finally, realization becomes liberation, and we embody everything.

I am laying out the journey to enlightenment, and we have almost reached the final stage of our journey. Ultimately, there is no longer any meditation to do, the meditation dissolves, and we become mindfulness and presence. It is from out of this presence that *rigpa,* the nature of mind, is revealed. The practice of dzogchen is to remain in and abide in the state of rigpa, in the state of nonmeditation. Why is this state called *nonmeditation?* Because there is nothing to do. We just are, and we remain undistracted.

The material we work with on our journey is the mind, but it is dirty at the moment, so we wash it again and again. Intelligence and heart reside within the mind, and from them can arise wisdom and compassion, because everything is already present within the mind. As we continue on our journey, the mind transcends duality and becomes free. When we learn how to ride a bicycle, we may fall over many times, but we slowly gain a sense of balance. In the same way, as mind is slowly matured, it will finally rise above duality.

Transcendent generosity

In the absolute state, mind sees things with tremendous humor. For example, if someone who has transcended his or her ordinary mind is involved in an act of generosity, he or she would know that the "I" does not exist, and neither does the act of giving, nor the one to whom the gift is given, as ultimately there is no separation or distinction. The mind that realizes this is called *transcendent*.

But we cannot say, "Okay, I don't exist, you don't exist, and giving doesn't exist, so why bother giving?" Such an attitude is just an excuse to avoid the practice of generosity. In fact, if we have truly realized the nature of transcendent mind, we become more and more generous.

Ordinarily, the way in which we give maintains an idea of "me," "gift," and "you." We also expect to receive thanks in return for our generosity, and if we are not thanked we are hurt. But as we continue to give, what we give is the giving itself; we forget the act of giving and simply give. That doesn't mean that we give mindlessly; it means that we gradually let go of the idea of giving.

We also shouldn't congratulate ourselves too much, or think that our generosity is exceptional. The ability to give is itself a great gift, because the act of generosity enriches us. As we realize this, the idea of doing good dissolves, and whatever good we do is transcendent, a bodhisattva action in which there is no "I," no "you," and no action. To consider that there is a subject, an object, and an action is dualistic. True giving is nondual and transcendent.

Maintaining the purity of mind

Normally, we talk so much that we cloud our understanding. We pollute our mind by storing in it absolutely everything we experience. Therefore, our discipline is to keep mind pure and unstained by impurities. Even though impurities arise, we no longer hold on to them. It is our tendency to hold on to our negativity that gives negativity so much power: we are what we are as a result of our own actions.

Our realization is obscured and made unstable by the sheer volume of our thoughts. Just suppose that our mind is empty, spacious, and free of discursive thought; if this were the case, a single realization would be quite sufficient for us. If one pure thought were to arise in the total silence of the purity of our mind, we would recognize it with utter clarity. As it is, although we do often have pure thoughts and realizations, they are completely outnumbered by thoughts that we have grasped and made dualistic.

Initially, if we have an insight into our true nature, we might lose it very easily. This could make us despair, and we might wonder what use an experience is when it disappears so rapidly. But if our attitude is right—if our attitude is nondual and beyond hope and fear—we can let go of our regret and no longer crave the return of our experience. We simply go on; we remain in and abide in the purity of the nature of mind.

Losing contact with a wonderful experience is just one of the many things we might go through. We might also encounter boredom, because an ego mind that is always seeking entertainment will sometimes perceive boredom.

It is extremely important to remember the view of the nature of mind. The point at which we forget the nature of mind is the point at which we need to remember it, and when we forget again, we must remember again. We shouldn't give up simply because we sometimes forget; if we continue to remember, we will ultimately become remembrance.

By following and practicing the spiritual path with diligence, our study and practice will eventually melt into our mind. For great masters such as Dilgo Khyentse Rinpoche and Dudjom Rinpoche, all the teachings are present in their being. They have realized everything; they don't have to remember a thing, because they have it all within themselves. But until we are able to do this, we need to remember.

The Buddhadharma is constantly showing us that there are very many stages to the path of enlightenment. If we manage to realize something that we haven't seen before, we also see that there is so much more to realize, and this recognition teaches us humility. But if we were to understand that there is so much more to realize in the wrong way, it could make us despair. If this is the case for us, then it is important to look back and see how far we have actually progressed on the spiritual path. When we are humbled by our realization, we are inspired to go further; and if we do look back, we will see that it has not all been for nothing. We *have* accomplished something.

31. THE FUTURE OF BUDDHISM: ENLIGHTENMENT IS REAL!

Dzigar Kongtrul Rinpoche

Buddha's teaching began some 2,550 years ago in Asia. Now it has come to the West. How relevant is it to the needs of people in the modern world? And what does it take for Buddhism to become established here?

QUESTION: *Many of us in the modern world have difficult emotional lives, and we somehow hope that spiritual teachings might help. But some people doubt that the ancient wisdom of Buddhism has anything to offer in terms of easing emotional problems that are particular to urban living in this day and age. Do you agree?*

RINPOCHE: The Buddhist teachings certainly do address the problem of emotions. According to Dharma, emotions are generated by thoughts and concepts; thoughts are likened to fire and emotions to a flame. By working with our conceptual mind to try and dispel our ignorance, we quite naturally develop a clear understanding of how to work with our emotions.

I feel it's very unfortunate that people think the Buddhist tradition offers little practical help on how to deal with emotions. Actually, we have many practices that work with emotions. There are the four immeasurables, for instance—developing loving-kindness, compassion, sympathetic joy, and equanimity. The Buddhist method of working with them is twofold and very thorough: we study the Dharma to develop an intellectual understanding of each one of these four immeasurables, and we engage in contemplation and meditation practices that enable us to embody them.

Buddhism also teaches that all negative emotions spring from two tendencies: cherishing the self, and protecting the self. Both these tendencies are rooted in clinging to the self. From the Buddhist point of view, clinging to the idea of self is the fundamental cause of all the suffering and misery we experience in everyday life, as well as all our past suffering. Transforming this suffering is very much a matter of observing our thoughts and emotions and working with them, rather than an intellectual process of studying the mind. As we observe our minds objectively in meditation over a long period of time, we can see for ourselves how self-clinging creates all the suffering we go through. A sense of renunciation then arises naturally and inspires us, emotionally rather than intellectually, to let go of the self.

QUESTION: *Westerners find it particularly difficult to trust themselves, but it seems that this problem is not so common in Asia. Is Buddhism able to help with this?*

RINPOCHE: I think Westerners are very intelligent and have a tremendous capacity to analyze phenomena with logic and reasoning. But sometimes I have found that you don't trust what you discover through your research, and find it difficult to be content with your conclusions. Perhaps you imagine that if you believe your understanding and conclusions to be good, and rest in that belief, you are naive or immature. As a result, there is a general tendency to doubt and question systematically and continuously, which is also fueled by a fear of being overconfident and arrogant. However, all this just becomes a way of perpetuating doubt in your own ability and in your wisdom, and this, in itself, creates problems.

Basically, if we are to develop trust in ourselves, we really have to believe that this mind of ours is fundamentally intelligent. Having the confidence that you are an intelligent person and have the wisdom to meet the future with an open mind, unencumbered with fears and hopes and preconceived plans, is very important. Developing such confidence is, I think, nothing other than developing confidence in our own innate buddha nature—our basic, primordial intelligence. This is actually what Buddhist practice is all about. Developing this trust is helpful not only in terms of trusting your own reasoning but in all aspects of everyday life.

QUESTION: *Could you explain how traditional Buddhist methods take us from a state where we lack trust and conviction to one where we have both?*

RINPOCHE: In Tibetan Buddhism, we begin by studying the view of the emptiness of self and phenomena of the Madhyamaka school. After detailed analysis using logic and reasoning, we come to the conclusion that phenomena and self are empty by nature and cannot exist intrinsically. However, the fact that everything is empty in nature does not mean that things do not exist and function on the relative plane.

When we understand and are convinced by the Madhyamaka view of emptiness, we apply ourselves to the practice of shamata meditation by following the instructions given by an authentic master. Then our meditation benefits from the blessings of the lineage masters, as well as the blessings of our teacher. What we need to contribute is a conviction that we have the ability to realize what we have studied. We will arrive at this conviction once we see that students of the past attained realization by using the very same methods that we are using, and once we have complete confidence in the realization of our own master and the belief that his or her guidance will help us. We have to have trust in all three, otherwise we cannot fully test the process experientially, nor are we giving ourselves completely to the path through which, ultimately, we can attain realization.

If we practice in this way, a change takes place within us quite naturally, and we attain a certain realization. Realizing emptiness even a little bit, whether conceptually or nonconceptually, helps us tremendously. Not only does it transform our lives, but it also leaves us with a feeling of freedom, of being able to just relax and be. At last our studies have turned into a living experience.

But the experience does not end there; it opens up so many possibilities for seeing how helpful and unhelpful our past habits and actions have been, as well as how much others are suffering, how they themselves are causing that suffering, and how they could be liberated from it. Then, with skill and a sense of genuine, not conceptual, loving-kindness toward people, we reach out and help them. I think we really can benefit others through genuine loving-kindness and compassion. When people are approached by someone who is truly compassionate, they feel a kind of power touching them. They sense that the person is really there for them. Sometimes you can help in a big way, but I feel that even a small amount of help can be a great help. This is the amazing magic of the study and practice of the Dharma.

QUESTION: *So, should we study first, before engaging in meditation?*
RINPOCHE: This depends on the individual. Some people choose to study first and practice later, others choose to practice and study at the same time. In my experience, engaging in study and practice together seems to be much more helpful than doing them separately. For instance, if you are studying the complex Madhyamaka arguments that establish emptiness but you cannot quite integrate emptiness into your practice, even simple shamata meditation will help you enormously. Although shamata is not the practice of emptiness, it helps the mind to relax and the intelligence to flow, and will connect you with what you are studying, so that your academic study is not so dry. True Dharma is not food for thought but food for well-being.

QUESTION: *You have said that studying and practicing emptiness can lead to an ability to help people more compassionately, but in the current discussions around "engaged Buddhism," it is often assumed that helping people is radically different from study and meditation, and that in practice the two are in opposition.*
RINPOCHE: It all depends on how much you believe you are helping people by doing formal practice, and whether you really practice meditation in order to attain enlightenment yourself so that you can bring all others to enlightenment. Each individual is different in this respect. Some people have very clear and confident bodhichitta, and all their practice, the whole of their lives, is dedicated to expressing that; while in others bodhichitta might not be so clear, and they may not have strong confidence in it.

From the point of view of people without clear and confident bodhichitta, they are not beyond suffering and obscurations, and they lack the wisdom, knowledge, and skillful means to benefit others. If you try to engage prematurely in benefiting others, it is something of a waste of time for you, and might not be of much benefit to others.

But then again, if Buddhists have the opportunity to benefit others, I feel very strongly that they should do so. We shouldn't say that we only open our minds in formal practice and do not engage in social work to help people. It all depends on the situation. There are good situations, when circumstances come together naturally and we can help, and there are others when they don't. If they do, we should take advantage of that, but if they don't, we should not try to seek such situations, become "professional" helpers, as it were, and get distracted from our personal path of study, contemplation, and practice.

QUESTION: *For many people, the ideal of religion is the ideal of Christian charity: to be more compassionate and loving, and a better human being. There can be a tendency to favor Mahayana Buddhism because it is seen as a path of compassion in this sense, and to consider Vajrayana as too esoteric.*

RINPOCHE: In some sense all religions, even Christianity, believe that bringing true benefit to others means teaching them. Christians will teach about Jesus, for example, and invite the person to believe in Jesus as a savior. A Christian will also feel that anything given prior to that in terms of care or material generosity is only of relative benefit. Similarly, in the Buddhist tradition, there are three types of generosity: material generosity; the transcendental generosity of a bodhisattva, who will give his or her very life for another's happiness; and ultimate generosity, which as in Christianity, is to give the teachings. The point of the teachings is to make people aware of their obscurations and their ultimate nature, and to show them how to purify those obscurations and realize their enlightened nature. In that way, Buddhism is no different from Christianity. The only difference, of course, is that Buddhists do not believe anyone can save you, or that God is creator of all beings. Ultimately you save yourself, and the law of interdependent origination is the creator of the illusory suffering of samsara.

QUESTION: *There can be a certain quality of narcissism in the way we practice meditation. As a result, when we see other people being more active and doing good, it can appear as if this kind of activity is closer to what spirituality is really all about. How do we avoid these two extremes?*

RINPOCHE: Cultivating the heart of compassion and loving-kindness, so that compassion and loving-kindness permeate our everyday actions, is very important. That is the courage and the practice of the Buddhist Mahayana path.

But that's not really what we are talking about here. What we are talking about is whether we will be able to establish a large organizational structure that includes a systematic way of benefiting others. If the right circumstances and conditions come together, and it is possible to create an organization like this that can continue to develop long term—perhaps over decades and centuries—then I think we should be interested. However, we should give equal emphasis to study, contemplation, and meditation practice. If we just go with one and not the other, especially if we go with study and not with meditation, we are in danger of losing our path to enlightenment. We will be so busy creating our organization, and those systematic ways of benefiting people, that we might not be able to contemplate and meditate. Then we will only be benefiting in social terms, not as a Buddhist.

The issue here is not so much whether we need to cultivate loving-kindness and compassion, or whether they should permeate everyday life and conduct; we're talking about something beyond that. But Buddhism is not to blame if we haven't yet managed to create systematic ways of benefiting others. It is a very young religion in the West, and people are still learning how to practice it and how to establish it here.

QUESTION: *What do you see as being really necessary for Dharma to become established in any country?*

RINPOCHE: Generally speaking, if we are able to establish the tradition of the Vinaya, the tradition of Sutra, and the tradition of Abhidharma, then the Dharma is established. The Vinaya helps to establish the ground, the Sutra helps to establish wisdom, and the Abhidharma helps to establish knowledge.

The question in everyone's mind at the moment is whether we're going to be able to establish all these traditions in the West, in exactly the way they were established in Tibet and India. Also, there is the question of whether establishing all these traditions in the West will be effective or not. For example, it is not that we don't need the monastic tradition of the Vinaya in the West, but will it be possible to establish it here?

From my own point of view, the Dharma has already come to the West, and people are already studying and practicing—especially Tibetan Buddhism, which is Mahayana Buddhism. Many teachers have given teachings, and many people are inspired to practice. What we need now is for people to bring their practice to fruition, and to exhibit their understanding, realization, qualities, and inspiration. We need *siddhas*— realized beings, or saints. I think that if we have siddhas who manifest qualities that are the fruition of their practice, even if there are only a few, then the Dharma is secured and well established in the West. So that's what I'm waiting for. And I'm very optimistic that it will happen.

QUESTION: *What do you see as the problems preventing us from establishing the monastic tradition in the West?*
RINPOCHE: No problems. But I'm not so sure that people are interested. Monastic life is a choice, and it is chosen when someone has an interest in that way of life. I'm sure there are a few individuals who are interested, but the vast majority is not.

QUESTION: *Do you think that might be a temporary thing? A few centuries ago in Europe, there was an extraordinary monastic institution with thousands of people in monasteries, and it was enormously successful and strong. If interest is rather limited at the moment, maybe it is because the idea has not taken off in people's imaginations.*
RINPOCHE: Exactly. By the end of the next century, we hope that Buddhism will be well established in the West, that some people will have accomplished the Dharma, and that all aspects of Buddhism will be established here.

QUESTION: *For a religion to become established, it has to touch all sections of society. In Tibet, Buddhism attracted people from all walks of life, including people of simple faith, but in the West it seems to interest mainly the middle classes and the well educated.*

RINPOCHE: In the future, as the tradition becomes established, it will not be so exclusive. The way Buddhism became established in Tibet was unique: it developed through the monastic and householder traditions at the same time. Lay people could study and practice just as the monastics could. That is the wonderful contribution that Tibet made to Buddhism.

QUESTION: *You said that the key to the development of Buddhism lies with its siddhas, or saints. What qualities should we find in a siddha?*
RINPOCHE: Don't imagine that only Western culture includes habits that are contrary to Dharma. All cultures, including the Tibetan culture, have habits that are strongly contrary to Dharma. So when we speak of the qualities, realizations, and lifestyle a person should exhibit as a siddha or realized being, they have to be the qualities of Dharma. They have nothing to do with culture. There should be no difference between the siddhas of India and Tibet and those in the West, between Eastern siddhas and Western siddhas: a siddha is simply a person who is totally transformed by the Dharma.

If a person is still influenced by his culture and that culture's neuroses, then he or she is not a genuine siddha. Whether he is within the Mahayana tradition or the Vajrayana tradition, if a person is to be respected as someone who upholds the Dharma, that respect must be based on his knowledge, understanding, and realization of the Dharma, and not on his social outlook, or outward activities aimed at benefiting people. Of course, if the person engages in such activity as well, that is wonderful, but the basic quality has to be that of the Dharma.

There is a universal wisdom that is contrary to all cultural habits, and Dharma is universal wisdom. The Indians had to transcend this difficulty when Buddha taught the Dharma in their country. The same happened when the Dharma went to Tibet. The same will happen now Dharma is coming to the West. If you stick to your views, saying "This is not our habit, this is not our culture, therefore I don't want to do this or practice that," then you are simply looking for a convenient path. Dharma is not a convenient path.

As far as I am aware, what we call "Tibetan Buddhism" came from India, down to the smallest detail. Even the choice of colors representing the five buddha families, for example, came from India. People think that Tibetans created all these rituals and ceremonies, but Tibetans weren't that smart. It all came from India.

So what did the Tibetans bring to the Dharma? As a people they are open, nonjudgmental and very devotional. They were receptive to the teachings, they studied and practiced, and they cultivated the Dharma in their lives.

QUESTION: *A prominent Western historian has said that in two hundred years' time, when people look back on the twentieth century as a whole, they will say that the most important thing that happened was the introduction of Buddhism to the West. What do you think Buddhism will bring?*
RINPOCHE: Liberation. Liberation is not just a theoretical concept. It is liberation from one's ignorance and delusory traps.

QUESTION: *There is a problem with the idea of liberation. For most it is just a myth, and those who believe it is possible think that it happened in the past but doesn't happen any more today. Some Theravada writings say that liberation no longer happens at this time, and the Dalai Lama has been quoted as saying that the truly great masters lived in the past, and there are no enlightened masters alive today. People take this literally, so in some circles there is disbelief in enlightenment as a possibility for us. This is reinforced by the fact that we feel so far away from it, that it's unreal.*
RINPOCHE: I personally believe that liberation is possible, as long as you study and practice. I think it is possible for me to attain enlightenment if I myself don't fail. I also believe that my teacher, Dilgo Khyentse Rinpoche, was enlightened. For me, liberation is not a myth or a vague goal, it is a truly living tradition that we are in touch with. We're so fortunate to be connected.

I understand that this is sometimes unclear for people. I'm not quite sure where the lack of clarity about enlightenment comes from. I always wonder about that.

QUESTION: *There is a sense of separation between path and goal, so that enlightenment becomes rather abstract. It is something we develop all kinds of attitudes toward, and we think the path is something else. I have been very struck when you talk about human growth, and the quality of freedom and empowerment that comes from the path as ignorance begins to shrivel. Can you say how we can work with this misunderstanding that enlightenment is something other than the path?*

RINPOCHE: In Mahayana, and in Vajrayana, there is a real possibility of attaining enlightenment. Our enlightened nature has a definite power, and what we're talking about here is making this present in ourselves by purifying and pacifying our obscurations. It is easier to see whether the path is powerful from this standpoint: if it is possible to pacify obscurations, then it is possible to gain enlightenment. Our illusions are transient, and if there is a path powerful enough to counteract them, we can wake up from that illusion and attain enlightenment. We can see through observation that this is indeed possible. So in my understanding, and in my judgment, the possibility of enlightenment is a very realistic one.

32. ADVICE TO WESTERN DHARMA FRIENDS

His Holiness the Dalai Lama

 At the official opening of Dzogchen Monastery in South India in 1992, the Dalai Lama gave advice to Rigpa students on how to practice the Dharma and integrate it into daily life.

QUESTION: *Many students who aspire to follow the dzogchen teachings, the highest esoteric teachings of Buddhism, seem to believe that there is nothing to do in this approach except "rest in the nature of mind." Could you please comment on this?*

THE DALAI LAMA: That doesn't seem very realistic. First we need to develop our minds deeply before we can accomplish this kind of practice. At this initial stage, two factors are important: We need to *practice* analytical meditation (reviewing the points of the path in meditation), and to develop a firm *understanding* of the Madhyamaka view of emptiness. We should study the commentaries by such masters as Nagarjuna and Asanga and really sharpen the sword of our good intelligence.

At the same time, we should strive to refine and deepen our *motivation* for practice, our vast aspiration to benefit beings. Both these elements cause us to accumulate tremendous positive merit, which really means that our minds become freer and freer, vaster and vaster. Then, when all these factors come together, it is possible to gain some personal experience of rigpa, the nature of mind, itself. At that moment, you meditate without using the usual mind, and you have a certain kind of experience that is beyond words.

Then in that state it would be wrong to carry out analytical meditation. This does not mean that the practitioner of dzogchen never practices analytical meditation, but rather that he or she practices it as a preparatory stage to nonconceptual meditation. So, if we compare analytical and dzogchen meditation, analytical meditation is definitely the inferior of the two, but it is nevertheless essential because without it, without that preliminary, dzogchen meditation would not even be possible. I would therefore like to remind you of the importance of the preliminaries, and of the complete and gradual path that is dzogchen practice.

QUESTION: *What advice would you have for people who are trying to follow the dzogchen teachings, particularly those of us in the West?*
THE DALAI LAMA: One of the most important points is to practice the tantric preliminary practices. I am always telling people that spiritual experience will not develop within a short period. In the scriptures, you see, it says that enlightenment is essentially within us at every moment, but in reality it takes time to manifest. Perhaps in the past there were some exceptional people for whom amazing and miraculous experiences happened suddenly, but this cannot be expected of ordinary people like us. For us, therefore, it takes time, and it is very important to know and understand that. For example, Tibetan medicine cannot produce a good result immediately but takes a few weeks or months to prove really effective; and likewise, when Tibetan Buddhism is practiced month after month, year after year, gradually our whole attitude and outlook undergoes a real and profound change. It is by practicing in this way that we can develop a personal experience of the teachings, and discover their value for ourselves.

QUESTION: *How can someone who is seriously trying to follow the teachings find a balance between the need for intensive practice and the need, according to the bodhisattva ideal, of contributing to society? This dilemma really perplexes many people in the West.*
THE DALAI LAMA: I think the answer will be different for every individual. In the Tibetan community, for instance, the majority of people are Buddhist practitioners and they each study and practice in whatever way they can, but most of them remain part of society. Many are monks and nuns, who naturally practice whenever they have the time, but

meanwhile remain part of the monastic community and carry their individual share of responsibility and work. Lay practitioners live and work within their own communities, too.

There are a few individuals—both monastic and lay—who have special potential in the spiritual field. Everyone has spiritual potential, of course, but these people have an immediate ability to achieve spiritual attainment. It is very worthwhile for such individuals to remain completely isolated, in retreat. If they can do this, then most of their time will be spent on spiritual practice and as a result, many—though not all—can have extraordinary experiences and attainments.

However, most people do not readily have such ability, and indeed it would not be beneficial for the majority of a population to be in retreat! They should remain part of their society and community, and live and work as productive, useful citizens. As Buddhist practitioners, they should even become good examples within their community. There is no need for them to make a show of the external signs of religion; rather what they need to do is develop a good heart.

QUESTION: *In the West, people seem to find it especially difficult to maintain their commitment to the teachings, maybe partly because society is not supportive. In your experience, how can Buddhist centers and groups best support individuals in their efforts to integrate the teachings into their lives?*
THE DALAI LAMA: That is a good question. I don't know! Perhaps there are differences according to the nature of people's jobs. If a practitioner works as a teacher, doctor, or lawyer, for example, and carries out his or her professional work with the compassionate motivation of a bodhisattva, then job and Dharma practice can go together very smoothly. On the other hand, certain types of work carry a negative karma, such as working in a slaughterhouse, and such work would be unthinkable for a Buddhist practitioner. Of course, there are also many nonviolent and nonharmful types of job or business that can be integrated into one's practice if they are carried out with sincere motivation and the aim of helping others.

Business usually involves competition, but I do not think competition is necessarily negative. With the right motivation, competition can be positive. Similarly, it is important to know that all desire is not necessarily negative; there are good desires and bad desires. Even what we call the ego is not necessarily negative. For example, a bodhisattva must have such a strong sense of "I," or ego, to accept to carry the responsibility of alleviating the suffering of all beings on his own! A bodhisattva's sense of "I" must be very powerful, otherwise he could not face the challenges of life with such determination! At the same time, this sense of "I" has no connection with the negative or selfish "I." Therefore, through practice, it is possible to develop strong determination based on the positive ego, and to carry out your business or your job, in whatever field, in that spirit.

QUESTION: *Finally, do you have a brief message for all the Dharma students who are not able to be here at this time?*

THE DALAI LAMA: My greetings. I appreciate your motivation and admire your effort. Buddhism is a different religion, from a different continent and a different tradition, and especially in the case of Tibetan Buddhism, it is also in a language that is foreign to you. More than this: Even though some individual Tibetans may not be especially inclined to religion, the whole atmosphere of Tibetan society draws them to it. But in the West, it is just the opposite! So, when I see Dharma friends putting their effort into practicing and studying the Dharma, and maintaining a keen interest in it despite all these difficulties, I admire it all the more.

I would also like to express my appreciation to all those of you who develop a genuine interest in Tibetan culture. If you practice Tibetan Buddhism, then automatically you will have some sense of responsibility to see how to preserve that culture, that spiritual tradition, and the country and people it comes from. I would like to appeal to you, and, through you, to all your friends, and point out that this spiritual culture that you value so much is actually dying. There is now a real danger of it disappearing not only from its country of origin, but also from this planet.

I am sure you know that the Tibetan national struggle is not merely a political struggle—quite clearly if that were the case, as a Buddhist monk I would not take any part in it at all. But the Tibetan struggle is actually a struggle to help preserve one of the world's ancient cultures, and one of the most complete forms of Buddhadharma. So, with sincere motivation, and on the basis of this realization and awareness, I hope that helping the Tibetan struggle can also be part of your Dharma practice.

Prayer for the Long Lives of All the Teachers

May the lives of the glorious masters be secure,
And may all beings enjoy happiness and peace;
May we all accumulate merit and wisdom,
purifying all negative karma,
And swiftly reach enlightenment!

We pray for the good health of the teachers,
We pray for their precious lives to be long,
We pray for their activities to spread and increase.
May we be blessed never to be separated from them![29]

NOTES

1. Thinley Norbu Rinpoche, *Magic Dance: The Display of the Self-Nature of the Five Wisdom Dakinis* (Boston: Shambhala Publications, 1998), p. 87.
2. These are said to have been the Buddha's first words following his enlightenment. Quoted from Sogyal Rinpoche, "Natural Great Peace," chap. 3 of this collection, p. 21.
3. Quoted in Patrul Rinpoche, *The Words of My Perfect Teacher* (Boston: Shambhala, 1998), p. xxxi.
4. From *The Excellent Path to Enlightenment,* an unpublished text developed by Siddhartha's Intent, which is an organization directed by Dzongsar Khyentse Rinpoche.
5. sGam.po.pa, *The Jewel Ornament of Liberation,* ed. and trans. by Herbert V. Guenther (Boston and London: Shambhala, 1986), p. 31.
6. Alexander Berzin, *Relating to a Spiritual Teacher: Building a Healthy Relationship* (Ithaca, NY: Snow Lion, 2000), p. 81.
7. Quoted in Sogyal Rinpoche, *The Tibetan Book of Living and Dying.* (San Francisco: HarperSanFrancisco, 1992), p. 134.
8. Sogyal Rinpoche, *The Future of Buddhism* (London: Rider, 2002).
9. Sogyal Rinpoche, *The Tibetan Book of Living and Dying,* p. 133.
10. Sonada, India, March 28, 1989, courtesy of Drajur Dzamling Kunchab.
11. Jigme Lingpa was strongly influenced by the teachings of Longchenpa even though nearly four hundred years separated them. During a three-year retreat he frequently called to him in his own words during guru-yoga practice, and Longchenpa appeared to him in three visions, during which he blessed Jigme Lingpa and gave him transmissions of wisdom body, speech, and mind. Longchenpa gave him the responsibility of protecting and spreading the meaning of his teachings.
12. Sogyal Rinpoche, *The Tibetan Book of Living and Dying,* p. 133ff.

13. In Maezumi Roshi, *Appreciate Your Life.* (Boston: Shambhala, 2001).
14. Sogyal Rinpoche, *The Future of Buddhism,* in Rigpa Journal 2000, p. 11.
15. Dzigar Kongtrul Rinpoche, "On the Responsibility of Our Generation for the Complete Preservation of the Tradition"; a talk given at Lerab Ling in France, July 7, 1997.
16. *The Tibetan Book of Living and Dying.*
17. There is a tradition in Tibet in which the most precious texts are signed with author names that seem comical to us. The convention of using such nicknames was widespread and perhaps demonstrates an author's lack of desire for honor and renown.
18. This reference is to Padmasambhava, who in the Vajrayana practice of guru yoga is seen as inseparable from the teacher.
19. The prayer to be born in Zangdok Palri (Copper-Colored Mountain), the pure realm of Guru Rinpoche, in one's next life.
20. Quoted in Matthieu Ricard, *Journey to Enlightenment: The Life and World of Khyentse Rinpoche* (New York: Aperture, 1996), p. 90.
21. *The Tibetan Book of Living and Dying.*
22. *The Tibetan Book of Living and Dying.*
23. Cited in *The Tibetan Book of Living and Dying.*
24. The eight practice lineages of Tibet are, according to Jamgön Kongtrul's *Sheja Kunkhyab:* Nyingma, Kadam, Sakya, Marpa Kagyü, Shangpa Kagyü, Shijé and Chö, Jordruk, and Dorjé Nendrup.
25. Message of greeting to the conference "Dying, Death, and Living," Munich, 1996, program notes, p. 4.
26. Quoted in *The Tibetan Book of Living and Dying,* p. 98.
27. Message of greeting to the convention "Unity in Diversity: Buddhism in Europe," held in Berlin in July 1992 under the auspices of the German Buddhist Union. Published in Deutsche Buddhistische Union, ed., *Einheit in der Vielfalt—Buddhismus im Westen* (Munich, 1993), p. 9.
28. Sogyal Rinpoche, "The Significance of the Sangha on the Spiritual Path." Unpublished transcript of a talk given to the German Buddhist Union's convention in Freiburg, Germany, October 23, 1998.
29. Prayer for the Long Life of All Teachers; from *Daily Practices,* (London: Rigpa, 1992).

SOURCES

CHAPTER 1. Sogyal Rinpoche, "It's Under Our Very Noses." Excerpt from a teaching given in Paris, 5 November 1996. *View Magazine,* October 1997.

CHAPTER 2. Patrick Gaffney, "The Spirit of Tibet." *Rigpa Rundbrief,* February 1994; talk at London Wesak celebration 1992.

CHAPTER 3. Sogyal Rinpoche, "Natural Great Peace." From *The Rigpa Journal,* September 2000.

CHAPTER 4. Ringu Tulku Rinpoche, based on a talk given at Shambhala Centre, Munich, October 10–12, 2000; © Ringu Tulku Rinpoche and Bodhicharya, 2001; printed with permission of the author.

CHAPTER 5. Sogyal Rinpoche, "The Guru Principle." Excerpt from Sogyal Rinpoche, *Dzogchen und Padmasambhava,* Rigpa Publications, 1990. *Rigpa Rundbrief,* February 1990.

CHAPTER 6. Francesca Fremantle, "Saints or Scoundrels?" In *Buddhism Now,* 1994; *Rigpa Rundbrief,* January 1995.

CHAPTER 7. Gyalwang Drukpa Rinpoche, "The Guru Question." *View Magazine,* September 1997; *Rigpa Rundbrief,* January 2000.

CHAPTER 8. Dzongsar Khyentse Rinpoche, "Distortion." From the *Shambhala Sun,* September 1997.

CHAPTER 9. Dzogchen Rinpoche, "Taming the Mindstream." Excerpt from a teaching at Lerab Ling, August 28, 1997. *Rigpa Rundbrief,* March 1997.

CHAPTER 10. Philippe Cornu, "Karma, Truth, and Emptiness." *View Magazine,* November 1998; *Rigpa Rundbrief,* March 1998.

CHAPTER 11. Chökyi Nyima Rinpoche, "Cutting Dualistic Thinking." Teaching given in Cologne, Germany, September 1994. *Rigpa Rundbrief,* February 1995.

CHAPTER 12. Orgyen Tobgyal Rinpoche, "Pure Buddhism, Authentic Transmission." *View Magazine,* November 1998; *Rigpa Rundbrief,* January 1999.

CHAPTER 13. Dzogchen Pönlop Rinpoche, "The Buddhist View of Reality." Excerpt from a talk given on November 18, 1994 in Munich, Germany. *Rigpa Rundbrief,* January 1995.

CHAPTER 14. H.H. Dudjom Rinpoche, "Meditation and Peace." Excerpt from a teaching given in London in May 1979. Copyright Rigpa 1987. *View Magazine,* October 1999; *Rigpa Rundbrief,* February 1993.

CHAPTER 15. Dilgo Khyentse Rinpoche, "Shamata, Vipashyana, and the Nature of Mind." Excerpt from a teaching given on August 23, 1990 in Prapoutel, France. Translated by Matthieu Ricard. *Rigpa Rundbrief,* March 1990.

CHAPTER 16. Nyoshul Khen Rinpoche, "Awareness—The Mirror of Mind." Unknown source. *Rigpa Rundbrief,* January 1994.

CHAPTER 17. Jamyang Khyentse Chökyi Lodrö, "Heart Advice in a Nutshell." Translated from the Tibetan by Sogyal Rinpoche, 1981. Rigpa *Rundbrief,* January 1993.

CHAPTER 18. Nyoshul Khen Rinpoche, "The Benefits of Dzogpachenpo." Excerpt from a teaching given at Brunissard, France, on August 6, 1989. Translated from the Tibetan by Sogyal Rinpoche. *Rigpa Rundbrief,* January 1990.

CHAPTER 19. Khetsun Sangpo Rinpoche, "Toward the Nature of Mind." Excerpt from a teaching given on August 23, 1990 in France. *Rigpa Rundbrief,* January 1992.

CHAPTER 20. Kalu Rinpoche, "The Unity of Mahamudra and Dzogchen." Excerpt from a teaching given in Paris in 1987. *Rigpa Rundbrief,* January 1990.

CHAPTER 21. Sogyal Rinpoche, "Losing the Clouds, Gaining the Sky." Excerpts from talks given in Paris and Lerab Ling in 1996. *View Magazine,* July 1996; *Rigpa Rundbrief,* January 1997.

CHAPTER 22. Dzigar Kongtrul Rinpoche, "Our Motivation: Different Kinds of Laziness and Their Antidotes." Excerpt from a teaching given on August 25, 1990 in France. *Rigpa Rundbrief,* February 1991.

CHAPTER 23. Sogyal Rinpoche, "Finding the Thread." *View Magazine,* 1996; *Rigpa Rundbrief,* February 1996.

CHAPTER 24. Frank Ostaseski, "Learning How to Serve." Talk given at the "Dying, Death, and Life" conference in Munich, Germany, on November 23, 1996. *Rigpa Rundbrief,* February 1998.

CHAPTER 25. Christine Longaker, "Transforming Suffering Through Compassion." Talk given to the German Buddhist Union, September 4, 1995. *Rigpa Rundbrief,* February 1996.

CHAPTER 26. Sogyal Rinpoche, "The Art of Dying." *Rigpa Rundbrief,* March 1996.

CHAPTER 27. Sakya Jetsun Chimey, "Women on the Spiritual Path." Interview with Dominique Side. *View Magazine,* April 1995; *Rigpa Rundbrief,* January 1996.

CHAPTER 28. Orgyen Tobgyal Rinpoche, "Diligence and Contentment." *View Magazine,* November 1998, as part of "Pure Buddhism, Authentic Transmission." *Rigpa Rundbrief,* January 1999.

CHAPTER 29. Sogyal Rinpoche, "Journey to Liberation." Teaching given on January 9, 1996 in Paris, France. *Rigpa Rundbrief,* January 1996.

CHAPTER 30. Dzigar Kongtrul Rinpoche, "The Future of Buddhism: Enlightenment Is Real!" Interview with Ian Maxwell and Dominique Side. *View Magazine,* October 1998; *Rigpa Rundbrief,* January 1998.

CHAPTER 31. H.H. the Dalai Lama, "Advice for Western Dharma Friends." Interview with Ian Maxwell. *View Magazine,* 1995; *Rigpa Rundbrief,* February 1995.

Abhidharma (Skt.). "higher teaching." The third section of the Buddhist canon. The Abhidharma is the earliest collection of Buddhist philosophy and psychology, and is a systematic presentation of the teachings on spiritual phenomena to be found in the discourses of the Buddha and his leading disciples.

aggregate. *See* skandha

alaya (Skt.). The primordial state of the mind. The fundamental clear nature of awareness. Synonymous with *buddha nature*.

alayavijñana (Skt.). "store consciousness." The deepest level of consciousness, which goes from life to life and which stores the imprints of karmic activity.

bardo (Tib.; Skt. *antarabhava*). "the between state." Usually refers to the state a being undergoes between incarnations, though can refer to any "between" state. Sogyal Rinpoche and others describe four bardos: (1) the natural bardo of this life, (2) the painful bardo of death, (3) the clear-light bardo of dharmata, (4) the karmic bardo of becoming.

bhumis (Skt.). The stages of development, usually enumerated as ten, that a bodhisattva must go through on the way to buddhahood after achieving the direct perception of emptiness.

bodhi (Skt. and Pali). "awakening." Enlightenment or buddhahood, or a direct realization on the path to full enlightenment.

buddha nature (Skt. *tathatagagarbha*). The essence of consciousness, which is utterly clear, luminous, and compassionate. The nature of the mind that ripens as a buddha mind in enlightenment.

Chittamatra (Skt.; Tib. *semtsam*). "mind only." The name of a philosophical school of Mahayana Buddhism that says that there is no difference between the objects of consciousness and the mind that perceives them. The Chittamatra school also developed the theory of the *alayavijñana,* or store consciouness. *See also* Yogachara.

dakini (Skt.; Tib. *khandroma*). "sky dancer." Female deity, in iconography often depicted in wrathful or semi-wrathful form. Represents compassion and emptiness, and embodies wisdom. On one level of meaning, dakinis are the third of the three roots in which one takes refuge (*see* refuge). Dakinis in some contexts also represent inspiring or auspicious circumstances.

dharmakaya (Skt.). "Dharma body." The true nature of a buddha, identical with the transcendent reality.

dharmata (Skt.). The nature of dharmas, the essence of all things. Philosophical concept in the Mahayana, similar in meaning to "suchness" and "buddha nature."

dzogchen, dzogpachenpo (Tib.; Skt. *mahasandhi; mahasampanna; maha ati*). "great perfection." The central teaching of the Nyingma school of Tibetan Buddhism, brought to Tibet from India by Padmasambhava and Vimalamitra in the eighth century. Longchenpa organized it into a unified system in the fourteenth century. Jigmé Lingpa (1730–98) presented the teaching anew, and this version stands as the definitive presentation to this day.

five aggregates. *See* skandha

guru yoga. Relying on a spiritual teacher, the foundation within Vajrayana Buddhism for success in actualizing the practices. One sees the teacher as a manifestation of the Buddha himself, and offers service and makes prayers to the teacher, fully trusting his or her advice and wisdom.

Hinayana (Skt.). "lesser vehicle." A term used by the Mahayana to describe Buddhist practices and orientations focused on individual liberation alone.

Kagyü (Tib.). One of the four main schools of Tibetan Buddhism, of which the central teachings are mahamudra and the Six Yogas of Naropa. The central masters of the Kagyü tradition are Tilopa, Naropa, Marpa, Milarepa, Gampopa, and the Karmapa.

klesha (Skt.). "disturbing emotions." Passions that cloud the mind, leading to negative actions, which bind a person to samsara, the wheel of birth and death. Common kleshas include attachment, aversion, ignorance, pride, and envy.

lojong (Tib.). "mind training." Refers especially to practices aimed at awakening bodhichitta, the mind that aspires to buddhahood for the sale of all sentient beings. Originally brought to Tibet and systematized by Atisha Dipamkara (ca. 980–1055), the founder of the Kadam school of Tibetan Buddhism.

Madhyamaka (Skt.). "Middle Way." Buddhist philosophical school founded by Nagarjuna (fl. ca. 150 C.E.), a philosopher of genius from Southern India whose chief work is the *Mulamadhyamakakarika*. Alongside the theory of universal relativity, Nagarjuna differentiated between the *two truths* (see entry below): (1) relative truth, where things arise on the basis of causes and conditions, and (2) ultimate truth, or emptiness *(shunyata):* the lack of inherent existence of all phenomena. Tibetan Buddhists recognize two subschools of the Madhyamaka: Prasangika and Svatantrika.

mahamudra (Skt.; Tib. *chagya chenpo*). "great seal." Practice aiming at the realization of one's own buddha nature. The central meditation transmission of the Kagyü school.

mahasiddha (Skt.). A great *siddha,* or adept. The mahasiddhas of classical Indian Buddhism, often numbered as eighty-four, were often known for their anti-conventional methods.

mala (Skt.). A string of beads with 108, 28, or 21 beads that is used for, among other things, counting the recitation of mantras.

mandala (Skt.). Symbolic representation of universe in two- or three-dimensional form. Also refers to the abode of a tantric deity. Making mandala offerings, i.e., offering the universe, is an important preliminary practice.

merit (Skt. *punya;* Tib. *sonam*). Wholesome tendencies that permeate the mind as a result of positive actions of body, speech, and mind, and that later arise as fortunate experience. The accumulation of merit is an important aspect of Buddhist practice, for it provides a crucial foundation for the development of realizations.

Middle Way. *See* Madhyamaka

mind training. *See* lojong

nirmanakaya (Skt.; Tib. *trulku*). "form body." The visible form of a buddha.

Padmasambhava (Skt.). "Lotus Born." Also known as Padmakara and Guru Rinpoche. The historical Padmasmbhava lived in the eighth century and is regarded as the founder of Tibetan Buddhism. He shaped the teachings primarily of the Nyingma school, where he is honored as a second Buddha. Padmasambhava has since become an almost legendary figure; for the Nyingma tradition he embodies the ultimate master, and is synonymous with the nature of mind.

paramita (Skt.). "That which has crossed over to the far shore." The paramitas are often referred to as "perfections;" they are the virtues that a bodhisattva develops in the course of his or her development. They are most often enumerated as six: *dana paramita* (generosity); *shila paramita* (moral discipline); *kshanti paramita* (patience); *virya paramita* (energy, or effort); *dhyana paramita* (meditation/concentration); and *prajna paramita* (wisdom).

prajña (Skt.). "transcendent wisdom." The direct, intuitive realization of ultimate knowledge, impossible to communicate in concepts. The distinguishing mark of this wisdom is insight into emptiness *(shunyata)*, the true nature of reality. The attainment of prajna is synonymous with enlightenment and is one of the essential characteristics of buddhahood.

Prajna is also one of the perfections *(paramita)* that bodhisattvas must realize in the course of their development.

pratyekabuddha (Skt.). "solitary realizer." A being who realizes enlightenment but who does not teach others. A pratyekabuddha, though enlightened, lacks the omniscience and the ten powers of a buddha.

rainbow body (Tib. *jalu*). Complete transformation into a body of light at death, which results from advanced practice of dzogchen. The practitioner leaves nothing behind except hair and fingernails.

refuge. In its simplest form, an outward ackowledgment of oneself as a Buddhist, and a daily recitation of a Buddhist. One takes refuge, or places one's hopes and trust, in the Three Jewels: the Buddha, the Dharma, and the Sangha. The Buddha is firstly the historical Buddha Shakyamuni, but refers to all enlightened beings. The Dharma is the teaching of the Buddha. The Noble Sangha is anyone, lay or ordained, who has directly perceived emptiness, but Sangha also means ordained monks and nuns or, more generally, the community of practitioners who support us in our practice.

renunciation (Skt. *naiskramya/prahana;* Tib. *nejung/pangwa*). A mental attitude free of compulsive craving to various worldly forms and qualities, and clinging to a favorable rebirth. The Tibetan term *nejung* literally means "definitive emergence," irreversible liberation from the fetters of our narrow-minded attachment to worldly pleasures. For Mahayana practitioners, renunciation can mean no longer creating the causes that lead to suffering.

rimé (Tib.). A nineteenth-century renaissance of Tibetan Buddhism that valorized a nonsectarian approach to the various lineages. The approach was championed in particular by Jamyang Khyentse Wangpo and the first Jamgon Kongtrul.

Samantabhadra (Skt.). "All-Embracing Goodness." (1) The primordial dharmakaya Buddha; (2) The bodhisattva Samantabhadra, who is known for having perfected the making of extensive offerings.

samaya (Skt.; Tib. *damtsig*). The Vajrayana principle of commitment, in which the whole experience of the disciple is bound to the path. Samayas essentially consist of the outer maintenance of harmony in relating to the master and co-disciples, and the inner commitment not to slacken in the continuity of one's practice.

sambhogakaya (Skt.). "enjoyment body." The dynamic body buddhas have in what are called buddha paradises, created by the massive merit of their own wisdom and compassion.

Sautrantika (Skt.). One of the philosophical schools of the so-called Hinayana. The Sautrantika school developed deeply the understanding of mental causality.

Sarma (Tib.). "new schools." Refers primarily to the Kagyü, Sakya, and Gelug schools, connected because they follow the later translations of the Indian canon into Tibetan, as distinguished from the Nyingma ("old") school.

shravaka (Skt.). "hearer." Original title of the personal disciples of the Buddha, or of students generally. In the Mahayana this is the title given to those who seek only their own enlightenment, and who attain this by hearing teachings and by gaining insight into the four noble truths and the unreality of phenomena.

shunyata (Skt.). "emptiness." The central view of Buddhism, which teaches that all compounded phenomena are impermanent, unsatisfactory, and empty of a findable essence. Both things and persons are thus "empty," which means that, although they exist in relative terms, they have no permanent, self-defining essence.

siddha (Skt.). An enlightened master in the tantric tradition, one who has attained the siddhis.

siddhi (Skt.). In the context of Buddhist yoga, especially as practiced in the Vajrayana, siddhis are special attainments that result from perfect command of physical energies. The Vajrayana distinguishes between ordinary siddhis—things like clairvoyance and flying—and the extraordinary or highest siddhi of enlightenment.

skandha (Skt.). "group," "heap," "aggregate." Refers to the five aggregates from which the entire person is composed: (1) physical form, (2) feeling (pleasant, unpleasant, or neutral), (3) perception, or memory, for example the immediate recognition of something as a telephone, based on past experiences of it functioning and being thought of as such, (4) mental formations, of which there are fifty, (5) consciousness: namely, eye consciousness, ear consciousness, taste consciousness, smell consciousness, touch consciousness, and mental consciousness. The aggregates are sometimes called "aggregates of clinging," because all those who are not fully free cling to the experiences thrown up by these different elements and senses and conceive a personhood, an "I," around them.

tantra (Skt.). "thread," "continuum." Buddhism's esoteric practices and texts; synonymous with Vajrayana.

tathagatha (Skt.). "one thus gone." A perfected one, who has reached the very end of the path: perfect full enlightenment. One of the epithets Shakyamuni Buddha used when referring to himself or to previous buddhas.

two truths, the. The Buddhist teachings understand reality from two perspectives, the relative and the absolute: (1) The absolute perspective of emptiness, in which all phenomena are empty of inherent existence; (2) The perspective of relative reality, in which all phenomena exist in relative terms, dependent on other factors to exist. There is no contradiction between the two realities: relative things "work" even though from the absolute perspective they are empty. On this subject, see especially the teaching by Chökyi Nyima Rinpoche in this book.

Vaibhashika (Skt.). One of the philosophical schools of the so-called Hinayana. This Buddhist school maintains that consciousness perceives an object when it comes into direct contact with it, and that the object is different and separate from the consciousness perceiving it. The Vaibhashika school holds that atoms and indivisible moments of consciousness both have ultimate existence, and that the three times (past, present, and future) also have solid existence.

vajra (Skt.; Tib. *dorje*). Diamond, diamond thunderbolt. Symbol of immutable and imperturbable wisdom, which can penetrate all things.

Vajrayana (Skt.). Tantra. Mahayana Buddhism's esoteric teachings and practices, which harness the energies of the emotions and which take the result as the path, using deity meditation in the generation stage and formless meditation in the completion stage.

yana (Skt.). Literally, "vehicle." A coherent system of teachings and practices. The most popular classification of Buddhist yanas is the hierarchical set of three vehicles—the Hinayana, the Mahayana, and the Vajrayana—which progresses from more gradual approaches to the more direct methods of tantra.

ABOUT THE CONTRIBUTORS

The Tibetan Teachers

CHÖKYI NYIMA RINPOCHE is the oldest son of the late Kyabje Tulku Urgyen Rinpoche, and was recognized at eighteen months old as the seventh incarnation of Gar Drubchen, a Drikung Kagyü master and an emanation of Nagarjuna. Soon after, he was enthroned at his predecessor's monastery, Drong Gon Tubten Dargye Ling Monastery in Nakchukha, Central Tibet. At age thirteen he entered Rumtek Monastery and spent the next eleven years studying the Karma Kagyü, Drikung Kagyü, and Nyingma traditions under the guidance of H.H. the Sixteenth Karmapa and other eminent masters. Rinpoche has a good command of the English language and has been instructing a growing number of Western students in meditation practice since 1977, mostly at his institute in the Kathmandu Valley.

DILGO KHYENTSE RINPOCHE was born in Eastern Tibet in 1910 and was widely regarded as his generation's most extraordinary poet, scholar, philosopher, and meditation master. He was one of the main lineage holders of the Dzogchen *Longchen Nyingthig* tradition and was the head of the Nyingma school of Tibetan Buddhism from 1987 until 1991. At the age of twenty-eight he completed his retreats and thereafter took teachings from Dzongsar Khyentse Chökyi Lodrö. He then decided to spend the rest of his life in solitary meditation. Khyentse Chökyi Lodrö had other ideas, however, and Dilgo Khyentse instead began a teaching career that lasted for the rest of his life. Although a Nyingma master, he was an exponent of the *rimé* movement and was well known for his ability to teach each Buddhist lineage from within its own tradition. In the last year of life he gave transmissions and empowerments to H.H. the Dalai Lama. His Holiness Dilgo Khyentse Rinpoche died in Bhutan on September 28, 1991.

DUDJOM RINPOCHE, Jigdral Yeshe Dorje, was one of the most outstanding yogins, scholars, and meditation masters of recent times. After the flight into exile, it was Dudjom Rinpoche who was the first master to be accorded the title of Supreme Head of the Nyingma School of Tibetan Buddhism. Dudjom Rinpoche was born 1904, was recognized as the incarnation of Dudjom Lingpa (1835–1904), and studied with some of the most outstanding masters of the time. He became renowned throughout Tibet for the depth of his realization and spiritual accomplishment, as well as for his unsurpassed scholarship. After leaving Tibet, Rinpoche settled in Kalimpong, Sikkim, and later in Nepal. In the final decade of his life, he founded many major centers in the United States and France, and settled in the Dordogne area of France. He passed away in 1987.

DZIGAR KONGTRUL RINPOCHE was born in 1964 in Northern India to Tibetan parents. He was recognized by H.H. the Sixteenth Karmapa as one of the five emanations of Jamgön Kongtrul the Great, one of Tibet's most influential spiritual teachers of the nineteenth century. Until the age of twenty-one, Kongtrul Rinpoche lived in a monastic environment and received extensive training in all the traditional teachings of Buddhist doctrine, primarily of the Nyingma lineage, with his root teacher H.H. Dilgo Khyentse Rinpoche. Kongtrul Rinpoche also studied with H.E. Tulku Urgyen Rinpoche, Nyoshul Khen Rinpoche, and the scholar-yogin Khenpo Rinchen. Dzigar Kongtrul Rinpoche came to live in the United States in 1989, and travels throughout the United States, Canada, and Europe teaching at various Buddhist centers.

DZOGCHEN RINPOCHE, Jikme Losel Wangpo, the seventh incarnation of Pema Rigdzin, was born in Sikkim in 1964. His father was the late Tsewang Paljor, whose family lineage is of Tertön descent traced back to Dudul Nuden Dorje of Khatog Monastery. This seventh incarnation of the Dzogchen Rinpoche was recognized by the Fourth Dodrupchen Rinpoche and was enthroned in October 1972 at Gangtok. At the invitation of his brother, Sogyal Rinpoche, he made the first of what has become a regular series of visits to the Western world, teaching in Europe, America, and Australia. In recent years Rinpoche has worked selflessly to improve the quality of life for the Tibetan refugee community in India, while at the same time he has continued to care for his monastery, the education, training, and welfare of its monks, and the spiritual needs of the local community.

DZOGCHEN PÖNLOP RINPOCHE was born at Rumtek Monastery in Sikkim, India. His father was Damchö Yongdu, General Secretary of H.H. the Sixteenth Karmapa. H.H. the Karmapa immediately recognized him as a reincarnate lama, and he was enthroned at Rumtek Monastery in 1968. Rinpoche was ordained as a novice monk in 1974. In 1981 he entered the monastic college at Rumtek, where he was schooled in the traditional scholastic curriculum of Buddhist philosophy, psychology, logic, and debate. In 1990 Rinpoche graduated as Ka Rabjampa, "one with unobstructed knowledge of scriptures," equivalent to the geshe degree, and also simultaneously earned the degree of acharya, or Masters in Buddhist philosophy, from Sampurnanant Sanskrit University. Rinpoche has been Visiting Professor at Naropa University, Colorado, since 1996. Fluent in English and well versed in Western culture, Rinpoche is also an accomplished calligrapher, visual artist, and poet. He serves as abbot of Dzogchen Monastery, a Nyingma institution, and in 1979 H.H. the Sixteenth Gyalwa Karmapa formally empowered and officially proclaimed him a lineage holder of the Karma Kagyü school as well.

DZONGSAR JAMYANG KHYENTSE RINPOCHE was born in Bhutan in 1961 and was recognized as the main incarnation of the Khyentse lineage of Tibetan Buddhism. He has studied with some of the greatest contemporary masters, particularly H.H. Dilgo Khyentse Rinpoche. From a young age he has been active for the preservation of the Buddhist teaching, establishing centers of learning, supporting practitioners, publishing books, and teaching all over the world. Dzongsar Khyentse Rinpoche supervises his traditional seat of Dzongsar Monastery and its retreat centers in Eastern Tibet, as well as his new colleges in India and Bhutan and is responsible for the care and education of approximately 1600 monks living in six monasteries and institutes in Asia. He oversees Siddhartha's Intent, an organisation of six teaching and practice centers around the world, as well as two nonprofit organisations, Khyentse Foundation and Lotus Outreach. He wrote and directed the films *The Cup* and *Travellers and Magicians.*

GYALWANG DRUKPA RINPOCHE, His Holiness the Twelfth Gyalwang Drukchen Rinpoche, is the supreme head of the Drukpa Kagyü lineage of Tibetan Buddhism. He is considered an emanation of the buddha of compassion, as well as an incarnation of several great masters of the past, including Naropa and Gampopa. Rinpoche's teachers include H.E. Thuksey Rinpoche, Kyabje Dudjom Rinpoche, H.H. the Dalai Lama, H.E. Trulshik Rinpoche, H.E. Bairo Tulku Rinpoche, and Pawo Rinpoche. He has reestablished a home for the Drukpa Kagyü lineage in exile at his monastery in Darjeeling. He oversees many monasteries in this tradition in Ladakh, Tibet, Bhutan, Nepal, Sikkim, and the far East, and now has centers in the West. Rinpoche speaks excellent English, and his teaching is noted for its directness, frankness, and freedom from convention.

HIS HOLINESS THE DALAI LAMA, is the head of state and spiritual leader of the Tibetan people. He was born Lhamo Döndrub to a peasant family on July 6, 1935, in a small village called Taktser in northeastern Tibet. His Holiness was recognized at age two, in accordance with Tibetan tradition, as the reincarnation of his predecessor. He began his education at age six, and completed the geshe lharampa degree in 1959. In November 1950, His Holiness was called upon to assume full political power as head of the Tibetan state and government after the Chinese Communist army invaded Tibet, following which he was given political asylum in India in March 1959. In December 1989 His Holiness was awarded the Nobel Peace Prize, and he accepted the prize on behalf of oppressed peoples everywhere. His numerous books and public appearances give special attention to the dialogue between Buddhism and modern science, world peace, and harmony among the world's religions.

JAMYANG KHYENTSE CHÖKYI LODRÖ (1896–1959) was one of the most outstanding Tibetan master of this century. An authority on all traditions and holder of all lineages, he was the heart of the ecumenical *rimé* movement. He was recognized as activity incarnation of Jamyang Khyentse Wangpo (1820–92), a notable rimé pioneer. He studied and practiced the teachings of all schools of Tibetan Buddhism under more than eighty masters. Rinpoche opened Dzongsar Khamje University and Karmo Tagtsang Retreat Center, as well as restoring other monasteries, constructing images, printing books, and teaching extensively. In 1958 he settled in Sikkim, where he passed away. He was the master of many notable Tibetan lamas, including Dilgo Khyentse Rinpoche, Dezhung Rinpoche, Kalu Rinpoche, Sogyal Rinpoche, Trungpa Rinpoche, and Tarthang Tulku.

KALU RINPOCHE was one of the great masters of our age. Born in Eastern Tibet in 1905, he was raised by his father and mother, both Dharma practitioners. The root guru of both his parents was the great Jamgön Kongtrul Lodrö Tayé. After his three-year retreat Kalu Rinpoche spent almost twenty years alone in the mountains. Before the Chinese takeover of Tibet, H.H. the Dalai Lama sent Kalu Rinpoche to Bhutan. He later moved to Northern India, in the Darjeeling area. At Sonada, Rinpoche was given a small monastery and immediately began to rebuild, add on, and start a three-year retreat. In the early 1970s, the Sixteenth Karmapa sent Kalu Rinpoche to the West. He traveled many times to many parts of the world and established many centers and three-year retreats. Kalu Rinpoche passed away in 1989.

KHETSUN SANGPO RINPOCHE is among the most senior lamas and dzogchen masters in the Nyingma tradition, and perhaps the most eminent Nyingma historian alive today. He was born in 1920 in central Tibet and came to India in 1959. Soon thereafter he was asked by H.H. the Dalai Lama to represent Dudjom Rinpoche, head of the Nyingma School, in Japan. Khetsun Rinpoche spent ten years (1960–70) in this capacity, teaching in Tokyo and Kyoto universities and becoming fluent in Japanese. In 1971 he returned to India and founded a school to educate Tibetan monks in his tradition. Over the last twenty-five years he has accepted numerous invitations to teach in Japanese and U.S. universities, and to teach students in retreats in Dordogne, France. Khetsun Rinpoche's writings feature a thirteen-volume history of all the Tibetan

Buddhist traditions. He is also the author of *Tantric Practice in Nyingma*, used by thousands of Western students as a guide to the foundational practices.

NYOSHUL KHEN RINPOCHE (Jamyang Dorje Nyoshul Khen Rinpoche) was born in 1932 in Kham. Khenpo counted twenty-five great masters as his principal teachers, of whom the most central in his life was Shedrup Tenpé Nyima, the reincarnation of Nyoshul Lungtok. He received the teachings of *Longchen Nyingtig* and the *Great Oral Lineage of Pith Instructions of Dzogpachenpo*, a lineage that passed back to the primordial buddha in an unbroken line. In 1959 he made a narrow escape from Tibet. In India his life veered between extremes, begging on the streets of Calcutta and living among the sadhus, and then giving empowerments to huge assemblies and to incarnate lamas. He later fell ill and then spent eight years in the Dordogne area of France. As his health improved, he traveled and taught throughout the world. Nyoshul Khen Rinpoche passed away in France in August 1999.

ORGYEN TOBGYAL RINPOCHE. As the oldest son of Tekchok Tenphel, the third incarnation of Chokgyur Lingpa at Neten, Orgyen Tobgyal Rinpoche has received many transmissions from Dzongsar Khyentse Chökyi Lodrö, and especially from Dilgo Khyentse Rinpoche, his root guru, for whom he has often served as close attendant. After his father's death, he assumed responsibility for completing the monastery at Bir, Himachal Pradesh, and overseeing the upbringing of the tulku of his father. Orgyen Tobgyal Rinpoche is renowned for being naturally learned, and is well known for his grasp of and ability to explain the Vajrayana teachings.

RINGU TULKU RINPOCHE is a Tibetan Buddhist master of the Kagyü order. He was trained in all schools of Tibetan Buddhism under many great masters such as H.H. the Sixteenth Karmapa and Dilgo Khyentse Rinpoche. He took his formal education at Namgyal Institute of Tibetology, Gangtok, and Sampurnananda Sanskrit University, Varanasi, India, and has served as Professor of Tibetology in Sikkim for seventeen years. Since 1990 he has been traveling and teaching Buddhism and meditation at more than fifty universities, institutes, and Buddhist centers in Europe, the United States, Canada, Australia, and Asia. He founded Bodhicharya, an international organization that coordinates activities to preserve and transmit Buddhist teachings and to promote intercultural dialogues and educational and social projects.

SAKYA JETSUN CHIMEY. Born in 1938 as the sister of the current head of the Sakya lineage, one of the four main sects of Tibetan Buddhism, she received much of her training alongside her brother, H.H. Sakya Trizin, from such legendary teachers as Jamyang Khyentse Chökyi Lodrö. Devoting herself to Buddhist practices from an early age, she completed her first retreat at age ten. Many more important retreats like Hevajra and Vajrayogini were to follow, enabling her to become one of fewer than a dozen masters who are qualified to transmit the *Lamdré* or "The Path with the Results," the central system of practice of the Sakya school. Jetsun Kushok gave her first transmission of the Lamdré, along with all the necessary empowerments, at age seventeen. In 1959, she left Tibet and, by way of India, eventually settled in Vancouver, Canada, with her family in 1971. Struggling to care for her children and make a living in a new country, she had to partition her time between working as a knitwear designer and keeping up her meditation practices, often to the point of staying up all night. At the repeated request of Sakya Trizin, Jetsun Kushok selflessly started to teach in Vancouver in the early 1980s, and now teaches all over the world. Beloved by all her students, Jetsun Kushok is both strict and warm, transmitting only genuine Buddhadharma in the traditional way, seasoned by her pragmatic experience of practicing and working in the West.

SOGYAL RINPOCHE. Born in Kham in Eastern Tibet, Sogyal Rinpoche was recognized as the incarnation of Lerab Lingpa Tertön Sogyal, a teacher to the Thirteenth Dalai Lama, by Jamyang Khyentse Chökyi Lodrö, one of the most outstanding masters of the twentieth century. Jamyang Khyentse supervised Rinpoche's training and raised him like his own son. In 1971, Rinpoche went to England where he received a Western education, studying Comparative Religion at Cambridge University. He went on to study with many other masters, of all schools of

Tibetan Buddhism, especially H. H. Dudjom Rinpoche and Dilgo Khyentse Rinpoche. First as translator and aide to these masters, and then teaching in his own right, he traveled to many countries, observing the reality of people's lives and seeking ways to translate the teachings in order to make them relevant to modern men and women, by drawing out their universal message while losing none of their authenticity, purity, and power. Out of this was born his unique style of teaching and his ability to attune the teachings to modern life, demonstrated so vividly in his highly-acclaimed and groundbreaking book, *The Tibetan Book of Living and Dying,* now regarded as a spiritual classic, with two million copies sold in thirty languages and fifty-nine countries. This book has been adopted by colleges, groups and institutions, both medical and religious, and is used extensively by nurses, doctors and health care professionals. Rinpoche is also the founder and spiritual director of Rigpa, an international network of 106 Buddhist centres and groups in twenty-three countries around the world. One of the most renowned teachers of our time, Rinpoche has been teaching for over thirty years, and continues to travel widely in Europe, America, Australia, and Asia, addressing thousands of people on his retreats and teaching tours.

The Western Teachers

PHILIPPE CORNU was born in 1957 and is a translator of Buddhist works from Tibetan and Chinese. He is the author of several works and translations on Buddhism and Tibetan culture, especially on the Nyingma tradition and on dzogchen. He has studied and practiced Tibetan Buddhism for more than twenty years with Dudjom Rinpoche, Sogyal Rinpoche, Namkhai Norbu Rinpoche, and other teachers of the Nyingma tradition.

FRANCESCA FREMANTLE received her doctorate from the School of Asian and African Studies at London University. She studied Sanskrit and Tibetan before meeting Chögyam Trungpa, whose student she was for many years, and with whom she collaborated in translating the *The Tibetan Book of the Dead.* Since then, Dr. Fremantle has continued to combine the practice of Buddhism with research into ancient Buddhist texts. A Buddhist teacher and practitioner, she lives in London.

PATRICK GAFFNEY was born in England and studied at Cambridge, where he first met Sogyal Rinpoche. He is one of Rinpoche's oldest and closest students, having served as his personal assistant since the mid-seventies and as co-editor of *The Tibetan Book of Living and Dying*. Patrick is closely involved with the work of Rigpa—the international network of Buddhist centers and groups founded by Sogyal Rinpoche—and he participates regularly in events at Rigpa centers around the world.

CHRISTINE LONGAKER is Training Director of the Spiritual Care Education and Training Program, and author of *Facing Death and Finding Hope: A Guide to the Emotional and Spiritual Care of the Dying*, now translated into nine languages. Since 1980 Christine has studied with Sogyal Rinpoche. An early pioneer in the hospice movement, she helped establish a hospice home care program in Santa Cruz County, California, and served as its director and staff trainer. Christine has devoted her life to the care of the dying and to training others to do the same, offering seminars internationally on the emotional, practical, and spiritual care of the dying.

FRANK OSTASESKI founded the Zen Hospice Project, the first Buddhist hospice in America, in 1987. He currently directs the Institute on Dying, the Project's new educational arm. Through lectures, retreats, and workshops, he has introduced thousands to the practices of mindful and compassionate care of the dying. His work has been featured in the Bill Moyers series *On Our Own Terms*, the PBS series *With Eyes Open*, the *Oprah Winfrey Show*, and numerous national publications. In addition to being a Buddhist teacher, Frank is a consultant to several healthcare organizations, and co-chairs the Robert Wood Johnson Foundation's Last Acts Spirituality Committee. In 2001 Frank was honored by the Dalai Lama for his years of compassionate service to the dying and their families, and he was recently named one of America's fifty most innovative people by the American Association of Retired Persons (AARP).

Editor

DORIS WOLTER, the editor of this book, was born in 1953, and studied German literature, comparative religion, and fine arts, and she currently works part-time as a school teacher in Berlin. For her first teacher, Sogyal Rinpoche, she helped develop Rigpa Germany, and acted as its secretary and later national director for more than sixteen years. She wrote for and edited a number of Buddhist publications, founding and serving as chief editor of *Rigpa Rundbrief,* a magazine published from 1988 until 2001. She became a member of the board of the German Buddhist Union from 1993 to 2001, and in 1992 was coordinator of the EBU conference "Unity in Diversity" in Berlin. In 1996 she initiated and organized "Dying, Death, and Living," a conference on spiritual care for the dying. Since 2004 she has been coordinating The Richness of Buddhist Knowledge, a study program of the German Buddhist Union in the spirit of inter-Buddhist dialogue. Doris has been a student of Dzongsar Khyentse Rinpoche since 1990 and supports his charities Khyentse Foundation and Lotus Outreach in Germany. She lives in Berlin and can be contacted via doriswolter@compuserve.com and doris@khyentsefoundation.org.

About Wisdom Publications

WISDOM PUBLICATIONS, a nonprofit publisher, is dedicated to making available authentic works relating to Buddhism for the benefit of all. We publish books by ancient and modern masters in all traditions of Buddhism, translations of important texts, and original scholarship. Additionally, we offer books that explore East-West themes unfolding as traditional Buddhism encounters our modern culture in all its aspects. Our titles are published with the appreciation of Buddhism as a living philosophy, and with the special commitment to preserve and transmit important works from Buddhism's many traditions.

To learn more about Wisdom, or to browse books online, visit our website at www.wisdompubs.org.

You may request a copy of our catalog online or by writing to this address:

Wisdom Publications
199 Elm Street
Somerville, Massachusetts 02144 USA
Telephone: 617-776-7416
Fax: 617-776-7841
Email: info@wisdompubs.org
www.wisdompubs.org

The Wisdom Trust

As a nonprofit publisher, Wisdom is dedicated to the publication of Dharma books for the benefit of all sentient beings and dependent upon the kindness and generosity of sponsors in order to do so. If you would like to make a donation to Wisdom, you may do so through our website or our Somerville office. If you would like to help sponsor the publication of a book, please write or email us at the address above.

Thank you.

Wisdom is a nonprofit, charitable 501(c)(3) organization affiliated with the Foundation for the Preservation of the Mahayana Tradition (FPMT).

Mind in Comfort and Ease:
The Vision of Enlightenment in the
Great Perfection
The Dalai Lama
Foreword by Sogyal Rinpoche
384 pp, Cloth * ISBN 0-86171-493-8,
$24.95

"One of the absolutely best and richest books on meditation practice that I have ever read, offered by His Holiness with remarkable precision and clarity, and with astonishing humility and candor. This book has it all."—Jon Kabat-Zinn, author of *Coming to Our Senses*

"This beautifully translated book is a treasure of great value to practicing Buddhists, philosophers, scientists, and everyone interested in fathoming the nature and potential of the mind."—B. Alan Wallace, author of *The Attention Revolution*

"All who wish to be at ease in the awakened, boundless, sublime nature of their own minds—buddhahood—should read this book."—Tulku Thondup Rinpoche, author of *The Practice of Dzogchen*

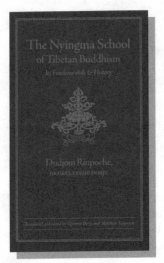

The Nyingma School of
Tibetan Buddhism:
Its Fundamentals and History
Dudjom Rinpoche
Translated, edited, and annotated by
Matthew Kapstein and Gyurme Dorje
1584 pp, Cloth, ISBN 0-86171-199-8,
$90.00

Two treatises form the present volume, namely the *Fundamentals of the Nyingma School* and the *History of the Nyingma School*. Among the most widely read of all His Holiness Dudjom Rinpoche's works, these treatises were composed during the years immediately following his arrival in India as a refugee. His intention in writing them was to preserve the precise structure of the Nyingma philosophical view within its historical and cultural context.

Beautifully presented, this single-volume edition features illustrations in both black and white and in color, plus maps, bibliographic information, and valuable reference material and annotations.